eDistribution

F. Barry Lawrence

Daniel F. Jennings

Brian E. Reynolds

Australia · Canada · Mexico · Singapore · Spain · United Kingdom · United States

eDistribution

F. Barry Lawrence, Daniel F. Jennings, and Brian E. Reynolds

Editor-in-Chief:
Jack W. Calhoun

Team Leader:
Melissa S. Acuna

Senior Acquisitions Editor:
Charles McCormick

Developmental Editor:
Taney Wilkins

Marketing Manager:
Larry Qualls

Production Editor:
Margaret M. Bril

Manufacturing Coordinator:
Diane Lohman

Compositor:
Lachina Publishing Services

Printer:
Phoenix Color
Hagerstown, Maryland

Internal Designer:
Chris Miller

Cover Designer:
Chris Miller

Cover Photograph:
Digital Vision (a stock house)

Library of Congress Cataloging-in-Publication Data
Lawrence, F. Barry
    Edistribution / F. Barry Lawrence, Daniel F. Jennings, Brian E. Reynolds
    p. cm.
    Includes bibliographical references and index.
    ISBN 0-324-12171-7 (pbk.)
    1. Electronic commerce. 2. Internet marketing. I. Title: E-distribution. II. Jennings, Daniel F. III. Reynolds, Brian E. IV. Title.
    HF5548.32 .L386 2003
    658.7'88'02854678—dc21
        2002070346

This book is dedicated to our wives, Lisa, Kay, and Suzanne, for the love and friendship on which we depend in every aspect of our lives.

Contents

part 2

Chapter 4
The E-business Model 38

Chapter 5
Distribution Sales and Marketing
Under E-business 55

Chapter 6
Using E-business Partners to Integrate
the Customer into the Distributor's Operations 69

Chapter 13
E-distribution Strategy

Preface

The full scope of the opportunity associated with the Internet is still unclear. At the beginning of the 21st century, most people believed it would revolutionize business by eliminating redundancies associated with classic distribution channels. As this book will demonstrate, that view both over- and underestimated the impact the Internet would have on industry. Distribution channels and, for that matter, all forms of commerce as well as our day-to-day lives will be impacted. The value will have more to do with connecting the world than eliminating any specific functions or intermediaries. Properly managed, real-time information makes all processes function better with less expense. The Internet, therefore, will not come to replace business sectors such as distribution but will only serve to make them function more effectively.

The implications of having the potential to improve all business activity are profound. Lower production costs, less inventory holding costs, more timely delivery, and greater product selection are only a few of the potential outcomes. The world became wealthier with the Total Quality Management and Just in Time movements at the close of the 20th century. People everywhere enjoyed the rewards of these programs through the introduction of new technologies and higher quality products at a lower cost, which raised the income of everyone. The impact of the Internet will be even more stunning if we can only harness the power we already understand. The extent of what industry leaders and dreamers such as ourselves currently envision is but a tiny fraction of what will result from a more fully connected world.

We did not write this book to canonize the Internet as the new way of doing business. The Internet is a tool that can offer great opportunities to all firms but carries great peril to those who would use it incorrectly or before they fully understand the implications of their actions. The Enterprise Resource Planning (ERP) systems failures of the 1990s and the dot-com disasters of the early 2000s are excellent examples of the results derived from poorly understood e-business initiatives. Our goal is to shed additional light on the possibilities and perils associated with e-business. This book is intended to add to the understanding of the true potential of a connected world.

The Internet allows communities such as academia and industry to collaborate in solving many problems. The impact of this collaboration is already being felt worldwide and is accelerating. We are pleased to join the efforts of the many talented academics and practitioners who seek to harness the power of the Internet.

This book represents the experiences and thoughts of many industry practitioners and a few academics. We want to thank the business partners of Texas A&M University's Industrial Distribution Program without whose vision and support we could not have written this work. In particular we wish to thank Tim Miller, Barry Marrs, and Terry Slattery and all the hard-working people at Master Halco for their continued support, tremendous insight, and courage to face the hardest of problems. We also wish to thank Keith Rainwater for his intelligent approach to information systems problems and for including us in his journey.

There are more people to thank than can be included in this preface, but the efforts of our many business partners are thoroughly interwoven into this text. We also want to thank our wives, Lisa, Kay, and Suzanne, for their tireless support, counsel, and patience as we went out on the numerous adventures that created this book. A special thanks goes to our good friend Ramesh Krishnamurthi whose wisdom and management skills in bringing these projects to their successful conclusion touch every part of this book. We also want to thank Charles McCormick and Taney Wilkins together with their associates at South-Western Publishing/Thomson Learning for their assistance in making this book a reality.

About the Authors

F. Barry Lawrence

Dr. Barry Lawrence is the director of the Information Systems Consortium and holder of the prestigious 3M Fellows Award at Texas A&M University. As a faculty member of the Industrial Distribution Program and Thomas and Joan Read Center for Distribution Research and Education, he is involved in graduate, undergraduate, and professional continuing education teaching activities, funded research projects, journal publication, academic society meetings and publications, service, and industry contact. His teaching activities surround classes in logistics, Supply Chain Management, distribution information systems, and distribution strategy. He is a frequent speaker for distribution associations and private firms on topics ranging from logistics and inventory management to information systems for distribution channels (e-business). He has also served as an advisor to the Professional Association of Industrial Distribution (PAID), student chapter, since 1997.

Dr. Lawrence's research interests include ERP/e-business implementation and logistics (inventory and other asset management) redesign for distribution operations. He has worked on many large industry projects generating millions of dollars in funding for the university and its students. Some of his major initiatives include the Information Systems Consortium for Supply Chain Integration, the Supply Chain Information Systems Laboratory, and the Consortium for ERP Benchmarking and Standardization. These initiatives have enjoyed high visibility and enormous success in increasing the understanding of e-business and in forging significant strategic partnerships with more than 20 information technology and supply chain solution providers.

Dr. Lawrence holds a Ph.D. in Information and Operations Management from Texas A&M University, an M.B.A. from Southwest Texas State University, and a B.B.A. in Finance from the University of Texas at Austin. He has more than 10 years of industry experience in sales and retail business.

Daniel F. Jennings

Dr. Jennings is a full professor at Texas A&M University and was formerly the Industrial Distribution Program Coordinator and Director of the Thomas and Joan

Read Center for Distribution Research and Education at Texas A&M University. He has held three endowed professorships in his academic career.

Jennings' corporate career includes engineering, corporate planning, and managerial positions with Armstrong World Industries, Kaiser Aluminum and Chemical Corporation, Olinkraft, Inc., Boise Cascade Corporation, and Certainteed Corporation in the United States, Canada, and South America. His industry experience involves manufacturing and distribution activities.

Dr. Jennings has served as a visiting professor at universities in Russia, France, Canada, Mexico, and Australia and has conducted executive development programs in the U.S., Canada, France, Mexico, and Italy. Dr. Jennings has performed consulting assignments for a variety of firms, labor unions, and governmental agencies in five areas: strategy formulation and implementation, value chain analysis, management development, organizational change, and human resource issues that are vital to a client's business. He also conducts economic loss analysis for a variety of organizations as well as participating in numerous workshops, programs, and seminars for industrial distributors, manufacturers, and trade associations.

Dr. Jennings has published over 130 articles in academic and practitioner journals and has authored 10 textbooks. His research has been described in both *The Wall Street Journal* and *The New York Times,* and he has received several best paper awards from the Academy of Management, New York University, Baylor University, Prentice-Hall Publishing, and McGraw-Hill Publishing. He also received the Outstanding Researcher Award while a faculty member at Baylor University. Dr. Jennings received a B.S. in Industrial Engineering (with honors) from the University of Tennessee, an M.B.A. in Finance from Northeast Louisiana University, and a Ph.D. in Strategic Management from Texas A&M University and is a Registered Professional Engineer.

Brian Reynolds

Brian Reynolds is the associate director of the Thomas and Joan Read Center for Distribution Research and Education, a part of the Texas Engineering Experiment Station. He holds a B.S. in Management from Pepperdine University and an M.B.A. from Texas A&M's Lowry Mays Graduate School of Business. Brian is affiliated with Texas A&M University's Industrial Distribution academic program.

He has more than 20 years of experience in the distribution industry, ranging from field sales and branch management to general sales management for a $75 million industrial distributor. He served as the director of the Quality Process and, following that, as director of marketing and integrated supply for a $200 million distributor. He was also the project team leader for selecting and implementing new distribution software and hardware, which went live on schedule and under budget.

Brian has designed and conducted training in field sales, sales management, branch operations, quality improvement, database marketing plans, statistical process control, and integrated supply. He has served in several volunteer capacities on industry trade association committees and task forces, including serving as a co-chair on a joint Industrial Distribution Association–Industrial Supply Manufacturers Association committee on Total Quality Process.

He has made presentations to the Industrial Distribution Association (IDA), the Industrial Supply Manufacturers Association (ISMA), the Institute for Supply Management (ISM), formerly NAPM, the International Quality & Productivity Center, the Institute for International Research, the National Association of Steel Pipe Distributors, and the Construction Equipment Manufacturers Association. He has also made numerous presentations, and conducted workshops, for industrial distributors and manufacturers.

New Distribution Strategies

part 1

The Changing Face of Distribution

Distributor Perspective

Ed Greene is the president of Tri-States Electrical Distributors headquartered in Atlanta, Georgia. Tri-States, with annual sales of $210 million, has sixteen branches located in the Southeast. Major suppliers include such manufacturers as the Allen-Bradley Division of Rockwell Automation as well as Siemens Energy and Automation. Major customers include electrical contractors as well as major manufacturing firms that use electrical products in the maintenance and operation of their facilities. These products include motor control centers, switches, variable speed drives, and a variety of other electrical components. Greene attended the University of Georgia, where he was an all-Southeast Conference (SEC) quarterback and a four-year member of the varsity golf team. During Greene's senior year in college, the golf team won the SEC Championship, and he was voted the team's most valuable player. Greene began working for Tri-States in sales after graduating from the University of Georgia. After twenty-five years of excellent achievements in a variety of sales positions, Greene was promoted to president. The Dunne family owns Tri-States, and four of the family's members are presently employed by the company. Greene has been given an ownership position in the firm in recognition of his past performance and now owns approximately 8% of Tri-States. Greene's effectiveness in sales has been attributed to his relationships with Tri-States suppliers *and customers. Greene plays golf with suppliers and customers on a regular basis and hosts them at a variety of sporting events. For the past four years, the profitability of Tri-States has declined. Inventories have increased, but shipments to customers have been late. In many instances, the wrong product has been shipped to the wrong place at the wrong time. Robert Peters, a son-in-law of the Dunne family, and the president of the Georgia Trust Company, a large banking institution, has recommended that Tri-States embrace Supply Chain Management techniques to improve the declining profitability of Tri-States. Greene does not understand Supply Chain Management and is concerned that Peters may force him out as president of Tri-States unless the profitability of Tri-States improves. Greene is concerned about developing an action plan that will improve the profitability of Tri-States.*

Introduction

The end of the 1990s revealed a different way of looking at distribution. A new movement called Supply Chain Management had been slowly redefining the distributor's role in the channel. The market was changing, and distributors were expected to cooperate with suppliers and customers to decrease total channel costs.

While increasing customer expectations were nothing new, they were unfolding at an alarming rate. The tasks required of distributors in order to satisfy customer expectations were not necessarily the ones that distributors would have chosen. For example, a paramount requirement was to provide logistics and inventory management services, which most distributors performed as a support function, not as a core competency. A core competency is something a firm either does so well it provides a competitive advantage, or something it must do for its customers in order to remain in business. Distributors did not ask to be the supply chain's inventory manager, but because they had the largest inventory, the task just naturally fell to them. Inventory became a core competency whether distributors wanted it or not. In a Just in Time (JIT) world, inventory is the hot potato, and the distributor is "it."

As if the inventory manager designation were not disturbing enough, more trouble was brewing. *E-commerce* (later renamed *e-business* to be more inclusive) became the buzz phrase by 1999, and pundits predicted it would not only revolutionize distribution but eliminate the distributor altogether. So distributors in the late '90s were first expected to handle the supply chain's inventory and then go away as the inventory disappeared, being replaced by data warehouses that managed customer demand in "real time."

These opening remarks introduce new terms that may confuse some readers. *Real time,* for instance, means that up to the microsecond, every time something happens in product movement anywhere in the supply chain, that occurrence has instant visibility to all supply chain members. If a customer buys a product from a branch warehouse, the product is scanned as it is taken off the shelf, and all supply chain members know that the product has been picked. The product is scanned as it is loaded on the truck, so everyone can now see it is on the truck and through Global Positioning Systems (GPS) they can even follow it down the highway.

Only a few years ago these concepts were not being utilized in most distribution channels. However, many applications that closely approach the preceding scenario have been described in both academic and practitioner journals. As a result, distributors who do not have the capability to utilize real-time concepts are greatly concerned because the lack of such capability places them at a competitive disadvantage. Moreover, beyond concerns about the lack of the capability to manage customer demand in real time lies the fundamental question on every distributor's mind: If the channels get to real time will distributors cease to exist?

The argument that distributors will be eliminated or severely downsized in the supply chain hinges on one fundamental premise: e-business will eliminate inventory, and the supply chain will no longer need distributors. The premise relies on two fundamental assumptions: First, e-business will eliminate the need for physical inventory. Second, elimination of inventory eliminates distributors.[1] The purpose of this chapter is to address the validity of these assumptions by reviewing both the development of the e-business movement and its potential future directions.

The Disintermediation Myth

Disintermediation is a term that means elimination of the distributor; it was first suggested for distributors in the early 1990s as a response to new technology and increasing pressure on the supply chain to cut costs.[2] Distributors were perceived as middlemen who added cost to the supply chain through redundant inventory, services, and information handling. It seemed logical that if suppliers and end users could "automate out inefficiency," they could eliminate the distributor. This logic follows from the reasoning that a shorter supply chain is inherently more efficient.

Until recently, most distributors described their core competency as "relationships." The statement covers the need for the following two roles. First is that of a channel leader, who determines where the sources of supply are and how to access them. The second role is that of a manager of customer information for manufacturers. Inventory management, financing for small customers, and supplying technical information were all considered as support functions that were necessary to carry out the key activity of building relationships. As such, the classical relationship of these functions became unchanging or "frozen." Today, the classic business relationship has become "unfrozen" by business forces like Just in Time (JIT), the technological revolution caused by the Internet, and advanced information management systems. Traditional relationships are in flux. It is unclear how new channels and new business models will be structured.

To eliminate the distributor from the supply chain, channel members must eliminate the services the distributor currently supplies. That means eliminating some services and outsourcing others. The activity that is singled out the most is inventory management. Inventory exists for only three reasons: forecast error, lead-time variability, and transportation cost. If the end user knew what was needed, exactly when it was needed, and exactly when it would be delivered from the supplier, and could get it delivered at no cost, there would be no need for inventory. The end user would only need to match up the information flows and have products shipped direct from the supplier. The same information-handling relationship would exist between the supplier and the supplier's vendors.

Forecast error will never be completely eliminated since natural disasters will remain difficult to predict, as will other events, so distributors will always carry some inventory. Most forecast error could be eliminated, however, by faster, more reliable information exchange. Because e-business promises to collapse information-exchange cycle times and dramatically increase data integrity, most academics and business practitioners expect inventories to drop dramatically.[3] As much as 40% or more of a distributor's inventory can be attributed to forecast error.[4] Thus, better forecasting has the potential to tremendously reduce the amount of inventory carried by distributors.

Transportation will also continue to create some inventory in the supply chain. In an effort to capitalize on economies of scale, manufacturers and distributors will ship more than what is exactly necessary to satisfy demand, which creates more inventory. Freight costs, however, are also dependent on information. Transportation planning, for instance, can be greatly facilitated by matching incoming shipments with outgoing ones to capture the freight company's "back haul." Opportunities such as these will lower the per-shipment cost, which in turn lowers the need to ship more for economies of scale. Smaller shipment sizes are consistent with Just in Time principles that lead to smaller inventories.

Lead-time variability should also be greatly reduced as information flows more freely. Manufacturers suffer from the "Bullwhip Effect," where inaccuracies and delays in the movement of information get multiplied as it passes through its stops in the supply chain.[5] By the time information reaches the manufacturer, it is so confused that the manufacturer can only guess at actual end user demand. Manufacturers are forced to serve whatever demand they can through capacity planning and lot sizing designed to minimize manufacturing costs. This process sends the wrong amount of goods into the marketplace at the wrong time. Distributors and their customers protect themselves by compensating with larger purchases at intervals that may or may not match up with actual end use. This further confounds manufacturers' understanding of the market, and soon they lose all touch with the end user.[6] Figure 1.1 depicts the "Bullwhip Effect."

An example of a supply chain that may suffer from the Bullwhip Effect is a building materials manufacturer/distributor. The distribution arm of the firm does not get Point of Sale (POS) data from customers. Instead, distribution tries to respond to

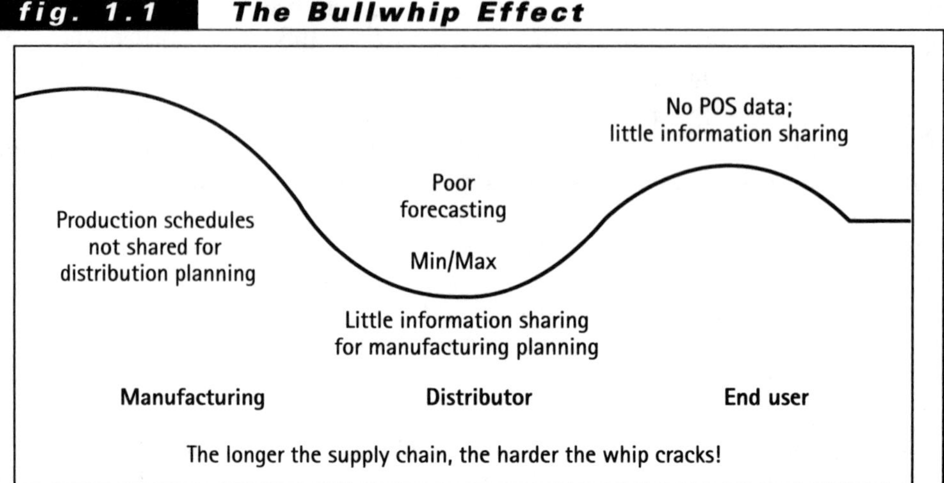

Source: Graphic created at Texas A&M University; based on the Bullwhip Effect theory cited in the text.

customer inquires as they happen with little lead time and a poor understanding of the customer's customer. The lack of real-time customer information causes forecasting to degrade to the point that most in the firm have little confidence in forecasts and demand larger inventories be maintained to protect customer service. The larger inventories buffer the customer demand so that the firm orders from manufacturing less often and in larger quantities. Since the time between orders is long, the seasonal movement of product is lost, and the manufacturing division does not get a clear picture of what actual demand is at the distribution facilities. This lack of understanding causes manufacturing to set schedules that minimize its costs without regard to distribution's true needs. The schedules do not always match distribution order needs, so distribution will carry more inventory to protect against manufacturing's inability to supply product on demand. The larger inventories further remove manufacturing from the customer in a never-ending cycle.

Manufacturers are, therefore, desperate to gain more end-user information. Distributors are sometimes perceived as an obstacle to this effort because of their failure to provide such information to manufacturers. Both the distributor and the manufacturer should be aware of the increased costs that occur from the failure to share end-user information. In essence, the inability of manufacturers to plan leads to larger minimum buys which, in turn, forces distributors to carry more inventory. Poor information exchange hurts every supply chain member. E-business will open up the opportunity for manufacturer access to end-user data and possibly more extensive analysis of market needs. The result will be more efficient markets with fewer assets (inventory). The question is whether the distributor will contribute to this information flow or slow and distort the process.

An argument is that e-business carried to its extreme (real time) should produce dramatic decreases in inventory. In fact, the manufacturer may already carry sufficient inventory to respond to demands of the supply chain if information is handled efficiently.[7] The problem with this scenario, however, is the difference between what the channels are currently capable of in terms of information management and what they must do to achieve those inventory reductions.

The State of Distribution Channels

Most distributors started as hardware stores or as small providers of hard-to-procure parts for a few local manufacturers. The value of the function became critical over the next forty or so years, and these businesses grew to include many more products and a suite of services based on their customers' needs. This evolutionary growth process led to considerable variation among distributors and their processes. Processes differ considerably not only from distributor to distributor but even between business divisions within a single distributor.

The major driver for most distribution operations is customer service. Ask a distributor for a special service, and odds are they will try to meet the need. Distributors have long been criticized for not maintaining a clearly defined "core competency." In fact, distributors have long employed the statement "I can do that" as their core competency. This implies tremendous flexibility. In distribution, flexibility means larger inventories, more services, and other expenses. Flexibility implies the distributor will be able to respond to virtually any scenario. Responsiveness requires capacity. Inventory is stored capacity. Services require an investment in personnel to respond to customer needs. Both entail a number of expenses that may or may not be compensated for by the customer.

All in all, distributors sound like a rather noble bunch—always rising to the occasion for the customer, willing to deal with uncertainty, provide flexibility, and focus on customer service. This environment, however, is a complete nightmare in which to implement information systems. Distributors are faced with an environment that is difficult to automate at a time when automation of information is critical to success. The end user is now in control of the supply chain and expects this information infrastructure.

Manufacturer Direct Fallacies

Manufacturer-distributor relationships have been destabilized as new technologies appear to have opened new opportunities. Manufacturing has experienced "commoditization" of its products as new technologies in flexible manufacturing systems are reducing competitive advantage. Mass customization is a relatively new concept that pushes manufacturers toward the ultimate in flexibility: give the customer what they want, in the amount they want, now![8] In this environment, no product is distinctly different and competitive advantage is lost. While the concept is idealistic in the extreme, many manufacturers are concerned that maintaining brand equity will be more difficult in the SCM/e-business environment. Brand equity comes from distinctive products that cause customers to request your brand. Manufacturers look to distributors to assist them in protecting their brand.

The automation equipment market has experienced tremendous change in recent years. Major manufacturers went to great lengths to control their respective markets before the 1990s. Limited distribution, where distributors are tied to one manufacturer, was very strong in the U.S., with an installed base that protected the distributors' and manufacturers' position in many customers' operations. The franchise relationship protected the distributor through the manufacturer's promise not to use multiple distributors in a single market. The relationship protected the manufacturer through the distributor's promise not sell other manufacturers' products in their territory.

With the ground rules in place, the manufacturers and distributors could work together to build the "installed base" (those customers with the manufacturer's products installed in their plant). The manufacturer's responsibility then became to produce a reliable product that was up to date with new technology. The pressure to create new innovations was not as extreme, since the cost of customer brand switching was considered high due to the need to install a new system that would involve multiple connected systems. The distributor's responsibility was to provide strong service and keep the customer convinced of the value of the manufacturer's product so there would be no perceived need for switching. Limited distribution was not as common outside the U.S., and competition was more open. The companies that supported each approach (limited distribution versus non-franchised distribution) sparred constantly, but the "installed base," as these customers were called, barred entry by the competition. Customers who had one brand installed in their operations were unlikely to try another.

As the e-business movement came along, the technology changed. The hardware associated with the installed base for most firms was being replaced with software. The major competitors became software firms and tried to control their installed base by switching them to branded software. This branded software was originally envisioned to communicate only with the same brand-name equipment and higher-level programs. International standards-setting organizations like Profibus, however, insisted that software and hardware become standardized. Many customers pushed the manufacturers to embrace standards to simplify their processes. Once these systems were standardized, the installed base was more difficult to defend since multiple systems could be used in one plant. The software was going to be more difficult to defend from a brand perspective.

Many distributors have capitalized on this brand-equity phenomenon and pushed manufacturers for lower prices and more services where products have been reduced to commodities. A major distributor requirement is for the manufacturer to carry the inventory. If a manufacturer makes a commodity that can be easily found elsewhere, the distributor only needs to call for the lowest price with current availability. If the product is not available, the manufacturer loses the sale. The distributor, therefore, is able to force the inventory back on the manufacturer.

A good example is PVC pipe. PVC pipe is a "commodity's commodity," so to speak. Distributors in this market were able to force manufacturers to carry the inventory, deliver to customer's site, and maintain low prices all at the same time. When a contractor customer contacted the distributor, the distributor would merely contact several manufacturers to determine who had availability, could deliver, and had the lowest price. Since there was no major difference in the quality of most manufactured pipe, the distributor was able to manipulate the supply chain. The relationship was rocky but worked for the distributor. Most manufacturers will go to great lengths to avoid such an environment.

The inventory problem, combined with what some manufacturers perceive as a lack of distributor loyalty, has caused some manufacturers to look at alternative channels of distribution. Some manufacturers are truly upset with distributor behaviors such as carrying competitors' lines, lack of sales effort on manufacturer new product introductions, and pressuring suppliers for more services. Other manufacturers believe that eliminating the middlemen will result in an increased profit margin for themselves. Still others are merely opportunists who cannot penetrate their competitor's (another manufacturer's) distribution network and are looking for ways to circumvent it.

Opening a new channel is not easy. Even with the great promise of Internet marketing, the key issue is customer information. If the seller does not know who the end user is or how to contact them, an Internet site becomes little more than an online catalog that may or may not draw customers. It will, however, threaten distributors and many will retaliate. Underestimating distributor power is not wise. One manufacturer tried to go direct on 20% of the business that had gone through their key distributor. The distributor reclaimed 90% of that business with the products of the manufacturer's competitor within six months. The rest of the distributors immediately began to diversify their product offering out of a perceived need to protect themselves, throwing the manufacturer's survival in doubt. The marketing arm of the distributor, which was much more developed than its own, crushed the manufacturer.[9]

Most disaffected manufacturers are aware of this problem and, hence, are not looking to develop their own channel but to use an alternative one instead. The stakes are high, since their existing channel can strike back faster than a new channel can ramp up. The new channel would need to be fully developed with its own set of customers and possibly have inroads to existing customers being served through the current distribution channel.[10] Marketplaces, commonly called "dotcoms," have aggressively tried to fill this role with questionable success.

The difficulties faced by the marketplaces are many. First and foremost, the technology is not quite here yet. The marketplaces must sell a customer base that is not using their technology, either out of lack of need or because the technology is still not ready. This "vaporware" solution is a tough sell. Manufacturers and distributors should not take this too lightly, however, since the technology is only a few years away. When it arrives, the race will be on, and it may be too late to change strategies. A more interesting question revolves around who will be the marketplace survivors and what e-business tools customers will ultimately value. The two issues are interrelated since, the marketplaces with the right tools will most likely be among the survivors. Many existing marketplaces may not make the final cut, and no doubt new ones will arise before the final channel members become clear.

Other challenges for marketplaces include fulfilling the additional functions carried out by distributors. Inventory will not go away, and any marketplace that starts carrying inventory will simply become a distributor. Wall Street expected the marketplaces to be low-asset based. Any attempt to become a traditional distributor was likely to be punished in terms of stock price. Without the inflated stock prices, the marketplaces would not have the funds to build a distribution network. Amazon.com, for instance, has been able to build a network of distribution facilities in spite of an inability to demonstrate significant profitability. A more likely option will be for the marketplaces to partner with distributors or third-party logistics companies (3PLs) like FedEx or UPS. Many already have.[11]

The other key distribution functions are easier to manage. Technical support will decline in value as more creative methods of delivering it over the Internet are developed. Manufacturers have been quick to provide technical information through the Internet, a wise move since it increases their channel power (brand equity) and diminishes a fundamental distribution service. In the extreme case, third-party engineering firms could be hired to handle the more difficult problems the Internet cannot support.

Financing appears to be easier to manage because existing channels are already positioned. Banks and credit card companies are anxious to serve distribution markets. Manufacturers are unlikely to handle their own credit, since it could mean supporting thousands of small customers. The only problem would be the profitability of small-firm financing. Distributors support many customers through hard times that other creditors would not. The net result would be a loss in business for the manufacturer that may not be reclaimed if the customer recovers.

So, theoretically, the distributor could be eliminated by some combination of four or five outsourcing firms (marketplace, 3PL, engineering firm, and creditor). If four firms make a more efficient supply chain than one distributor, then it will happen. As previously discussed, disintermediation will be a complex process and will likely not materialize in most applications. The alternative is for the distributor to become a strong contributor to the e-business environment. The purpose of this book is to explore the premise that the current channel is efficient but will be modified by technology. The new channels to market are currently being determined. Manufacturers and their distributor partners will need to stop trying to outmaneuver one another and get busy preparing together for the technological reshaping of the channel which appears imminent.

The Distributor's Role in the Supply Chain: A Prescription

By the summer of 2000, the concept of the Internet as a marketing mechanism was in doubt. The early leaders in the field were still struggling, and Wall Street was withdrawing its support. Marketplaces were crashing, and IPOs (Initial Public Offerings) for new Internet ventures slowed to a trickle. There was some quiet jubilation among distributors as they received what seemed like a reprieve from the grim reaper of disintermediation. The celebration was premature, because the problem had less to do with the viability of virtual marketplaces and e-business than with timing. When the next generation of technology becomes available and computer-literate Generation X starts making purchasing decisions, e-business will shift into high gear.

The distributor must make those processes that can be regularized regular. Next, distributors have to determine which remaining irregular processes are strategic (essential) and which can be eliminated or absorbed into other processes. Finally, distributors must maintain their flexibility. They have to develop information technology (IT) solutions that are well understood by their people and changeable in response to customer needs. The first two goals will take considerable planning and strategic reasoning. Their implementation will take a great deal of time and effort. The last objective (maintaining flexibility) will require creativity and thorough consideration of customer processes and needs, now and into the future. IT systems are expensive to change, so distributors will want to get it right the first time!

The bottom line: *The IT firms cannot make the transition to information management for traditional channel members!* It does not matter how afraid of technology the distribution firm's people are, IT people do not understand distributor customer relationships as well as distributors. They do not, therefore, fully understand every distributor's processes. Processes can be mapped, but if a firm does not understand the objectives of the process, they will not understand the process. Firms that leave the automation of processes to IT providers will get processes that do not work with their customer base. If a distribution firm believes its processes are special, they probably are, and most distributors think that way.

The major part of the e-business solution is the adopting firm's responsibility. The company has to understand the technology and prepare for it. That means cooperation and communication between IT personnel and the distribution firm's people. The distributor's employees have to commit to working in cross-functional teams to solve problems. They have to defend the integrity of their processes while understanding the limitations of the IT systems. Most of all, they need to defend the strategic direction of the firm and its customer relationships. It is both an art and a science and will take a lot of time.

This transition will not be easy. Most distributors are lean organizations that do not have the time to pull key people into teams that work the long hours required by IT implementations. Communication will be critical and difficult. Typically a logistics expert from the warehouse and an IT person will not speak the same language. The communication gap between sales and IT is likely to increase. But the sales and logistics operations are what make up a distribution firm, and failure to bring the keepers of those processes into IT implementation guarantees failure.

If we can take the IT revolution as a strategic imperative, then outsourcing the entire program to an IT provider is the equivalent of turning the firm's strategic position over to the IT firm. At best, an IT firm is a hardware/software provider and advisor, not the architect of a company's channel to market. The firm must commit its best functional experts (sales, marketing, human resources, logistics, etc.) to the project, no matter how much it may hurt in the short term. Management is betting the future of the company when making e-business decisions.

Manufacturers and their distribution partners must start preparing for the new channel now. The process changes will take years to accomplish, and the technology will be available long before most firms are ready. If the company is not ready, many old and new competitors will gamble on the technology, and although many will fail, the damage they will do in the meantime could be significant.

All of the foregoing leaves us with many unanswered questions:

○ What processes need redesign?

○ How should they be redesigned?

○ How will inventory be reduced?

○ What services will distributors offer once inventory is reduced?

○ What, if any, role will marketplaces play?

○ What will the manufacturer/distributor relationship look like?

○ What will the distributor look like?

○ What technology do we need and how should we use it?

○ Will there be new competition, and if so, where will it come from?

○ How will end-user expectations change?

○ How will the new distributor systems interact with the customers and suppliers?

The following chapters will address these and many other questions. The purpose of this book is to provide a road map for distributors and their manufacturing counterparts to help them transform their operations in preparation for e-business.

Summary

On the other side of the dot-com craze, it is clear that information automation for distribution firms will bring great savings to supply chains. This savings, however, will most likely be achieved through the collaborative efforts of existing channel members like distributors and their manufacturing partners. Each has a great deal to contribute—and to lose, if the implementations are not successful. Distributors and manufacturers will have to team in ways they would not have considered in the past, and the benefits and risks for each will have to be considered by all parties.

The re-creation of existing distribution channels driven by information management (e-business) will be a complex, time-intensive process. This book outlines this new approach to the channel, providing examples of potential technologies and their use. In the process of demonstrating these technologies, we will use tools that have been developed within multiple disciplines. Many of these tools were developed specifically for information automation but have experienced only limited use due to the lack of a technological infrastructure to provide for their efficient use.

While many examples will use classic theory to demonstrate how e-business will make the application of that theory possible, the point of the text is to demonstrate the "connectivity" opportunities rather than teach the theory itself. The reader is encouraged to learn more about the theory before approaching applications that apply the tools. The book's central theme is making technology pay for itself by utilizing heretofore unavailable applications that can bring value to the supply chain. This connectivity requires the effective utilization of new e-business technology, supply chain tools developed from theoretical research, and alliances that facilitate the application of both.

Figure 1.2 describes the overarching purpose of this book, which is to completely connect the supply chain through e-business, with the distributor's responsibilities

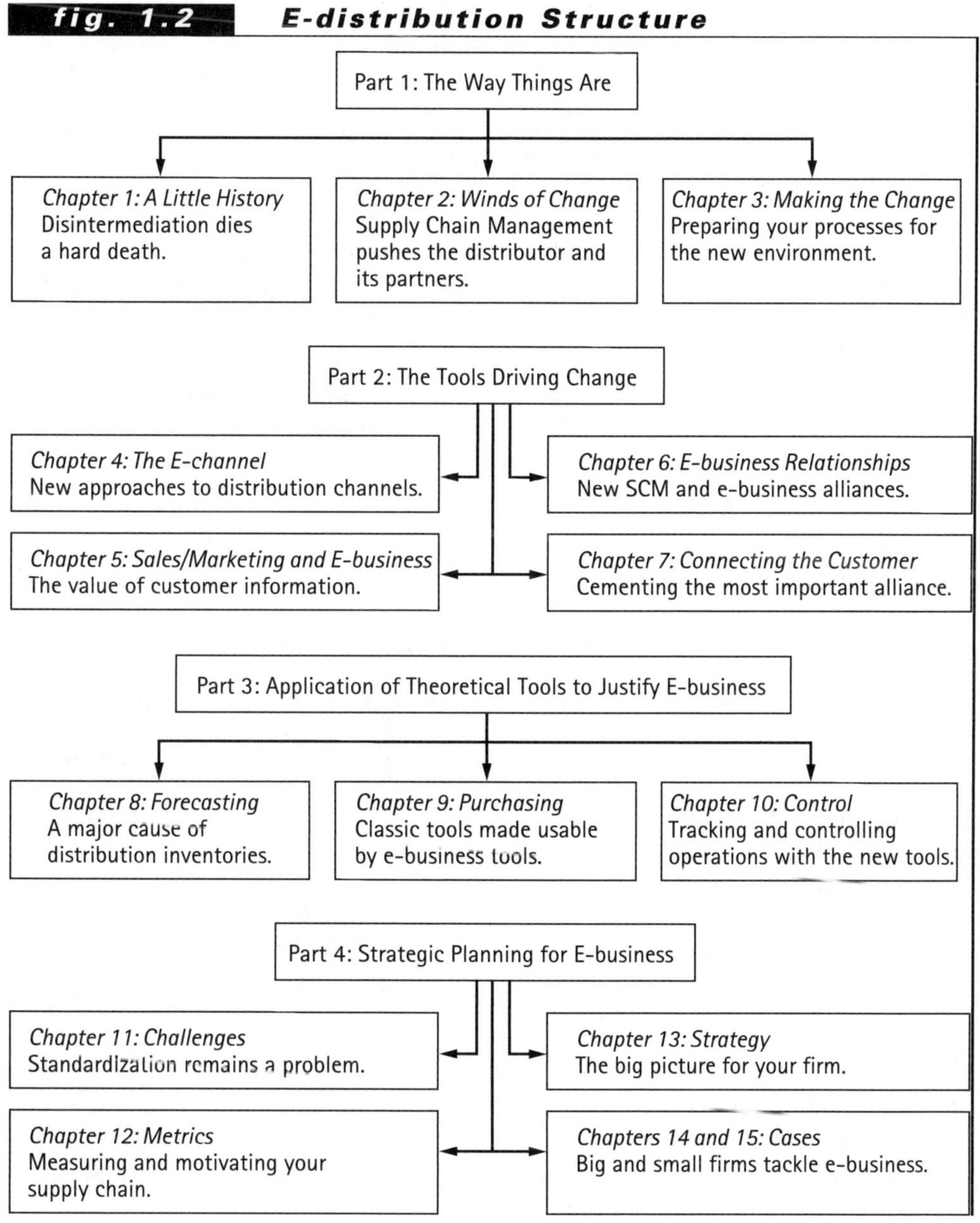

fig. 1.2　**E-distribution Structure**

as the central focus. The first part (Chapters 1–3) describes the existing relationships and existing processes and how to recast them into e-business. The chapters look at how we got to where we are in our current relationships and where e-business is likely to take us in the future. The chapters focus on understanding the value of current relationships and how to capture and preserve that value in the Supply Chain/e-business transition.

Part Two (Chapters 4–7) describes the e-business tools that parallel the existing customer-facing processes and relationships and details how new relationships will develop as the new tools are applied. Supply Chain Management theory focuses on end users and puts them first. E-business tools should start here too. We start with the end user and work backwards through the supply chain in our application of tools. The customer-facing tools and their effect on relationships are examined here.

Part Three is operations focused and, therefore, highly prescriptive, since many solutions have been developed and applied to modern IT systems. The chapters give many examples of how to apply classic operational theory to the new tools and thereby achieve the promised savings associated with e-business. The examples are by no means all-inclusive, nor are they intended to act as a substitute for intensive study of proper inventory or marketing theory. They are intended instead to demonstrate potential approaches to some of the "low-hanging fruit" expected to help justify e-business costs.

Part Four deals with global problems (standardization and relationship competition) that stand in the way of e-business and its redefined channels. Strategy and metrics to monitor the process are examined in depth.

Distributor Retrospective

Ed Greene has to learn that to be an effective Top Manager and to improve the profitability of Tri-States, he must be able to adapt to the principles of Supply Chain Management. Greene must realize that the manner in which he has managed in the past is not effective, and he must be aware of the changing aspects of distribution.

Issues to Consider

1. Should industrial distributors consider e-business as a threat or an opportunity? Why or why not?

2. What are the primary reasons that inventory exists, or is required, in the channel?

3. What forces in the channel could cause distributors to no longer be required to hold inventory? Is this likely or unlikely to occur?

4. How does improved information sharing offer the potential to reduce inventory in the channel?

5. What are the principal issues affecting the manufacturer/distributor relationship?

6. In theory, what current functions that the distributor provides could be outsourced? Is this likely to happen? Why or why not?

7. What must distributors do to prepare for e-business?

Notes

1. Gary J. Cross, "How E-business Is Transforming Supply Chain Management," *IEEE Engineering Management Review* 28 (3): 17–19 (2000).

2. R. Gellman, "Disintermediation and the Internet," *Government Information Quarterly* 13 (1): 1–8 (1996).

3. John Fallows, "Net Profits," *Manufacturing Engineer* 78 (1): 33–36 (1999).

4. F. Barry Lawrence, "The Forecasting Game" (unpublished programs, Texas A&M University, 1997–2001).

5. Richard Metters, "Quantifying the Bullwhip Effect in Supply Chains," *Journal of Operations Management* 15 (2): 89–100 (1997).

6. Frank Chen, Jennifer K. Ryan, and David Simchi-Levi, "Impact of Exponential Smoothing Forecasts on the Bullwhip Effect," *Naval Research Logistics* 47 (4): 269–286 (2000).

7. Karla E. Bourlanda, Stephen G. Powella, and David F. Pykea, "Exploiting Timely Demand Information to Reduce Inventories," *European Journal of Operational Research* 92 (2): 239–253 (1996).

8. David A. Soberman, "It's a Whole New Ball-Game," *European Management Journal* 17 (3): 290–295 (1999).

9. Observations made from research studies at Texas A&M University.

10. Leyland Pitt, Pierre Berthon, and Jean-Paul Berthon, "Changing Channels: The Impact of the Internet on Distribution Strategy," *IEEE Engineering Management Review* 27 (4): 108–116 (1999).

11. "Dot-Coms Continue Seeking Fulfillment Solutions," *Frontline Solutions* (UMI Article Re. No.: FRSE-9-32 UMI Journal Code: FRSE) 1 (12): 56 (2000).

2

Strategic Supply Chain Management for Distribution

Distributor Perspective

Fluid Dynamics, Inc., is a publicly held fluid power distributor headquartered in Los Angeles. Annual sales are $350 million. Profitability and stock price have declined for the past two years. Fluid Dynamics has twenty branches located on the West Coast and in the Midwest. Its major customers are large manufacturers that use fluid power components in the maintenance and repair of their facilities. Major suppliers include Vickers, Eaton Corporation, Gates Manufacturing, Sauer-Sundstrand, and SMC Pneumatics. In an attempt to increase sales and improve profitability, top management of Fluid Dynamics used an independent third party to conduct a customer satisfaction survey. Results of the survey indicated that (1) it is difficult for customers to do business with Fluid Dynamics, and (2) it is also difficult for Fluid Dynamics to do business with its suppliers. The difficulties described by both customers and suppliers include: excessive time required to develop quotations, inadequate information regarding available inventory, failure to ship products on time, and the inability to forecast properly. After obtaining the results of the survey, Fluid Dynamics formed an internal team consisting of individuals from sales, operations, purchasing, and engineering to develop a plan of action to resolve the problems identified by the survey. David Miller, director of operations for Fluid Dynamics, has been assigned the role of team leader.

Introduction

The supply chain consists of all contributors to a final product and its delivery to the consumer or end user. A sample supply chain would consist of a mining firm that extracts iron ore from the ground, a logistics carrier that delivers the iron ore to the steel mill, the steel mill that refines the ore, the logistics carrier that delivers bulk steel to a steel service center (a form of distributor), a logistics carrier that delivers smaller bundles of steel from the distributor to a manufacturer of drilling equipment, a logistics firm that delivers the drilling equipment to an equipment distributor, and the distributor who sells or rents the drill to a mining firm. This supply chain is circular, but typically supply chains are presented as linear in nature (see Figure 2.1).

The circular supply chain described above is not the only exception to the simplistic linear view of supply chains. Most supply chains, linear or not, are more complex than the theoretical model depicted in Figure 2.1. In addition to the circular supply chain's supplier, who is also a customer of the supply chain, there are other players who do not fit neatly into the picture. The steel mill, for example, has other suppliers that are competitors of the mining firm. It is a stretch for the mining company to consider the steel mill a partner in the supply chain, when the mill does business with its would-be "destroyers" (other mining firms), with obvious strategic implications.

The relationship problems between the steel service center and the mill are the same as those between the service center and the end user. The supply chain is not, in fact, linear. Each member acts as a nexus of crisscrossing supply chains. The supply chain planner must also consider service providers (insurance and accounting firms, for instance) and providers of ancillary products (maintenance, repair, and operations, commonly called MRO, products). While not recognized directly in the theoretical linear supply chain, they contribute to its success or failure tremendously.

Given that the supply chain is a complex, nonlinear environment, the cooperation concept that lies at the heart of Supply Chain Management (SCM) is challenging, at best. If the members of the supply chain can overcome the difficulties it poses, however, there is much to be gained. The goals and rewards of SCM are numerous, but they require the application of managerial strategy, new processes and procedures, and technology. Until recently, technology was not able to contribute as much as

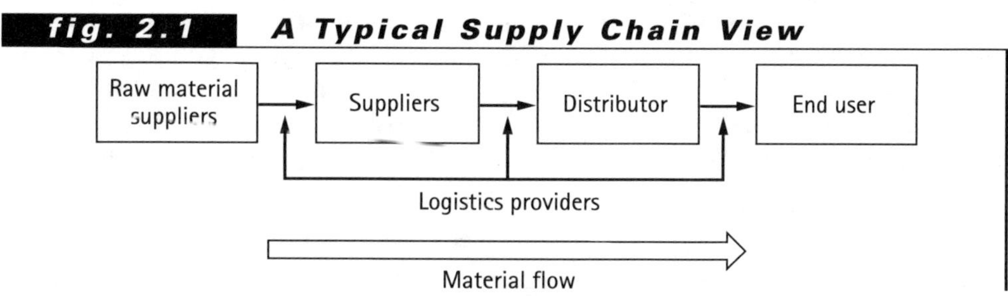

fig. 2.1 **A Typical Supply Chain View**

was needed to the SCM movement. In many ways, SCM was hampered by the lack of enabling technologies. E-business has stepped into this void. This chapter looks at the foundations of SCM, and at how e-business tools will be used by distributors to enable and enhance the new channel relationships.

The Evolution of Supply Chain Management

SCM goals are based on classic theory that until recently was either difficult to put into practice or poorly understood.[1] Most firms focused on their own operations and found that challenge more than sufficient. In addition, the business world did not define success along supply chains but on a firm-by-firm basis. A company could seek more profit by outperforming its competition or by outmaneuvering its suppliers and customers. The result was the same, so American firms focused on adversarial (bidding war) relationships with suppliers, and advanced sales and marketing efforts with customers. In this type of environment, cooperation between supply chain members is lost, since no one really recognizes the supply chain as a competitive unit.

Early attempts at SCM came mostly through vertical integration.[2] Henry Ford attempted to bring a complete supply chain together, from raw materials all the way through to the final purchase by the consumer. Such applications were rare, however, and outside of a few industries (oil companies are an excellent example) proved difficult to maintain. Manufacturers have different core competencies from distributors and logistics providers. The vertical integration movement lost momentum, as specialization proved more powerful than integration.[3]

Integration was far from dead, however, and would be revived halfway around the world. Scientific methods were being applied to business processes, and the value of integration was obvious. New techniques were being developed for purchasing procedures and manufacturing process control like Economic Order Quantity (EOQ) and Statistical Process Control (SPC), and while marketing- and material price-driven firms in the U.S. would be slow to adopt these techniques, they would find a home in Japan.

Japan emerged from World War II with its economy shattered. Industry did what it could to pick up potential markets, and a great deal of interest surrounded any method that could make Japan competitive with the rest of the world. Two major schools of thought, one new and one more well developed, came together in this environment. The first was led by Japanese thinkers like Toyoda, Ohno, and Shingo and became known as Just in Time (JIT) when it hit the U.S. The second was led by American theorists like Deming, Juran, and Crosby and became Total Quality Management (TQM). These two movements would reshape the business world.[4]

The U.S. was slow to take notice. Japanese firms quickly adopted TQM, since it eliminated waste (scrap), and JIT, since it saved space and financial resources (inventory reduction). In a country where space was at a premium and resources were dear after the war, the programs made a lot of sense. In the U.S., American manufacturers were finding that they could sell stuff as fast as they could make it. TQM and JIT did not appear to lead to increased capacity; in fact, JIT seemed to pose the risk of losing capacity, since inventory was typically used as a buffer against forecast error and manufacturing or logistics systems failures. Most U.S. firms focused on making what they could make the most money from, and the American marketing machine sold whatever the manufacturers could produce.

The world changed in the 1970s, however. The relative abundance of U.S. resources came to an abrupt halt with the Arab oil embargo of 1973 and the subsequent shocks associated with OPEC policy and the overthrow of the Shah of Iran. Suddenly, at least one resource (fuel) was not limitless, and the cost of operating manufacturing plants increased significantly. Reducing manufacturing waste should have taken center stage, but the oil embargo touched off an inflationary period that would mask the problem for nearly ten more years.

The inflation of the 1970s actually made it profitable to hold inventory. If the margin on a product was 30% and inflation was 10%, then a firm increased its margin as it held the product, at a rate of 33% the first year. Distribution was a good field to be in, since distributors by nature held inventory and it was appreciating at such high rates. The process encouraged large inventories and covered up a lot of sins. Low inflation in Japan, however, prevented the same phenomenon, and so the research on TQM and JIT continued. In particular, Japan was making great strides in the area of setup reduction.

Setup reduction focused on reducing the amount of time and expense it took to initiate an action like changing over a machine or issuing a purchase order. The most dramatic success was the work of Shigeo Shingo and others on reducing machine change over time.[5] The reduction in purchase or transaction costs was not emphasized to the same degree. Since distribution is a transaction-driven business, transaction cost reduction would have hit home sooner. Distribution was not emphasized in the Japanese research efforts, however, so American distributors were given a reprieve. American manufacturers, however, were in for a considerable shock.

The 1980s brought a new era for manufacturing. Inflation was reined in during the early eighties, so inventory profits went away; suddenly holding inventory cost money. In addition, for the first time since World War II, American manufacturers had competition to face, and it was formidable. Europe and Japan had recovered from the war, and there was now more capacity than demand. U.S. firms could no longer sell merchandise as fast as they could make it. What was worse, the competition had lower cost structures and better-quality merchandise. American firms fought back gamely, using marketing techniques, but the battle was a losing one. For the first time, American manufacturers took a serious look at JIT and TQM. It was not to be an easy transition, however.

As the manufacturing community suffered losses and worked through the TQM and JIT learning curves, distributors remained largely unaffected. Manufacturers were rushing to get out of the inventory business, and though inventory profits from inflation were gone, demand for distribution services (especially local inventory) soared. There was a cloud on the horizon, however: as the demand for local inventory and JIT delivery increased, margins started to narrow. Manufacturers also started to pressure distributors to adopt TQM and, in particular, ISO 9000 standards to fit in with their own quality strategies.

ISO 9000 standards were a European-initiated effort to bring quality-control measurement under a single umbrella. It was quite successful and went a long way toward introducing the distribution community to TQM. JIT was slower to mature. TQM was, in fact, an enabler for JIT, since poor quality led to stockouts (the bane of JIT). Until the TQM movement gained momentum, American manufacturers had great difficulty implementing JIT. Once TQM was well understood and widely adopted, JIT was the next logical step. While TQM and ISO 9000 were comparatively successful in distribution, JIT would prove to be one of the biggest challenges in distribution history.

Manufacturers typically handled JIT using a three-pronged approach. First, setup reduction and TQM were applied internally to production lines to eliminate the need for work in process (WIP) inventory. WIP is typically the largest inventory in a plant. Next, suppliers were asked to deliver directly to the manufacturing line Just in Time for processing. This forced suppliers to carry more inventory to avoid shutting down the manufacturing lines. The need for ready access to inventory increased the supply chain's dependence on distributors, and the increase in supplier inventories caused many to claim that JIT merely pushed inventory upstream.

The third point of attack was less controllable. Manufacturers tried as much as possible to "fix" production schedules to limit forecast error. This meant that customer demand could not be met in some cases, and those most likely to get left out were small customers. Those customers would have to either carry more inventory or rely on distributors. Distribution inventories had to expand again. Inventory was being pushed downstream as well as upstream, and most of it was going into distributor warehouses. Manufacturers showed tremendous success at reducing their own inventories, but the supply chain saw only marginal gains.

There was an obvious need to rethink the supply chain. SCM came about as a response to the failure of JIT to fully benefit the end user. Essentially, SCM is JIT on a global basis. The causes of distribution inventories were principally information based: poor forecast information and short response times under JIT were forcing distributors to carry large inventories. SCM would force distributors to look at how they applied forecasting and exchanged information with their customers and suppliers, and how they tracked and measured system performance. Information management would be the key to SCM. While SCM theory was being developed, the Internet and e-business were also being developed. The latter two would come together to change the way the supply chain looked at distribution.

Supply Chain Management Goals

Understanding the SCM goals requires starting with the end user and working backwards through the supply chain. The end user wants useful products, at the right time and place, at the lowest possible cost. These requirements have not changed much from the beginnings of commerce. SCM takes these goals and translates them to actionable objectives that are tracked throughout the supply chain, rather than having each member act as an island.

The first goal, useful products, requires that the entire supply chain understand the end user's needs. Distributors offer flexibility to the end user by aggregating many products across many manufacturers into one-stop shopping. The greater the flexibility, the greater the inventory cost as more products are added to the distributor's offering. If the supply chain has a poor understanding of the end user's needs, then either more products will be needed in the distributor's catalog or the end user will be forced to operate with less than optimal support. Each alternative is a loss for the supply chain, and each is information dependent. The end user's needs, both current and future, must be captured and passed up the supply chain to manufacturers and their suppliers. Part of the problem is effective capture of buying patterns and unsatisfied requests. The other issue involves extrapolating probable future needs from the end user's environment before they occur.

The second goal is to meet the end user's needs at the right time and place. This is a capacity-management issue. If sufficient capacity is made available and the appropriate lead time is provided, the supply chain can meet the end user's time window. Capacity comes in two forms: production and stored. Production capacity requires availability and a sufficient time window to produce and deliver. Stored capacity is inventory that is used to protect the firm from stockouts. Stored capacity can only be reduced if the causes of stockouts are reduced. Both are forecast dependent. If the forecast is 100% accurate for the time period in question and capacity is available, then the end user's order can be met. If the forecast is inaccurate and planned capacity is not available, then excess capacity will be needed to meet the end user's request. Excess capacity can be idle machinery, but more than likely it will be inventory (stored capacity). Excess capacity, either inventory or equipment, is expensive and increases cascading costs in the supply chain that ultimately affects the end user's cost. Forecasting and capacity planning are information based.

The process of getting useful products to the right place at the right time can run counter to the final objective: the lowest possible cost. TQM, however, has demonstrated that quality costs far less than many once thought and in many cases pays for itself.[6] The same may be true for distribution processes. A better forecast will reduce system costs through reduced need for inventory and reduced stockouts for the end user. Better forecasting allows for better capacity planning, which translates into better availability and less idle capacity, production or stored. SCM proposes better supply chain planning by starting with the end user's needs and setting up forecasting and capacity planning methodologies that target the end user instead of simply meeting the needs of the firm in question.

New Expectations for Distributors

What does all this mean for distributors? Put simply, distributors will have to manage their customers needs, transfer significant information up the supply chain in a timely fashion, and cooperate with other supply chain members in using that information to reduce cost for the end user. The distributor's role has not changed; these expectations have always existed. What has changed is the volume and speed of transfer of the information side of the distributor's business.

SCM seeks to decrease costs and increase customer service simultaneously. The only way to do so is to greatly improve information-related activities in the supply chain. Distributors will be asked to increase their information gathering, handling, and analysis.

The information-gathering expectation means that distributors will be expected to obtain greater information volume and/or quality from the end user. The ability to do so will vary from channel to channel, but, as this book will demonstrate, every channel will have both the need and the opportunity to improve end user data. Greater volume can take many forms, from increased use of customer feedback mechanisms like surveys to sales force automation, where information that formerly only resided in a salesperson's head is transferred to the distributor's information system.

Better quality means that sources of inaccuracy are reduced or eliminated, the first and most obvious being lack of timeliness. The older information is, the less reliable it is. Information automation will offer many opportunities to transfer data more quickly through the supply chain. Quality also applies to the types of information generated. Forecasts, for instance, can be greatly enhanced by the use of direct customer and salesperson input under controlled circumstances. Information that was formerly unavailable for sharing with suppliers will become available through new technologies as the e-business movement proceeds.

Information handling refers to the stress distributor systems will undergo as this veritable mountain of information is dumped into them. Many distributors have already discovered that e-business overwhelms their legacy or ERP (Enterprise Resource Planning) system. A legacy planning system is an outdated computer system passed on to IT personnel and managers, who apply it to planning problems that have changed, using awkward data linkages to newer systems.[7] An ERP system allows a company to replace inefficient legacy systems and to homogenize and integrate disparate corporate databases.[8] Collecting information is one thing—what to do with it when it becomes available is another. This is a technology issue and, therefore, somewhat short term in nature. Even so, skill in handling large volumes of data will be valued for some time to come.

Information analysis skills could become a differentiator for distributors. Suppliers have long counted on distributors to open up new markets, maximize opportunities with existing customers, and ensure that supply meets demand. From forecasting to marketing studies to new product development ideas, there are many opportunities for analysis that improves the efficiency of the supply chain. Other supply chain members will conduct their own analysis, but the distributor's unique position in relation to the end user will make distributor information different from that available to other supply chain members and should add considerable value.

The new expectations will, therefore, revolve around the distributor as information manager in either marketing or logistics. The distributors will continue in their role of marketer for manufacturers and logistician for end users, but that role will become information intensive and customer/supplier expectations will drive distributors toward better gathering, handling, and analysis of that information.

Customer Alliances

E-business is, in many ways, an outgrowth of Supply Chain Management. The SCM movement already existed, but few believed it would advance quickly, since information management needs were so high. E-business was quickly recognized as an enabler for SCM and was even seen as a substitute for distribution. As was explained in Chapter 1, this expectation was an oversimplification of distribution processes, but the belief that e-business would transform distribution was grounded in fact. The advent of e-business tools has thrown many SCM programs into hyperdrive.

Perhaps the most prevalent feature of SCM is customer and supplier alliances. Customer alliances have long existed in programs like Vendor Managed Inventory (VMI) and Integrated Supply (I/S). SCM rolls these programs under its umbrella. Alliances are key to information exchange. VMI and I/S, though principally outsourcing arrangements for customers, are major information opportunities for distributors. Any distributor in such an arrangement who does not take advantage of the increased quality of information available is likely to fail.

SCM programs are customer driven. Many customers perceive the exclusivity of such arrangements as a tremendous value to distributors. They have, therefore, negotiated hard over these arrangements, putting pressure on distributor margins. VMI and I/S have higher service requirements, inventory management (if not outright ownership) being foremost, which has put further pressure on distributor margins. If the additional volume and increased information quality cannot be capitalized upon, many distributors will suffer from extreme margin erosion (some already have).

Supplier Alliances

By the end of 2000, the e-business movement had increased supplier power. Alternative channels of distribution sprang up in the form of "dot-coms" at first, then evolved into channels that could be supplier dominated through the use of third-party logistics carriers (3PLs) in conjunction with e-business tools.[9] These channels have failed to materialize in all industrial sectors. However, the possibility exists for supplier-dominated channels to materialize in most supply chains.

This change in dynamics increased supplier power. The traditional business models had, in effect, become unfrozen. Most members of the channel recognized this fact and began scrambling to gain an advantage. This traditional "island" approach of adversarial relationships within the supply chain led to considerable breakdowns in channels. Many manufacturers sought to change the channel dynamics before the models "refroze."

One of the major objectives was a closer relationship with end users. Suppliers felt the distributor owned this relationship and frequently manipulated it to the manufacturer's disadvantage. The new environment offered the opportunity, and the tools, to change this arrangement. As part of their new distributor alliance, many manufacturers began to demand direct, unfiltered end user information. Manufacturers felt this information would increase their understanding of the market, leading to better planning.

Other channels had already experienced this sort of changed relationship. Channels that had already adopted e-business through the use of EDI had encountered these same issues and had arrived at different ways of dealing with the problem. In retail, the suppliers had been expected to carry out VMI as the customer (retailer) came closer and closer to a "hands off" inventory policy. In electronics distribution, the supplier developed franchise arrangements with distributors, with detailed expectations for information exchange and support for the manufacturer's products. In the latter arrangement, the manufacturer had become a customer. In the former, the manufacturer shouldered a major burden in the interest of getting closer customer contact.

Evolving Channels

The "unfrozen" business models caused great consternation in traditional channels as manufacturers, distributors, 3PLs, and customers jockeyed for position. It seemed likely that models developed in retail and electronics would be introduced in more channels but that other channels would take an entirely different direction. Integrated Supply for instance, popular in Maintenance, Repair, and Operations (MRO) supply, would have to be handled differently, but there were opportunities for e-business to have a tremendous impact on I/S. How these other channels would be handled and how manufacturer/distributor/3PL/end-user relationships would look was still unclear at the end of 2000.

This positioning had a worrisome backdrop to it as well. Those firms that had jumped into e-business were finding it could be extremely costly and that many issues were outside of just one supply chain member's control. Teamwork (alliances) with customers and suppliers would be essential to e-business success. The stage was set for the next step, a refreezing of the business models in their new form. Partnerships were going to be a key factor in e-business success. The SCM principles of alliances and cooperation in the supply chain would be the path to e-business. E-business was the enabler to SCM, and vice versa.

Distributor Retrospective

David Miller must understand that Fluid Dynamics has to manage the needs of its customers and transfer this information up the supply chain to its suppliers in a timely fashion. Fluid Dynamics has an excellent opportunity to decrease costs and increase simultaneously customer service. Also, Fluid Dynamics has the potential to differentiate itself from other fluid power distributors by developing the appropriate information analysis skills. The key for David Miller's team is to develop a plan of action and then successfully implement the plan.

Issues to Consider

1. To what degree will e-business enable supply chain management?

2. What were the two business movements in the post–World War II U.S. that reshaped the business world?

3. What was the financial environment of the 1970s, and what was its impact on distributors?

4. What have been the three principal elements of the manufacturers' response to JIT, and what were the likely reasons why their response was unsuccessful?

5. How will supply chain management help to reduce production and stored capacity?

6. What are the challenges, from the distributor's perspective, that e-business brings to customer and supplier alliances?

Notes

1. L. P. Bucklin, *A Theory of Distribution Channel Structure* (Berkeley, Calif.: Institute of Business and Economic Research, University of California, 1966). C. Scott and R. Westbrook, "New Strategic Tools for Supply Chain Management," *International Journal of Physical Distribution and Logistics Management* 21 (1): 23–33, (1991).

2. Lisa M. Ellram, "Supply-Chain Management: The Industrial Organization Perspective," *International Journal of Physical Distribution & Logistics Management* 21 (1): 13–22 (1991).

3. R. Johnston and P. T. Bolwijn, "Beyond Vertical Integration—The Rise of the Value-Adding Partnership," *Harvard Business Review* 66 (4): 94–101 (1988).

4. W. L. Currie, "Revisiting Management Innovation and Change Programs: Strategic Vision or Tunnel Vision?" *Omega* 27 (6): 647–660 (1999).

5. S. Shingo, *A Revolution in Manufacturing: The SMED System* (Stamford, Conn.: Productivity Press, 1985).

6. P. R. Crosby, *Quality Is Free* (Milwaukee, Wisc.: Quality Press, 1979).

7. J. F. Shapiro, *Modeling the Supply Chain* (Pacific Grove, Calif.: Wadsworth Group, Thomson Learning, 2001).

8. *Ibid.*

9. Gary J. Cross, "How E-business is Transforming Supply Chain Management," *IEEE Engineering Management Review* 28 (3): 17–19 (2000).

Tactical Planning for Modern Distribution

Distributor Perspective

Morgan Brown is the CEO and owner of Brown Supply Co., headquartered in Naperville, Illinois. Brown Supply is a specialty industrial distributor carrying items specifically for the woodworking industry. The range of items includes decorative and functional hardware and fittings, shop supplies, surfacing materials, board and panel products, and tools and machinery. Brown Supply catalogs and inventories over 65,000 stock keeping units (SKUs) for its customers who are involved in the fabrication and sale of cabinets and countertops. Brown Supply has twenty-four branch locations located in the Midwest, Southwest, and Southeast. Recently, Morgan Brown has considered the implementation of a "new" information technology system that will allow the customers of Brown Supply to place orders via the Internet. Morgan also wants to develop a protocol that will allow customers to view the inventory of Brown Supply via the Internet. An information technology system provider has advised Morgan that such an implementation can be accomplished without disrupting the existing business processes and that existing personnel within Brown Supply can effect the implementation. However, Morgan Brown has some doubts regarding the ability of his people and the impact the new system might have on his business.

Introduction

The distributor's position in the supply chain has not changed much. However, customer expectations and the functions of the distributor in the supply chain are changing rapidly. A distributor is now expected to be more of an information-based, as opposed to inventory-based, organization. Inventory management will continue to be an important activity, but the distributor will be expected to minimize inventory needs for all supply chain members and to enhance other opportunities that better information processing will provide. These new expectations will require distributors to rethink their approach to the market both strategically and tactically.

Strategic decisions will revolve around the services each distributor chooses to offer. Some distributors will choose to focus on high-level service environments like Integrated Supply (I/S) or Vendor Managed Inventory (VMI) and develop software/hardware solutions that largely automate those environments and serve the supply chain to maximum advantage. Other distributors will choose to focus on a more technically competent sales force that is supported by new technological tools. Thus, the number of potential strategies is limited only by the number of value-added services that distributors currently offer, as well as new value-added services that may become possible under new technologies.

Once the strategic decisions are made, tactical decisions will be necessary for strategy implementation. Tactical decisions are typically developed for one to three years and require that the organization have the necessary capability to meet its strategic goals. Tactical implementation is somewhat difficult because the e-business movement proposes to position expensive and complex technology, seamlessly integrate that technology into customer service operations, and then leverage the technology to decrease supply chain costs or increase customer value. For example, distributors who have undertaken the challenge of introducing e-business into their operations have discovered it to be very expensive and difficult to implement. Failure to develop and implement extensive tactical plans will doom an e-business initiative.

How E-business Will Reshape the Distributor

Distribution occurs through a looped activity that meets customer demand through certain physical processes.[1] From the customer's viewpoint, the Distribution/Logistics Loop provides a highly detailed picture of the principal functions provided by a distributor. Figure 3.1 depicts these functions.

The loop begins with a customer demand forecast, which with some degree of accuracy starts the replenishment process. Replenishment (purchasing) then utilizes the forecast and supply capacity to make a buy/produce decision. If stored capacity (inventory) is not sufficient to meet forecasted customer demand, then the replenishment planners will make a purchase or produce decision that depends on supplier (internal or external) capability to meet the order. If the supplier is limited in capacity or flexibility, the planners will be forced to carry additional inventory in safety

fig. 3.1 **The Distribution/Logistics Loop**

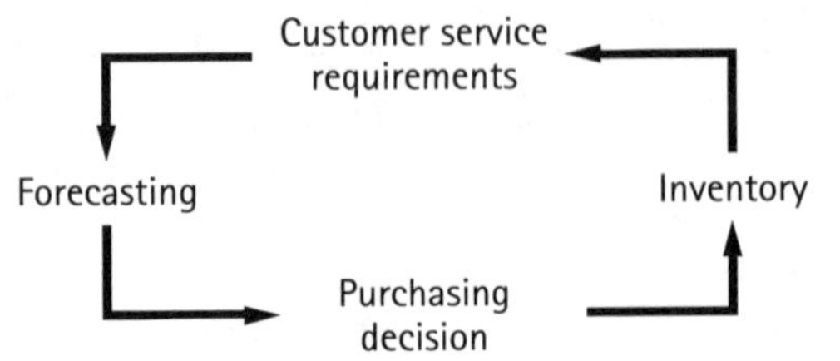

Customer service
requirements

Forecasting

Inventory

Purchasing
decision

Source: Reprinted with permission of APICS—The Educational Society for Resource Management, Alexandria, VA, *Production and Inventory Management Journal,* Vol. 1, No. 1, First Quarter, 1999.

stock to protect against stockouts (capacity-limited supplier) or to buy/produce in larger amounts to meet minimum order requirements (flexibility-limited supplier). Larger safety stocks or larger purchases both result in larger inventories.

Once the inventory arrives, it must be allocated and managed. Ultimately, either customer expectations are or are not met, and the process starts over with another forecast. Note how many opportunities there are for information system involvement:

1. The forecast is entirely information driven.

2. The purchasing decision is also entirely information driven.

3. Inventory management requires an understanding of where product is, how much is on hand, what the classification is, how it should be allocated, etc.

4. The customer service metrics, the outcome of the process, are entirely information driven.

In short, the entire physical-activity loop of a distributor is information driven. This implies that an information loop overlays (and controls) the physical process loop. The information loop, however, flows backwards and provides information on what has happened rather than what will happen. This second loop consists of metrics and tracking signals that can be used for evaluation and control of current operations or future decision making (see Figure 3.2).[2]

The key to transitioning into an information-driven environment involves capturing these information sources and putting them to work properly. The process of obtaining and properly utilizing information sources is highly tactical in nature, and a great deal of this book is devoted to such a process. Before information can be properly utilized it must be obtained, or captured. Such an activity implies that hardware/software assets and redesigned people-driven processes are in place to generate information for the system to capture.

Capture requires processes that store information as it is generated. There are two aspects involved in capturing information. On the one hand there must be physical information technology assets in place for capture purposes. On the other, there must be information handling processes in place that capture the right information,

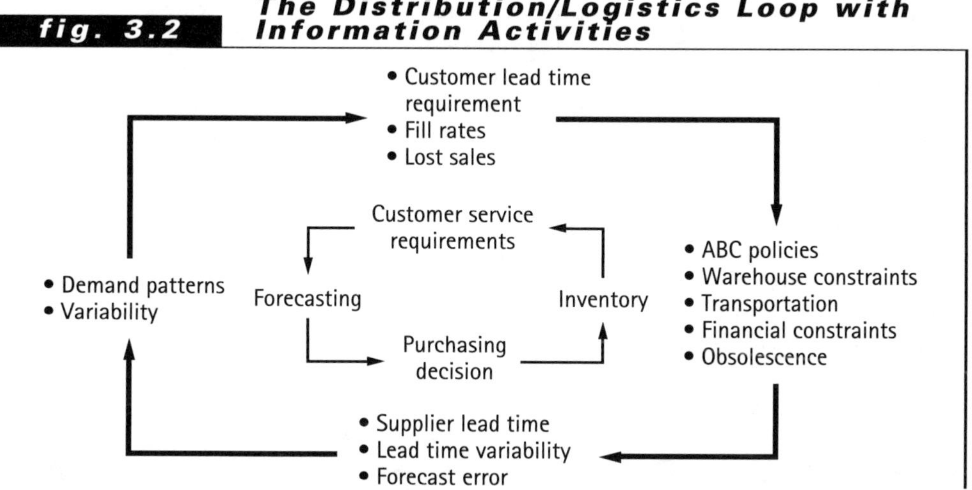

Source: Reprinted with permission of APICS—The Educational Society for Resource Management, Alexandria, VA, *Production and Inventory Management Journal,* Vol. 1, No. 1, First Quarter, 1999.

at the right time, in the right quantity, and in the right form. The nature of information technology is that physical assets will change quickly and that these assets must be evaluated at the time of adoption. A common mistake made by technology consumers is buying underpowered hardware or software solutions that are not adequate for their environment.

On the hardware side, upgrading is more expensive than making the initial investment. Thus, if a company is to err, it is best to buy more powerful hardware than the firm believes is needed. Information-processing expectations tend to increase exponentially, and system capabilities can be overwhelmed quickly. Distributors are in a particularly information-rich environment that will challenge information systems.

For software, the challenge is more complex. Software packages offer many different capabilities at varying levels of sophistication. What this means, simply, is that a firm may wish or need to increase its capability to forecast, buy, or manage inventory or physical processes and may have its effectiveness limited by its software. As an example, when this book was written, there were a number of software packages that depended on classic inventory theory for replenishment purposes, but some applied the theory more accurately or more extensively than others.

Some packages, for instance, allowed statistical estimation of safety stock dynamically in real time (see Chapter 9 for a description of setting dynamic safety stocks), while others required the firm to set safety stocks for all products and feed it into the system. If a firm had a large number of products with highly seasonal demand patterns, it had to reset all safety stocks twice per year to avoid carrying summer safety stocks in the winter (too much inventory) or winter safety stocks during the summer (potential stockouts). Even this is suboptimal, because the safety stock should increase or decrease with sales activity and should be different from week to week as demand and supply conditions change. Also, some software packages had several flaws. For example, they were incapable of setting safety stock dynamically and could not track supplier performance or forecast error. These software packages could not factor supplier performance and forecast error into safety stock calculations. Such flaws create serious problems because the only reason to carry safety stock is to prepare for lead-time variability (supplier performance) or forecast error.

The safety stock issue is only one among many weaknesses that may still exist in some software packages. If a distributor is to be the information/inventory specialist for the supply chain, such weaknesses should be avoided if possible. In essence, the distributor should understand the limitations of its software package and take into account these limitations.

Matching Distribution Processes to Information Technology

Positioning resources requires an understanding of what is needed. In the past, this decision was fairly simple once a strategic direction was established. Equipment speeds and personnel needs were well understood, and a cost/benefit analysis of new technology was straightforward. Economic and financial models for payback periods, net present value, break-even analysis, etc. were well established and understood by most firms. All that was required was for the organization to determine the potential financial benefits of their processes and then compare these benefits to the cost of new technology.

In contrast, e-business and internal information systems have little performance history associated with their implementation. Utilizing such systems may change processes so dramatically that past history is rarely representative of what the environment will look like after the new technology is introduced into the firm's operation. This lack of representative history has made benefit projections highly unreliable (difficult to forecast). Another problem is the fact that the new technology has been, for many industrial experts, a black box, presenting many firms with great difficulty in making e-business decisions. This seeming inability to apply traditional financial measures to information technology has caused many individuals to proclaim that traditional financial measures do not apply to e-business.[3] That has proven to be a dangerous approach.

Wall Street backed many failed e-business ventures with considerable funds. Many of those ventures (the dot-coms) failed because their business models did not appeal to buyers or suppliers. The failure of these e-business solutions had a number of root causes, including inexperienced management, lack of Internet utilization in purchasing decisions by potential customers, technology shortcomings, and a poor match between traditional business processes and the new technology.[4] The dot-com shakeout in the summer of 2000 was mostly driven by the first three problems, but the last one, matching traditional business processes with the new technology, will be the most significant problem facing distribution in the future.

Before addressing the process/technology match, it is important to consider why the other three issues will cease to matter in the near future. The problem of inexperienced management was an outgrowth of the belief that the dot-coms could replace traditional businesses such as distributors. Technology specialists who could "think outside the box" were considered better suited to building the new channels because they would not be constrained by old paradigms and they understood how the Internet worked. This view assumed that Internet technology was more difficult to understand than supplier/distributor/customer relationships. That belief is no longer widely held, and e-business is now driven by traditional businesses or by technology providers partnering with traditional business channels.

The lack of Internet utilization was related to technology shortcomings. The Internet did not take off in 2000 as a purchasing tool because it was still difficult to use for the following reasons:[5]

1. Lack of data standardization made setting up Web sites for selling product very expensive.

2. The Internet was not accessible enough because of bandwidth problems.

3. Business procedures used by many end users still required a written purchase-order process.

4. Trust and security issues hampered the process as firms jockeyed for position.

The standardization issue still looms large, but many industry associations and individual firms are attacking the problem. Solving the standardization problem will be expensive and difficult, but it will be solved in the next few years. The short-term ramifications of this issue are explored in greater depth in later chapters. The accessibility issue is a high priority for government and industry and should also be overcome in the fairly near future. When the Internet is as easy to access as a telephone, many firms will position themselves to take advantage of this new customer contact tool. Most firms are working toward a "paperless" environment, so end-user purchase-order problems should go away in due time. Trust and security will be discussed in detail in this book, and most companies are giving serious consideration to how their relationships will be handled by e-business. This issue will be difficult to solve and is an important component of this text.

In short, the technology problems should disappear over the next few years, leaving distribution firms with one essential task: getting ready. E-business is not an "out of the box" solution that a firm just buys and installs. As many firms learned with Enterprise Resource Planning (ERP) systems, connecting all information flows seamlessly within the company is a very work-intensive process. Most ERP adopters are still struggling with implementation issues because their internal processes do not match the ERP system.

What does this mean for companies that have not adopted ERP systems? It's simple—no company can achieve the full benefits of e-business without a seamless flow of information throughout the firm. So if a company has not adopted ERP, it will be forced to do so in order to be a major player in the e-business world. This does not necessarily mean everyone should rush out and buy the latest ERP technology; quite the contrary, it means every firm needs to determine how its processes can be information automated. How should distribution processes function in a connected (customer/distributor/supplier) business environment?

The distribution firm must look inward. Distribution processes must be identified, documented, and redesigned to meet information automation requirements. This will require a working strategy for what the firm wishes to accomplish through e-business that is then translated into processes that meet customer service objectives while being both efficient and programmable. First, the firm has to identify and thoroughly document its business processes. Second, it must determine how much value these processes generate for the firm's customers. Noncritical processes should be considered for elimination. Third, the firm must embark on a Business Process Redesign initiative to determine how processes that are critical to customers can be redesigned for the most effective information system automation. Those processes that are resistant to automation should be disassembled into base components that are automated where possible and documented into well-understood, consistent human processes where automation is not possible. The documentation and redesign process will take a great deal of time and cannot be cut short.

Process Mapping Distribution

The documentation of processes will be time consuming but rewarding for distribution firms. It should begin with the customer and work backward through the distributor's supply chain. This means the connection to the customer must be studied first, documented, and then redesigned for optimal performance. Next come the distribution customer support systems (inside/outside sales, transportation, call centers, etc.). Warehouse operations are next, followed by planning/replenishment all the way back to the supplier. Support processes (financial, human resources, etc.) should be considered where most logical, but information systems usually have better capability on these types of processes because efforts like GAAP (Generally Accepted Accounting Principles) normalized such activities before most information systems were written.

Documentation should start with the customer for several reasons. First, in tandem with the process mapping, the firm should be considering whether the process adds value to the customer. Any process that does not add value to the customer is a prime candidate for elimination. Second, as processes are mapped, the firm should also be considering how redesign would affect the customer-facing processes. The reverberations from process design changes upstream should always be thoroughly understood before they are connected to the critical downstream activities. Lastly, the new redesigned processes should maximize information that will be coming upstream from the customer. Knowing what that information will be, in what volume and form, gives the firm an advantage in designing upstream processes that capitalize on its value.[6]

This process-mapping exercise should capture all information activities that are or are not captured or supported by the information system. Detail is important, since programming requires exactness. Many existing software packages support process mapping, although conventions differ as to what different boxes or squares mean. The important point is not the form of the documentation but its thoroughness.

Figure 3.3 provides an example of a process map for a building materials supplier's sales process. The map demonstrates how one fairly minor operation that appears simple when carried out manually becomes incredibly complex when detailed for computer implementation. The reader will note the number of steps that could be eliminated if the process were completely rather than only partially automated. For example, consider the step that matches the computer-generated pick ticket with the handwritten copy. This step is followed by a long series of manual activities offline that could be eliminated if the pick ticket were 100% reliable. To achieve such reliability requires a level of accuracy that does not exist in most information systems, thus the process the company uses has many backups to protect customer service.

It is overly simplistic to state that the company should just trust the information system. Many errors get introduced into systems through poorly designed or only partially connected computer networks. Few companies can afford to leave customer service to a system with low levels of connectivity and poorly designed processes. The chapters in Part Three will address connecting specific distribution processes to information systems. The process map is the starting point detailing all activity.

From Process Mapping to Organizational Realities

Once processes are mapped, the company must go through the redesign activity and load the improved processes that are friendly to or compatible with the information technology system into their system or begin using the processes already programmed into the package. There will be changes in the way the company communicates with its customers and suppliers, and within its own four walls. These changes can reduce flexibility but will (if properly implemented) increase capability. The firm will be less able to adapt to odd requests. Changing customer needs will have to be anticipated in time to alter systems. On the other hand, the company will be able to reduce costs and increase supply chain reliability. This tradeoff will be a major management challenge for distribution firms.

In the current dynamic environment, the tactical decision to redesign systems and to put resources in place will determine the success and viability of distribution firms. This fact has always been clear, but with tools that are difficult to evaluate (IT systems) and rapidly changing customer expectations, the decision-making processes have become more complex. The chapters in Part Two will address the new tools, their true benefits and costs, and how to cost justify the expense of IT implementations. Most importantly, the questions of when to implement and what to expect from implementation will be addressed in greater detail.

fig. 3.3   *Sample Process Map for Sales Transactions*

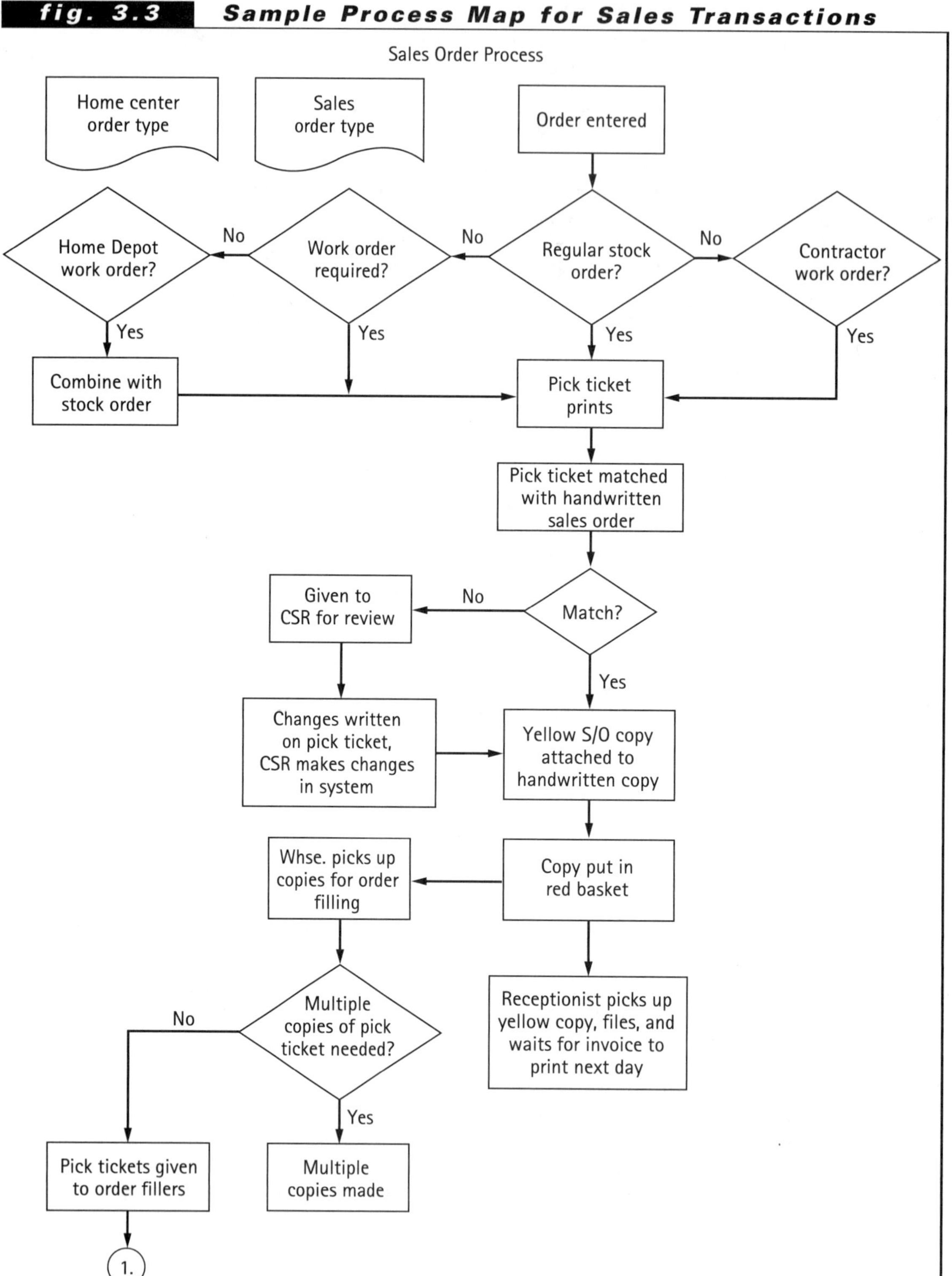

(*Continued on next page*)

fig. 3.3 *(Continued)*

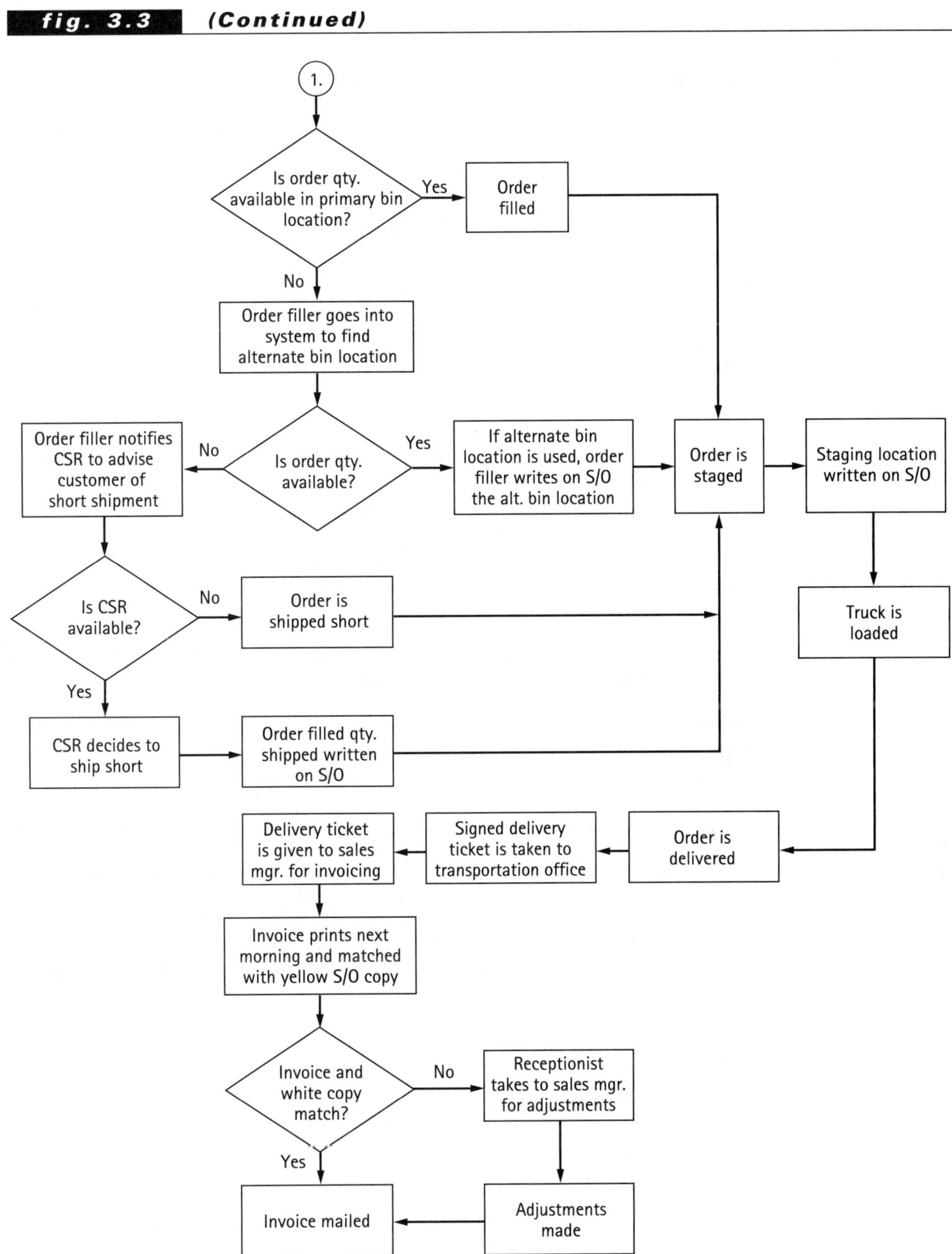

> ### *Distributor Retrospective*
>
> *Morgan Brown must consider how the new information technology system will impact existing processes. To what extent will operating expenses, customer service, customer satisfaction, and the customer value proposition be affected? Do the existing personnel at Brown Supply have the time and ability to implement the new information technology system?*

Issues to Consider

1. What are the two principal factors that drive up inventory levels in the supply chain? Discuss why this happens.

2. Describe the opportunities for applying information systems to improve inventory forecasting.

3. Discuss the root causes why some early e-business ventures (dot-coms) failed. Which of these has been the most significant and why?

4. Discuss what the technology shortcomings have been regarding the utilization of the Internet and how can they be overcome.

5. What steps should a distributor take prior to implementing an ERP system?

6. Why is it important to document physical processes? How can this process documentation be used to improve business processes?

Notes

1. F. Barry Lawrence, "Closing the Logistics Loop: A Tutorial," *Production and Inventory Management Journal* 1 (1): 43–51 (1999).

2. *Ibid.*

3. "News Focus: Analysts Still Can't Learn to Value Dotcoms" *Investor Relations Business* (UMI Article Re. No.: IVRB-54-2 UMI Journal Code: IVRB New York) July 10, 2000.

4. Albrecht Enders and Tawfik Jelassi, "The Converging Business Models of Internet and Bricks-and-Mortar Retailers," *European Management Journal* 18 (5): 542–550 (2000).

5. Michael P. Papazoglou and Aphrodite Tsalgatidou, "Business to Business Electronic Commerce Issues and Solutions," *Decision Support Systems* 29 (4): 301–304 (2000).

6. Martin G. Helander and Halimahtun M. Khalid, "Modeling the Customer in Electronic Commerce," *Applied Ergonomics* 31 (6): 609–619 (2000).

The E-channel

4

The E-business Model

Distributor Perspective

Alpha, Inc., a multinational manufacturer of electronic components with annual sales exceeding $50 billion, uses a strong network of independent distributors to distribute its products. These distributors can market Alpha's products and services to a substantially larger customer base than can be effectively handled by Alpha itself. These distributors provide engineering services, software/hardware configuration and integration, consulting, and a wide array of value-added services. Alpha's top management group is aware that major forces of change are at work in their channel. For example, customers and competitors continue to globalize their operations, and distributors are consolidating. Also, Alpha's top managers realize that the Internet can radically alter market dynamics as companies rethink their core business processes, consumers shop for and purchase goods and services online, and value created and distributed within industries is redefined. Thus, Alpha's top management team is concerned about the effect that e-business might have on Alpha's traditional distribution model. For example, will e-business become a channel that competes with Alpha's existing channel, or can e-business be utilized in such a way that the existing channel is improved?

Introduction

E-business models went through considerable change in the late 1990s and into 2000. The first models focused on e-business as a channel that competed with the physical channel. When this failed to materialize, the e-business channel (or e-channel) developed as a parallel channel that "mirrored" the physical channel and could be used to control, support, and improve the physical goods channel. Market makers that competed with the physical channel disappeared, and ones that supported the channel started appearing as Application Service Providers (ASPs), auction sites for dead or slow-moving inventory, and other infrastructure providers that came to serve the existing distribution channels. Some of the new players were old players who changed in time to stay alive.

Recasting the e-channel in a supporting role shifted the focus from supply chain competition and adversarial relationships to continuous improvement, with end-user needs as the driving force. Manufacturers and distributors began the process of connecting their systems. The process would be difficult and time-consuming, but the rewards would be considerable for all members of the supply chain.

Alternative Channels of Distribution

In its early stages, e-business promised to eliminate the distributor's channel or, at the very least, splinter it into more narrowly defined channels. The former has proved unlikely to occur in many channels, but many still believe the e-channel will allow for alternative channels of distribution. The splintering of these channels into multiple channels is based on the theory that while some distribution functions cannot be replaced by e-business entities (i.e. inventory, transportation, etc.), others could be (financing, customer relationship management, etc.). Logic dictates that those functions that carry the highest margins or offer the greatest benefits to the supply chain will be taken over first.[1] Distributors would see their businesses dissected piece by piece, starting with the most valuable parts. The first target was customer relationship management.

The problem with this reasoning was that it was premature from both a technological and marketing point of view. On the technology side, neither the customer nor the technology provider had systems sufficiently mature to carry out the process. On the marketing side, customers were not, as yet, convinced they needed to seek another channel. Distributors would be given a reprieve in which they could master the e-channel themselves. Even if the distributor would not be ripped apart for a while, the fact remained that alternative channels did exist, and e-business would have an impact on those channels.

In a study conducted at Texas A&M University, the alternative channels of distribution were identified and cast in e-business terms.[2] The resulting channels are described in the following sections.

Manufacturer Direct Sale to the End User

A manufacturer's website on the Internet enables direct transactions with end users (see Figure 4.1). Any end user can buy product from the company catalog through the Internet. This direct marketing technique has been successful in many high-profile cases like Dell Computers and Amazon.com. Although the success of this channel is well documented, industrial applications have been less common.

The lack of industrial applications can be attributed to a variety of factors. The following were some of the early obstacles to a direct channel:

○ Standardization

○ Technical sophistication of the supply chain

○ Distributor value-added services core proposition

  ○ *Inventory management*

  ○ *Transaction volume, multiple small orders*

  ○ *Technical knowledge and after-sale support*

  ○ *Financial support for small customers*

  ○ *Additional product modification*

  ○ *Local transportation*

  ○ *Counter sales and will call*

  ○ *Prospecting sales force*

  ○ *Reverse logistics, i.e. returned goods*

The standardization issue takes two forms: data and process. The data side involves matching all supply chain partners' information so that e-business transac-

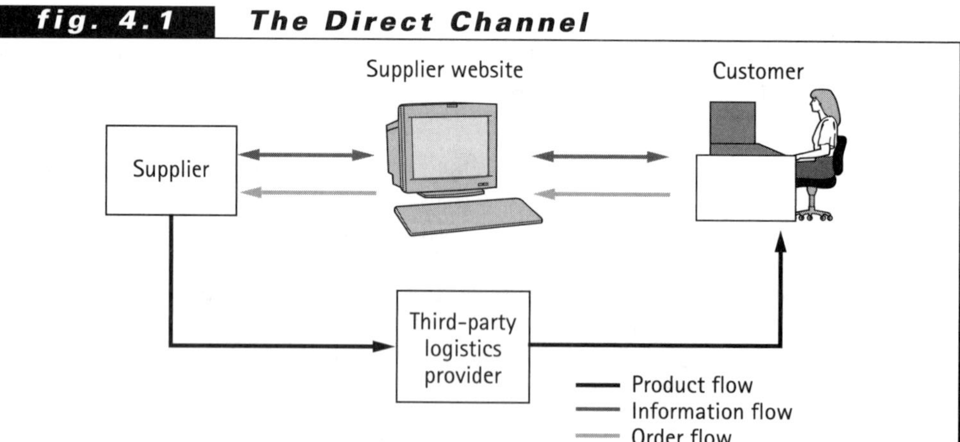

fig. 4.1 *The Direct Channel*

Source: Reprinted with permission of APICS—The Educational Society for Resource Management, Alexandria, VA, *Production and Inventory Management Journal*, Third/Fourth Quarter, 2001.

tions can occur with little transformation of data in the supply chain. The problem is analogous to using a translator in a discussion. A translator will take what one party says in their native tongue and translate it into the language of the listener. Imagine how long this would take if the translator were attempting to handle thousands of speakers all at the same time. The translator would have to be lightning fast and capable of handling any of the thousands of potential languages of each speaker. While speed is a very reasonable demand to make of computers (definitely their strong suit), the concept of handling a virtually endless number of languages is overwhelming when one considers that each language must be coded in its entirety, and many of these so-called languages are in a proprietary format to the transmitting party. Standardization is the subject of much debate in the industry, and there is evidence to suggest that progress is being made. Until standardization of part numbers, product descriptions, etc. becomes developed and widely adopted, this issue will remain a major hurdle to the industry's ability to reap the promise of e-distribution.

Point-to-point connection with every manufacturer and customer with a translation engine for each is therefore not an attractive option for most members of the supply chain. The options are to either develop a supply chain standard or follow a format created by a supply chain leader, with theirs becoming the standard. The technical aspects of standardization are discussed in detail in Chapter 11.

The second aspect of the standardization issue, process standardization, is even more difficult. If one system is to communicate with another, it must understand when and how conversation will take place, what the intent of that conversation is, what the appropriate responses are to different scenarios, and so forth. This standardization of processes so that they work in unison across multiple partners in the supply chain makes the data transformation issue look minor by comparison. The data transformation issue is more immediate, however. It is difficult to plan processes if those processes are unable to understand one another. Until data standardization takes place, the problem is similar to giving instructions in Japanese to an English-speaking person.

Information technology providers, industry associations, and large supply chain captains are hard at work on the data standardization issue. While Chapter 11 will offer insights on what every company must understand and address in data standardization, the majority of this book focuses on the huge task of process standardization.

The next obstacle for the Direct Channel was a lack of technical sophistication on the part of many supply chain partners. The technical problems started with the end user. The end user or the supply chain captain that controls the end user drives most successful supply chain programs. Wal-Mart is an excellent example of a supply chain captain that controls end users and represents their needs. The technical sophistication that has been applied in that channel was driven by Wal-Mart as part of its "Everyday low pricing" strategy. The end user (consumers) made it clear that the highest priority was lowest cost, and Wal-Mart responded with a more efficient supply chain.

The end user in most industrial channels was not immediately looking for supply chain solutions that involved e-business. The distributor would have to play the same role as Wal-Mart in determining what was best for achieving the end user's objectives. The problem was that the distribution channels were too fragmented. There were many industrial channels with many different distributors in each. In the rare cases where a dominant distributor was present, for example, Grainger a broad line distribution firm, the distributor was trying to introduce e-business into an environment where the customer's purchases were scattered across many channels (fluid power, electrical, power transmission, to name only a few) and did not have a consistent process for e-business applications.[3] The e-business processes would have an uphill battle to gain market share. Once the cost of such systems came down and the Internet became substantially easier to use, e-business initiatives would struggle for survival.

If the distributor, who had end-user access, had a problem launching e-business initiatives, others (manufacturers planning to go direct and dot-coms) would face even greater challenges. Displacing distributors also meant displacing their value-added services. Inventory management, counter sales, and will call sales could be outsourced to third-party logistics firms (3PLs) provided they or the manufacturer were willing to take possession of local inventory (neither side appeared anxious to do so). Some technical knowledge could come over the Internet, but the remainder would have to be supplied by third-party engineering firms. Banks and credit card companies could handle financial support for small customers, but, as was noted in the first chapter, many of these customers might be poor credit risks. Local providers could handle product modification and local transportation, but, as many manufacturers and distributors had already discovered, the capacity of these firms was frequently not up to the challenge. A prospecting sales force would also be necessary, since the Internet could not be used to reach some customers, but this would require a considerable expansion in the manufacturer's sales force.

All in all, the distributor was going to be difficult to replace, and, given the narrow margins associated with most distribution, it would be difficult for so many providers to make a profit in the process. A question still remained: If the distributor could not be eliminated in the short run, could the supply chain balance of power be altered in some other fashion? Many different variations are possible, and several were attempted in the late 1990s.

Manufacturer as Information Controller

Even if a pure Direct Channel was not possible, few doubted that information control was very important to one's position in the supply chain. The manufacturer could continue to rely on the distributor for customer information or seek to gain some control. However, the action was risky since any attempt to get closer to the customer might be viewed as a threat by their distributors. The concept of a manufacturer-controlled information network would involve a manufacturer-hosted website for information control of the ordering, and routing of end-user demand (see Figure 4.2).

The order is routed to the distributor who can give the best price quote and is allowed to sell in the corresponding area of the customer (if franchises are present). The order is placed directly with the distributor through the manufacturer's website.

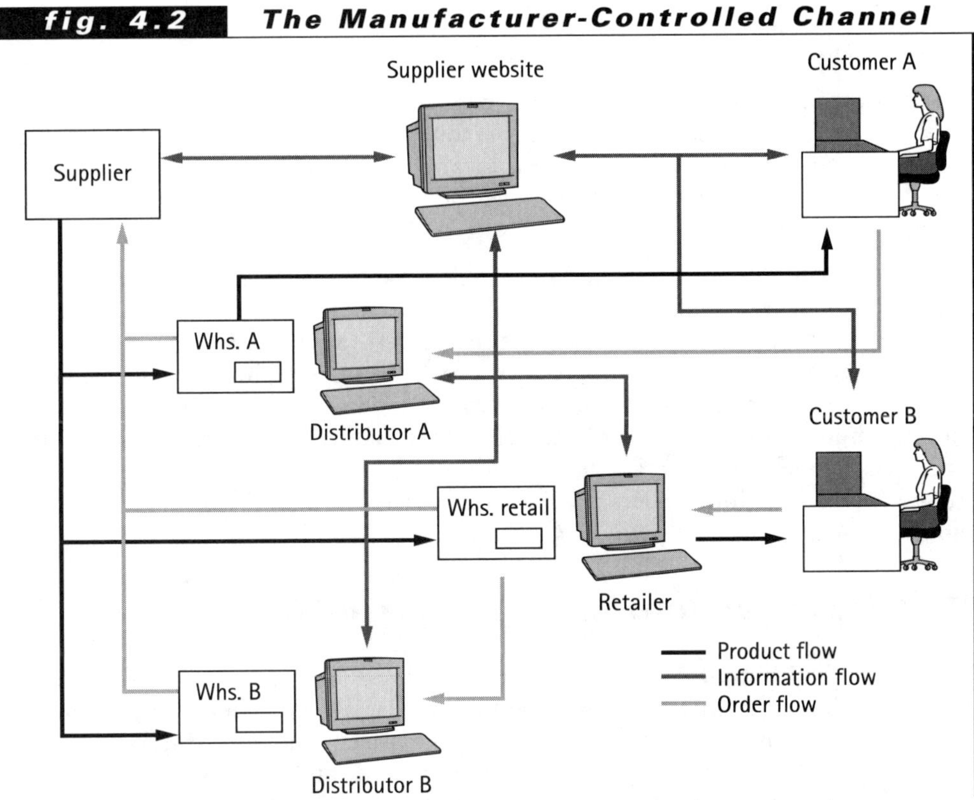

fig. 4.2 **The Manufacturer-Controlled Channel**

Source: Reprinted with permission of APICS—The Educational Society for Resource Management, Alexandria, VA, *Production and Inventory Management Journal,* Third/Fourth Quarter, 2001.

The distributor uses the manufacturer's site or an industry-supported database from the manufacturer's channel to get the updated product specifications and prices. The entire transaction takes place over the Internet. The transaction is immediately recorded by the system at all sites, giving the manufacturer point of sale (POS) customer information. POS information has long been a point of contention, even outright conflict, in the industrial distribution channel. In its basic form, POS information consists of the specific information about which end-use customer bought what specific item, in what quantity, and on what date. The value of this level of information, and the distributors' current reluctance to share it with the manufacturer, is one of the primary impediments to successful e-distribution. The distributor retains all basic functions except for order initiation and exclusive customer information tracking (the manufacturer now has access to customer information as well).

Some of the highest-profile cases of the manufacturer-controlled channel are the auto companies like GM and Ford who started websites to direct the customer to the dealers/distributors in a particular region. The customer can get complete specifications for the product, and even customize the car and get the corresponding minimum retail price. Deals can then be made with the local dealer using the website information.[4]

The effect of other distributor/retailer contributions to the supply chain listed as impediments to e-business are reduced in this model. Technical support, financial services, product value-added services, local inventories, counter sales, transportation services, and the prospecting sales force remain in place at the distributor/retailer operations.

Many distributors and retailers viewed this type of website as a threat. Information control, especially control of customer information, was perceived as necessary to their very survival, and manufacturers' attempts to gain control of it were quietly or, in some cases, openly opposed. In some channel struggles, manufacturers were threatened with complete loss of a distributor or retailer's business if they attempted to reach the customer directly.[5] The key differentiator in the short run was channel power. Franchise distributor/dealer/retailers could be forced to share information (auto dealers provide an excellent example), but others could and did resist.

Distributor as Information Controller

This model has manufacturers, distributors, and customers working in concert to develop an information center controlled by the distributor. The distributor acts as the supply chain information nexus, utilizing the principal manufacturers' and other suppliers' production schedules, customer data, and intelligent software to match customer needs with manufacturer capability. Distributors use their information to optimize their operations, then pass it through to manufacturers for their planning purposes (see Figure 4.3).

The strength of this strategy is that it leaves the inventory, financial, sales, and other distributor activities in place and, therefore, minimizes channel conflict. If transactional data only is passed through, the manufacturer may be viewed as a more benevolent supply chain partner than those that are attempting to control the channel and threatening disintermediation either in word or in deed.

The weaknesses are associated with the necessary financial commitments members of the supply chain must make to participate in e-business initiatives. It forces each to "pick" certain partners for e-business alliances (this may be positive as a motivator). For the manufacturer, it surrenders the role of information controller to the distributor. If a competitor seizes the channel with a direct approach, the manufacturer may be trapped in the distribution model (like Compaq was when Dell went direct).[6]

The Mixed Model

Most channels offer a wide range of products for different types of customers (see Figure 4.4). Those customers may require different distribution channels based on various types of products and transactions. Certain products or customer environments may lend themselves to e-business disintermediation while others may not.

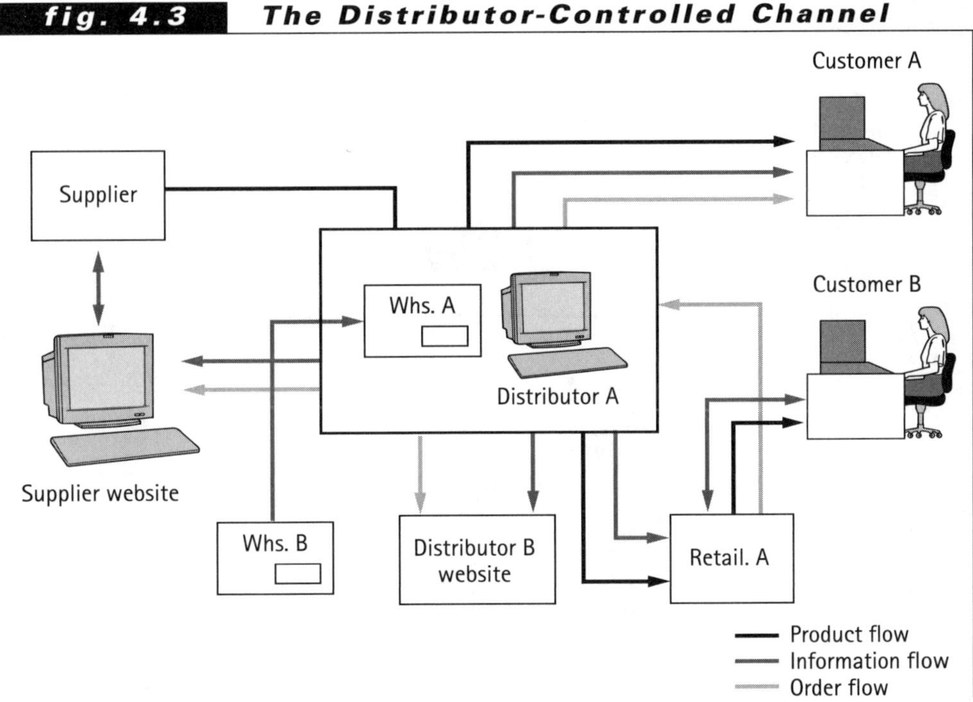

Source: Reprinted with permission of APICS—The Educational Society for Resource Management, Alexandria, VA, *Production and Inventory Management Journal,* Third/Fourth Quarter, 2001.

When considering the value-added services offered by distributors and retailers, some obvious disintermediation scenarios include large customers with technical sophistication in relation to the product, high consumption that meets critical mass for the manufacturer's system, a strong financial status, and the capability to customize product to their needs. A direct channel through a third-party logistics firm could serve this type of customer.

Other customers cannot use direct channels, since they require technical assistance, break/make bulk and local inventory (lack of critical mass), need financial support (small accounts), do not have the capability to customize product beyond the manufacturer's original product, or any/all of the above. These customers need a distributor or a retailer to provide these services. The Internet offers little transactional benefit for these customers. The mixed model reinforces the importance of the distributor/retailer role to these customers. This model, though, looks suspiciously like the one we have come to know as the current model. Have the widely touted benefits of e-business been grossly overstated? Will we continue to do business the same as we always have?

Not exactly. The issue is not simply about whether the direct channel will exist. It did before e-business and will continue afterwards. The question is whether distributor and retailer channels will lose business to the direct channel or vice versa. In

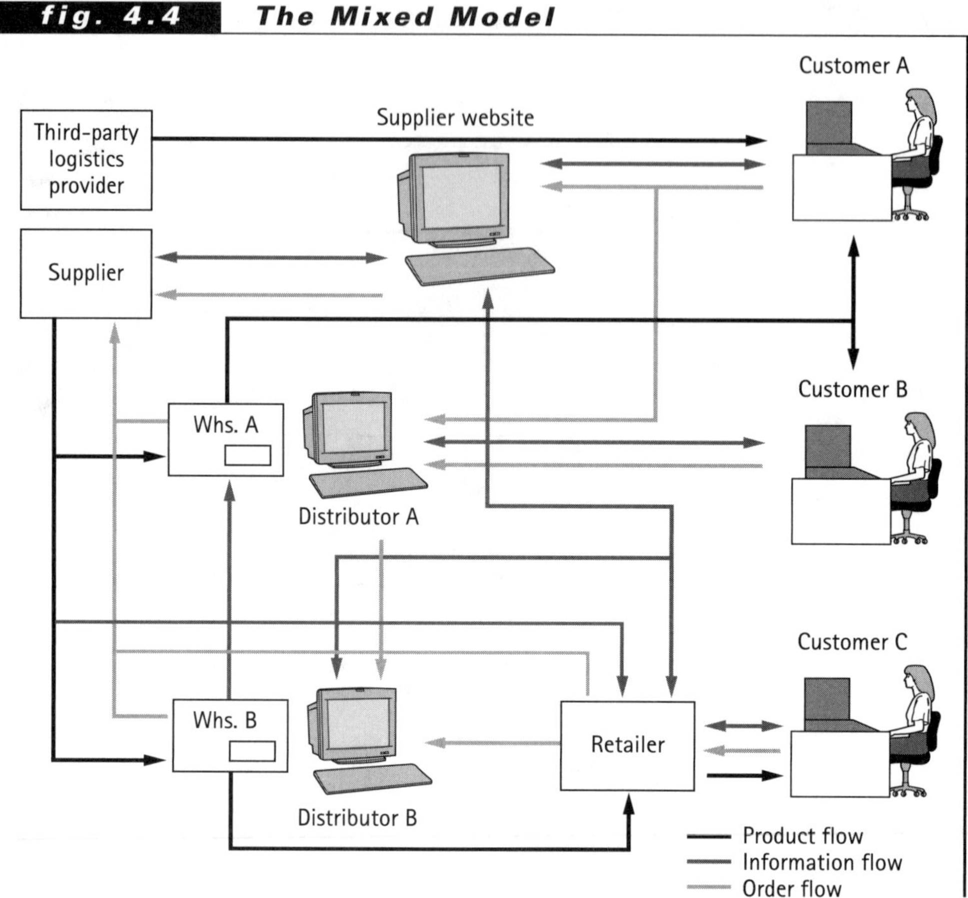

Source: Reprinted with permission of APICS—The Educational Society for Resource Management, Alexandria, VA, *Production and Inventory Management Journal,* Third/Fourth Quarter, 2001.

some markets, the majority of the channel itself could be e-business (stock trading or airline reservations for instance). Any product that can be digitized (information based) could be delivered over the Internet. The technology, though still somewhat insufficient, is evolving rapidly. Music, some books, movies, and all businesses involving pure information are in for dramatic change.

Thus the channels under the mixed model are in conflict—the classic business relationship has become unfrozen. Until it refreezes, there will be considerable tumult as the channels vie for competitive advantage. The manufacturer sees an opportunity to gain more customer control and possibly larger profit margins through the direct channel. Distributors see an opportunity to improve the efficiency of their operations, encroach on the retailer, and possibly use information to "own" the customer, while fearing growth of the other channels at their expense. The retailer faces the same scenario as the distributor.

If the mixed model is the most efficient, then whether the individual channels will prevail depends solely on the value they offer the end user. The value equation is dependent on tools employed in the channel; e-business is one such tool. If e-business is a channel (a distribution means) in a purely informational setting and just a tool in physical product channels, then distributors/retailers need only master the use of the tool to a greater extent than the manufacturer to continue in their role or maybe even grow against other channels. The tool itself is dynamic, however, with new uses evolving all the time. The channels may not refreeze. The ability to adapt may be the only differentiator.

The mixed channel simply suggests automation of current relationships. That scenario could change, however. In the meantime, this model requires all channel members to increase the efficiency of each individual channel. Since the channels are in conflict, this will be exceedingly difficult. Many manufacturers are struggling with strategy to apply to their direct channels while not offending their distributors/retailers.

The mixed model is currently the dominant one in non-information product channels. The failure of the dot-coms in the summer and fall of 2000 demonstrated an overestimation of the Internet as a delivery channel in physical goods markets. What is not clear is whether those models were ahead of their time or just poorly designed business models. As a near-term strategy, the mixed model is safer than others and does not preclude moving to other models when necessary. In fact, it will support migration to other models, since the infrastructure will be in place. If all channel members pursue the mixed model together, the channel will be more efficient, but relationships will remain dicey, since any one of the members will be positioned to make a move on the others.

The Independent Infomediary (The Cannibal)

The book *The Innovator's Dilemma* suggests another channel.[7] Popularly called the "Cannibal," this channel competes with existing channels independently of the company or its supply chain partners (see Figure 4.5). An independent website is supported by the parent company, which exercises no control over its actions. Christensen describes Monster.com (TMP) and eSchwab.com (Schwab) as examples. In each case the parent set up the cybercompany and specifically told it to go after any business it could, including the parent.[8]

The cannibal was introduced into industrial channels in the late 1990s. Its form was a little different from Monster.com or eSchwab, however. TMP and Schwab were 100% information-based firms that could have their principal business taken over by the cannibal. For industrial channels, a manufacturing firm cannot have its business taken over by a cannibal, since an Internet company produces no physical product. The infomediary, instead, cannibalizes the distribution channel. An infomediary is a channel information handler as opposed to a physical materials manager. Note that the entire channel cannot be cannibalized, however—only the information portion. Physical goods handling (logistics) would remain with the distributors and retailers.

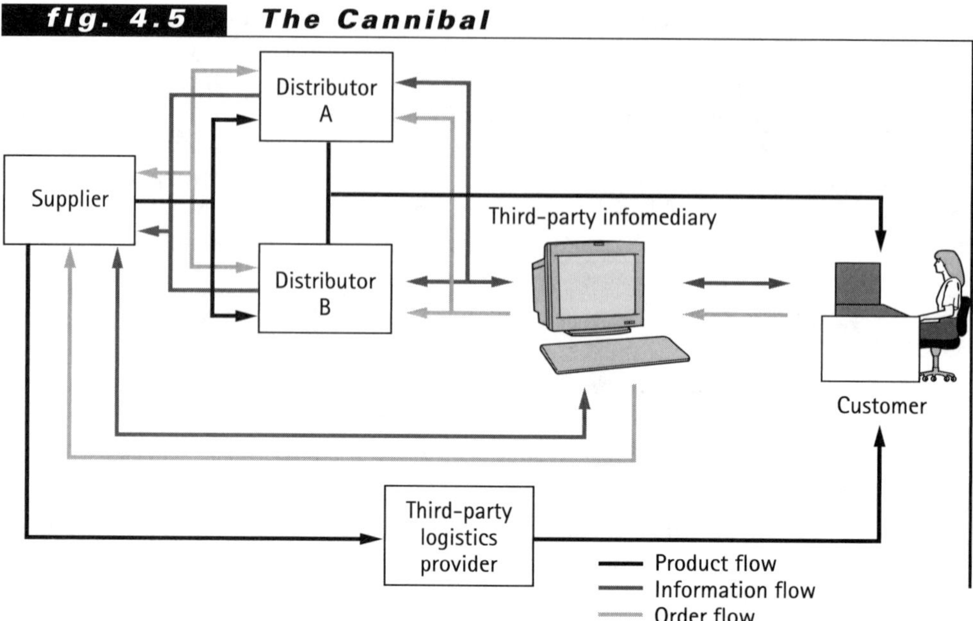

Source: Reprinted with permission of APICS—The Educational Society for Resource Management, Alexandria, VA, *Production and Inventory Management Journal,* Third/Fourth Quarter, 2001.

The concept was not appealing to distributors and retailers and so was most often introduced as a defensive move to prevent independent infomediaries from taking over the channel. If a manufacturer held a strong distribution position in a territory and an independent infomediary were to gain a foothold, the manufacturer could lose market share, and information share along with its distribution channel. Several cannibals were set up to prevent the potential loss of business. Manufacturers and distributors incubated infomediaries and then spun them off with instructions to support the existing distributors. Like the automaker model, the infomediary was to make the sale and then have the existing distributor network handle fulfillment.

Industrial channels accepted the cannibal begrudgingly at first, but when customers did not rush to it, they quickly abandoned the effort. The infomediary was then forced to evolve into an infrastructure provider for the channel (web hosting, website design, etc.). The demise of cannibals was swift, and the only remaining ones in industrial channels would deny ever being anything but an infrastructure provider.

The E-channel

All the variants on distribution channels brought about by e-business suggest the form of distribution channels is heavily dependent on information. There is, in fact, an information channel that leads, supports, and, in general, determines the efficiency of the physical channel. The existence of this channel is the reason for all the excitement surrounding e-business. The form of this information channel (the e-channel) offers considerable insight into the entire e-business movement and gives a shape to e-distribution. If the product is information, the e-channel can also serve as the distribution channel. If not, the e-channel will direct and control the physical channel, and a firm's competitive advantage will be derived from it.[9]

The e-channel works backward from the customer. In other words, information creation starts with the customer and, for the most part, flows upstream towards the manufacturer. There is much inefficiency in most channels, but the e-channel exists in every case. Each step has an information component, which may or may not be automated. The degree to which channel members are willing to allow the "unfiltered" flow of information remains to be determined. Channel members may elect to utilize information filters that separate what they consider to be mission critical information and then pass along only that information essential to the transaction. The number and density of filters are a function of the level of trust that exists among channel members. The completely automated channel is the ultimate goal of e-business.

The End-User Connection: E-marketing and E-sales

The front end of the channel is the customer's order system. This can vary from completely automated systems like Vendor Managed Inventory (VMI), where Point of Sale (POS) information is captured by the manufacturer/distributor and refilled automatically, to a phone call or fax from the customer's purchasing agent. We explore VMI in greater depth in the next chapter. Note, however, that whether the information is automated (VMI) or not (phone), it is still information and can, therefore, be automated when the appropriate technology and relationships exist.

The customer's order system interacts with the distributor through either an electronic connection that automatically collects replenishment information (VMI) or through human interaction. Many feel the automated and human-based systems are so different that the two will never meet in some environments. The best way to analyze that belief is to break the process down to its components.

Take a low-tech environment—sales to job-site contractors. Contractors vary widely in their operations, but most handle their replenishment needs on a personal basis with a distributor or a home center store. If the contractor needs only a few items that are easily picked up and dropped off at the job site, he may have someone drop by a home center store and pick up the items. If, however, the job can be planned in advance and/or large quantities of materials or difficult-to-carry items are to be delivered, he may use a distributor with a private fleet and experience in the handling of those types of materials.

The order will typically go by phone call or fax. How can this order be automated? First consider the customer's hardware, the phone or fax. To automate, the contractor will need a device that can deliver the order faster and with less opportunity for error. PDA or palm top technology looks promising here. The contractor can open up a PDA with cellular capability that has the distributor's catalog installed. After clicking through the radial buttons, the order can be made without any need for human interaction. Many providers are already working on this type of technology.[10] The question is: Will this be any better than the phone call or fax?

The issue breaks down into two components: efficiency and relationships. On the efficiency side, the PDA only requires the contractor to correctly select the item from the catalog. If a phone call is made, the contractor must describe what is needed to the inside salesperson. If the inside salesperson then makes a mistake in keying or understanding, the opportunity for error increases. While it may seem that the PDA cuts the error opportunity in half, however, the inside salesperson frequently will guide the contractor through the order and actually prevent errors. A potential downside aspect to automating the order entry process is the lost opportunity for the inside salesperson to make alternate product recommendations, suggest add-on products, and in general to optimize the sales order. A decrease in information handling may not lead to an increase in efficiency.

If the PDA device is equipped with a scanner to read a bar code on the product, then the error opportunity can be virtually eliminated. However, there are a few other potential problems here as well. First, the contractor may not have any of the desired material on hand to scan into the device. Second, even if he does, building materials products are frequently not bar coded. The difficulties associated with bar coding building materials are numerous and it will be a few years before the industry sees any substantial progress in this area.[11]

There is opportunity for efficiency improvements, however. The contractor can now place the order as soon as the need becomes apparent. This shortens the cycle time between orders. Shorter cycle times, as we shall see in later chapters, reduce stockouts and decrease inventory.

The bigger opportunity in the short run, however, is relationship based. A popular view in distribution is that "people want to deal with people." While that seems entirely reasonable, trends seem to be heading in the opposite direction. The inside sales force has grown rapidly in almost every industry, a trend based on time compression. People have less and less time to do more and more. There does not seem to be an end in sight. It takes far less time to interact with an inside salesperson over the phone than it does to interact with an outside person at your jobsite.

E-business seems well positioned to take advantage of this trend. As cold as it sounds, a customer does not have to ask a computer how its day is going or inquire after its health. Time pressure will cause many to move to more and more automated systems. This means the "relationship" with the customer could be at risk. With the distributor's catalog on a palm top, however, the customer may have an even stronger relationship based on the ease of ordering and reliability of the distributor's logistics systems. Some distributors have already started providing their largest customers with PDAs equipped with the distributor's catalog.

It seems likely that the distributor will continue to automate the customer relationship. If the contractor environment offers opportunities that will likely grow with technological change, then other environments will probably evolve even faster. The PDA is one opportunity area but may not be the optimal answer. An early (in Internet time, a few years is an eternity) application for communication was the website, which combined the e-catalog with e-sales.

The e-catalog is an electronic billboard of sorts. It announces to the world that your company is here on the Internet and ready to do business. The decisions and strategy surrounding the use of PDA or e-catalog technologies are placed in the category of e-marketing, or how your firm intends to market itself in cyberspace. As recently as 1999, this seemed an important innovation. In 2000, many had doubts after seeing the tremendous costs and failures associated with e-marketing.

As described in the direct channel section, many issues have hamstrung the e-marketing concept. The standardization issue looms large and will present many problems for e-business.[12] If a company can get past the back-office integration or translator problem, the next step will be e-sales, or the recording of the transaction in the distribution system.

A recurring theme throughout this book will be that e-business is more about automating existing processes than replacing them. The e-catalog exists as the distributor's current printed catalog. Back-office integration also exists in the current channel. Standardization is achieved through human-assisted processes. Take the data standardization issue. In the current environment, the data standardization translator is the inside salesperson. The customer calls and describes the need, and the inside salesperson "translates" that need into product numbers or SKUs (Stock Keeping Units) the distributor's system can understand.

The translation capability of the inside salesperson is a function of training, experience, and the knowledge of the salesperson, which in many cases limits the service capability of the distributor. The distributor's ability to efficiently and effectively process customer calls is constrained by the number and availability of capable inside salespeople. Automating many of the routine sales order transactions may offer the distributor the ability to have more inside salespeople available for technical, value-added customer phone calls.

Process standardization takes place as well. The customer knows the distributor's phone (or fax) number, hours of operation, delivery schedules, and principal product offerings. This knowledge about the distributor's operation allows the customer to communicate at the right time and in the appropriate way with the distributor. Customer information traditionally comes from standard sources like a phone book, references, and history of direct contact with distributors. Process standardization requires that all this information be captured and controlled by the distributor/customer system-to-system exchange. Standard sources (the phone number or dial-up) are easy for both the distributor and customer to automate. Customer needs and behavior are going to be very difficult.

Take the inside salesperson for our contractor. When the contractor calls, the inside salesperson may have to quote a special price based on the customer relationship (matrix pricing will be addressed later). In addition, there may be special delivery instructions for operations based on the customer's environment that the customer is not even aware of. Customers know what the delivery is but not necessarily how it will be carried out. The inside salesperson may need to handle a myriad of other issues such as suggestive selling (the customer may need to be reminded that hangers are needed for the light fixture), technical information, intervention on credit issues, special bundling or kitting needs, unusual product modifications, delivery time windows, and prioritization of orders. Automation of the process will be more difficult than planned for in most systems.

An important point to stress, however, is that complexity means opportunity. One plumbing distributor maintains a 30% margin in an industry that averages 12% margins. Typically the difference between high-performance and average firms is usually not very high (a few margin points). How does this plumbing distributor achieve this level of success? The answer lies in information automation, well-designed processes, and a complex environment. The distributor uses technology not commonly associated with his industry.

Electronic distributors are well known for using Statistical Process Control and real-time information to achieve high fill rates while minimizing inventory. This plumbing distributor uses the same technology in an industry better known for using paper-based systems and large inventories. The resulting fill rates increase sales, and the world-class processes decrease inventory. These techniques have been slow to reach other plumbing and building materials distributors because of how difficult they are to implement in such a complex environment. The complexity of the environment, however, means the savings typically associated with these programs are more significant if the systems are successfully applied. Electronics distributors fight for tiny increments of improvement in efficiency with advanced solutions that must be grounded in theory and rigorously applied. Other types of distributors can show dramatic success with minor changes if they overcome the complexity of their environment.

The Back End: E-resource Management and E-procurement

The distributor's information management function, commonly called the back office system, refers to whatever configuration of information tools the firm uses to manage its operations. It can range from a disparate group of information tools like spreadsheets and salespeople's day timers to a fully operational Enterprise Resource Planning (ERP) system.

ERP systems have been growing in use since the mid 1990s. The early adopters met with many challenges related to the lack of standardization of information flows and process design. The latter problem was the most troubling, since the early systems lacked flexibility, and domain experts who knew how to match distribution processes to information technology solutions were rare. Since the process design problem is the central theme of this book, ERP implementation challenges make an interesting study in terms of what the challenges and potential solutions will be for e-business.

If the ERP revolution had been complete before e-business started, it would be clearer what direction firms should take in implementing their e-business strategy. Unfortunately, many small and midsized firms have not even started ERP adoption, and many large firms have not completed their implementation. This lack of internal information integration will serve as a roadblock to supply chain integration. The ERP system integrates all internal information activities, and this internal e-channel will have to be connected before an external one can be developed.

Many will choose to connect their customers and manufacturers before they complete their own internal integration. This strategy may be necessary for relationship purposes, but, in the long term, the firm will not fully realize the benefits of supply chain integration until internal operations are fully connected to and participating in the e-channel. The lack of an ERP system introduces manual processes into the information channel, with all the inaccuracy and inefficiency that implies. We discuss ERP systems in detail in Chapters 8 through 12.

Finally, the manufacturer will have to be integrated into a system-to-system connection. Standardization issues similar to those experienced with end users will complicate the process, but the sophistication and motivation of supply chain partners will differ. The principal problem will be lack of trust between supply chain partners as they jockey for position in the alternative channels.

Conclusion

The e-channel information channel is a mirror image of the physical flow channel. Re-creating supply chains in cyberspace is work-intensive under the best of conditions. The channels of distribution have become unfrozen, however, leading to a dynamic environment fraught with the danger of channel conflict. If the channels refreeze quickly, the business of transforming the supply chain will be greatly simplified. The very nature of the e-business tools, however, is dynamic, so channel conflict will likely continue indefinitely, mandating that supply chain partners work their alliances to overcome the relationship problems. A concerted, cooperative approach with supply chain roles clearly defined will simplify e-channel management.

Distributor Retrospective

Alpha's top management group has to realize that physical channels of distribution will not be eliminated by e-business. Instead, the management of information will become a critical aspect towards determining which channel partner has a competitive advantage.

Issues to Consider

1. Discuss the early obstacles to the Direct-Channel model. Why are they considered obstacles and how can they be overcome?

2. From the distributor's perspective, discuss the advantages and disadvantages to the Supplier-Controlled Channel.

3. From the supplier's perspective, discuss the advantages and disadvantages to the Distributor-Controlled Channel.

4. Discuss why the Mixed model is likely to cause or increase channel conflict among the channel members.

5. Discuss why the Independent Infomediary (Cannibal) model was developed and what it was intended to accomplish.

6. Consider the end-user connection through e-marketing and e-sales and discuss the two principal components.

7. Discuss why the standardization, automation, and continuous improvement of existing processes are important to the effective utilization of e-distribution.

Notes

1. Philip Evans and Thomas S. Wurster, "The Unbundling of Information, Blown to Bits: How the New Economics of Information Transforms Strategy" (Boston: *Harvard Business School Press,* 2000).

2. F. Barry Lawrence et al., "Alternative Channels of Distribution: E-Commerce Strategies For Industrial Manufacturers" (*Production and Inventory Management Journal,* forthcoming).

3. Frederick F. Reichheld and Phil Schefter, "E-Loyalty: Your Secret Weapon on the Web," *Harvard Business Review:* 105 (July/August, 2000).

4. Terril Y. Jones, "California; Ford Motor Begins Online Sales Operation In 9 States," *Los Angeles Times,* April 3, 2001, home edition, section C, p. 2.

5. Bob Tedeschi, "E-Commerce Report: Traditional Manufacturers are Grappling with the Pros and Cons of Direct Sales on the Internet," *The New York Times,* Jan. 3, 2000, late edition, section C, p. 7, col. 1.

6. Editorial, "Explosive Small Business PC and Server Purchases Via the Internet Channel Propel Direct Vendor Share Gains," *Business Wire,* Sept. 11, 2000.

7. M. Clayton Christensen, "The Innovator's Dilemma" (Boston: *Harvard Business School Press,* 1997).

8. Jerry Useem, "Internet Defense Strategy: Cannibalize Yourself," *Fortune,* Sept. 6, 1999: 121.

9. F. Barry Lawrence and Brian E. Reynolds, "E-Commerce Hype: It's Not the Technology That Matters," *Progressive MRO* 5 (6): 52–56 (Nov./Dec. 2000).

10. Editorial, "Office Depot, Symbol Technologies and BarPoint.com Introduce Mobile Scanning Computer and Unique Shopping Applications," *Business Wire,* Jan. 8, 2001.

11. Editorial, "Home Centers Chain," *Store Age Inventory Management Supplement,* December 2000, pp. 13B–14B.

12. Editorial, "Standardized Web Technologies Needed to Connect Highly Fragmented Construction Industry, Says Construction.com's Chip D'Angelo," *Business Wire,* February 16, 2001.

Distribution Sales and Marketing Under E-business

Distributor Perspective

Jack Marshall is president and CEO of Omega, Inc., a general line distributor with annual sales of $750 million. Marshall is concerned about Omega's declining gross margin and the inability of his customers to accurately forecast their requirements. To compensate for their customers' inability to forecast, Omega anticipated customer requirements by purchasing products and placing these products into its inventory. Unfortunately, Omega over anticipated the requirements of certain large customers and is now faced with an excessive amount of inventory. Marshall is convinced that if Omega had better information, the company could improve its profitability. Thus, Marshall is interested in determining what is involved in obtaining better information.

Introduction

Distribution sales and marketing in industrial channels consists of connecting buyers who have very specialized product and service needs with suppliers of MRO or component parts and a distribution service mechanism that can meet those needs. The sales and marketing function relies on the key "core competencies" of the distributor. Sourcing (supplier/customer connections) and logistics (distributor service) are specific distribution core competencies and are at the center of the distributor value equation. Examining those activities further, one can see that sourcing is a purely informational activity and logistics is so heavily dependent on reliable information that successful operations without good information would be impossible. The supplier plays an important role as well through new product engineering and a highly technical sales force that supports the distributor.

The distributor is, in fact, an information organization that matches the manufacturer's supply capabilities with the customer's needs. The existence of large inventories in so many distribution channels is an indication that the effectiveness of current information handling by distributors has room for improvement. The e-business movement drives the distributor to trade information for inventory. E-business strategies are expensive, however, and justification for more efficient and extensive handling of information requires careful thought. To justify technology investment, the firm must look to the savings generated by that investment (the ROI or Return on Investment). That raises some interesting questions:

○ Just what is the value of information?

○ How do you measure it?

○ How does it behave?

    ○ *Does it increase at the same rate as investment?*

    ○ *Are there economies of scale?*

○ Can you put concrete numbers on the value of information, the actual benefits received, and match these benefits with actual investments in technology?

The Value of Information

Most executives, salespeople, and operations specialists—and even the average person on the street—have a sense that information is power, but what exactly does that power mean and how is it translated into profits? An electronics distributor with an aggressive e-business strategy held a conference with suppliers to determine how to successfully build relationships to support channel technology initiatives. The distributor had hired IBM to develop an extensive capability to collect and analyze customer information. The investment would be significant, and the distributor was wondering how to get compensated for its investment.

The electronics distributor had reasoned that more efficient handling of information and its increased market analysis capability would provide the suppliers with valuable information that could be used for new product development and marketing opportunities. The former had never existed before, and the latter was typically paid for through consulting services from third-party marketing firms or through attempts to contact the customer directly through the supplier's sales engineers. The electronics distributor explained the system's proposed capabilities and asked the suppliers if they would be willing to compensate the distributor for this information that had not been previously available. The answer was a resounding "No!"

The suppliers' response seems counterintuitive at first. Why not compensate the electronics distributor for a service if it adds value to the supplier's organization? The reasons are complicated. The first problem is valuing the information from the supplier's point of view. Marketing information is easier to evaluate than logistical information because suppliers merely need to examine how much they will pay a consultant for the same information. The other possibility is to look at the cost of the supplier's technical sales force and assess to what degree distributor information gathering could either add value to its efforts or reduce the need for the expense. The value added would be the cost and value of gathering information that the supplier did not have access to before. The cost reduction would be the reduced cost of personnel if some of the supplier's information gathering could be outsourced to the distributor.

The problem is that the electronics distributor in the previous example had never offered this kind of information to the supplier before—thus the new product was difficult to evaluate. There is reason to believe the distributor has better access to information than a third party would have had. For example, a distributor can obtain sales and customer relationship information, which is not readily available to a third party such as a consulting firm. However, there is some concern regarding a distributor's ability to obtain such information because distributors have not previously performed this information-gathering activity. Product development information was gathered by the supplier or by consultants. Market size, trends, and changing customer preferences were "filtered" by the distributor or not delivered at all and frequently had to be gathered by consulting firms.

Interestingly, the previously mentioned electronics distributor had access to this information but did not always choose to share it with suppliers. The sheer volume of information coming from various sources in a distributorship is both difficult to collect and to manage. In addition, most supplier systems could not make effective use of certain information even if it were available to them. The distributor would have to do the analysis for the suppliers, or the suppliers would have to invest in better technology before real information exchange could occur.

E-business now makes it easier to analyze and share customer data. However, the supplier may not trust the distributor as an information handler. The supplier may suspect the distributor will "filter" the information to gain power in the supply chain. Another issue is the distribution compensation scheme. Distributors have traditionally earned their income in two ways. One approach was charging a price to their customers that allowed distributors to make a profit margin in addition to absorbing their costs. The other approach was through effective purchasing. For a long time, distributors have speculated on inventory purchases to make larger margins during material shortages by manipulating suppliers' capacity.

Distributor Compensation

Inventory speculation is the process of buying when prices are low during loose capacity/low demand periods and selling at higher prices during tight capacity/high demand periods. This process was especially effective during the 1970s, when inflation reached double digits, and the 1980s, when Just in Time (JIT) programs caused many manufacturers to shed inventory and rely heavily on distributors to take up the slack when markets went awry.[1]

In the 1990s, however, distribution customers began to expect distributors to provide this inventory service at a lower cost. Distributors were expected to decrease supply chain costs but were unsure how to do so. The customer would not tolerate stockouts. JIT would cause a system to crash if a stockout occurred. So the increased inventory reliability expectation stayed in place, but the customer was no longer willing to compensate the distributor for the service. Local inventories and rapid small deliveries associated with JIT are expensive, and the distributor did not know how to maintain the service without compensation. Distribution margins narrowed as this inventory speculation method stopped providing excess profits and experienced increasing service costs. Worse yet, the delivery-time windows continued to narrow, and customer segments that one would not normally associate with JIT (contractors, for example) started expecting quicker, more reliable deliveries.

High inflation died a quick death in the early eighties, but the rise of JIT caused its demise to go largely unnoticed in many distribution channels. The change in climate caught many distributors by surprise in the early nineties, therefore, and margin pressure became a hot topic. Capacity shortages became less common as world production levels continued to increase and inventory speculation became possible only for a few "hot" products that would quickly see production increases once the shortages became obvious.

One of the few remaining purchasing advantages was a supplier rebate. Some suppliers used rebates to increase distributor incentive to sell their products. However, many suppliers were feeling the pinch in the early nineties as well, and rebates started disappearing. The impact was significant, since distributors could add their margin on top of the supplier's price and then get the rebate back at the end of the year. If the supplier took a 1% rebate back, the benefit to the supplier was a 1% increase in the purchase price. The distributor, on the other hand, lost the 1% plus the margin that would have resulted from that price differential. The purchasing function as a profit machine was waning at the same time that distributors were experiencing increasing margin pressure from customers. The distributor compensation scheme was breaking down, and it was as yet unclear how to restore profitability.

The compensation scheme was breaking down, largely because information was smoothing markets, eliminating capacity problems, and increasing expectations that high-service programs such as JIT could be maintained by the distributor with less inventory and, therefore, less cost. Suppliers had come to associate distributor compensation (rebates) with increased sales and did not see a need to pay for additional information that might or might not lead to increased sales. In addition, the distributor was expected to be the customer specialist and provide the information to the supplier at no cost. The connection between the value of information and distributor compensation schemes like rebates had not been established.

An important question to address is "What is the value of distributor-generated information?" The answer can be determined by one particular supplier's response regarding why they would not pay for information that should have improved operations or increased sales. The supplier simply stated that instead of paying the distributor for information analysis, they should handle it themselves. In other words, the information was so valuable that the firm did not trust others to provide information but preferred to obtain it themselves. The supplier was concerned that if information handling were turned over to the distributor, information could be manipulated or even turned over to the competition, since the distributor had relationships with multiple suppliers. The problem with this view is that the supplier is unlikely to develop this information without distributor assistance. The distributor and supplier would have to ally to determine what information processing and analysis should take place and what specific tasks each organization should provide. For entire industries to agree on such a thing before anybody invested in e-business was unreasonable, so distributors would have to take the plunge without a clear definition of how to get compensated for the new services they would provide.

Information Compensation

If a new compensation model was not immediately apparent, another approach was to use the traditional model of improving margins. Thus, trading information for inventory implied exchanging costs for technology implementation. One approach that the distributor could utilize would be to reduce costs through more efficient operations at a rate faster than that at which costs could increase from satisfying increased customer service requirements. That meant the technology investment had to pay for itself and add to the bottom line very fast. Another possible approach was to increase customer service (raise fill rates, for example) and increase sales. The trade-off between increasing customer service and broadening margins was very complex and would require extensive analysis, which would become easier if the technology investment made such analysis possible. Distributors would become more dependent on their information capability for strategic decision-making.

Increasing sales implied increasing power over suppliers. The distributor could convert the ability to increase a supplier's sales into rebates or into willingness to pay for information analysis in order to know what the distributor knew. In the short term, the distributor would have to pay for new technology with increased efficiency but in the long term could convert that capability into increased sales and supply chain power. Increased power could mean increased compensation. There are different forms of compensation, incidentally, and distributors with well-designed e business initiatives might be able to negotiate other compensation schemes such as franchise arrangements (exclusive or limited distribution) that would replace rebates entirely or provide new rebates.

Thus, the value of information can be identified through traditional methods. The distributor is offering a new service, so the rules governing new product introductions for manufacturers are instructive. The new service should be evaluated by the following criteria:

1. Does the customer really need the service? This issue was not well studied in the early days of the dot-coms, and companies set up virtual marketplaces that customers were either unwilling or unable to use. For distributors, the concept of better information handling can lead to lower logistics costs and/or better service levels. Depending on the market, either or both could be highly valued.

2. If the customer needs the service, how do you determine an economic return on investing in that service? Determining value depends on whether distributors decide to use the greater efficiency to decrease their own costs, to improve service levels and hence increase sales, or to pass on cost savings to the customer in an effort to drive larger market share. The former requires an understanding of how efficiency improvement reduces cost at a constant service level (we explore this concept in Part Three). The latter two require an understanding of how increases in fill rates or other customer value-added services increase sales and how increases in sales affect profitability at a given sales level. At lower sales levels, an increase in sales has a fairly large impact on profitability due to economies of scale. As sales increase, the impact is reduced, and reductions in costs may have a more significant impact. The best balance of internal savings versus increased sales should be determined to match potential value to the cost of implementing new information handling ability.

The issues involved in justifying e-business investments by reducing costs through operational efficiency are the focus of many of the remaining chapters. This chapter focuses instead on how to justify investments that make the sales force more efficient and/or increase sales. Sales increases can be achieved through new product introductions, increased market coverage, repositioning of the firm's marketing strategy, improvements in sales force capability, increased operational efficiency, and a general improvement in the manner in which specific firms conduct business.

Justifying Investments with Sales

Before addressing the question of how to increase sales under e-business, an important question is how to measure the effect of increased sales on the firm's cost structure. Such a determination provides a method for justifying the use of e-business tools to increase sales. The first problem is projecting the effect of new innovations on sales or forecasting. Forecasting the demand for an existing product or service offering is easier than forecasting demand for a new product or service because existing products or services have a history, which can be used to project the future. Demand for new products or services is very difficult to forecast because it is difficult to predict the future of something that has not existed before. Since historical projections are not available, market researchers will often rely on panels of experts such as customer focus groups or management teams. This expert forecasting methodology has a very poor track record.[2]

Methods exist for improving expert forecasts. The firm can examine related innovations and track the impact on sales after implementation, and benchmark results from early adopters in the same or other channels. These information sources can be compared with findings by expert panels to verify if the projection is realistic. Even under the best of circumstances, the expert forecast should be regarded as highly risky, and such risk must be considered in evaluating the new innovation. The risk that a project will not meet expectations and therefore be a money-losing venture is often counterbalanced by the risk that inaction will result in a loss in sales through allowing the competition a window of opportunity to offer an enhanced product and steal market share.

Outcome determination can be developed for existing products and services as well as for those products resulting from innovative activities. A common approach in determining the outcome for existing products is to develop three scenarios as follows: one scenario providing an optimistic projection based on events happening according to plan; the second providing a pessimistic projection based on the failure to forecast accurately, while the third is a most-likely scenario based on typical performance. Next, an estimated outcome is determined by applying weighted percentages to the preceding three scenarios. The same procedure for determining outcomes for existing products and services is used for new products, with the exception that the focus is on whether or not to adopt the innovation. Finally the two outcomes, for existing products and services and for new products and services from innovation, are compared to determine a course of action.

To compare scenarios, the impact of additional sales or loss in sales from inaction must be evaluated. Increased sales offer two opportunities for an improved return on investment. The first, profit margin on new sales, is straightforward and easily calculated by taking the additional margin generated through projected sales increases. The effect of the second, economies of scale generated through using existing facilities, personnel, and equipment to satisfy new sales, is often overestimated (see Figure 5.1).

The "economy of scale" logic is based on the assumption that margins increase as sales increase, or that increases in efficiency provide an Internal Rate of Return (IRR)

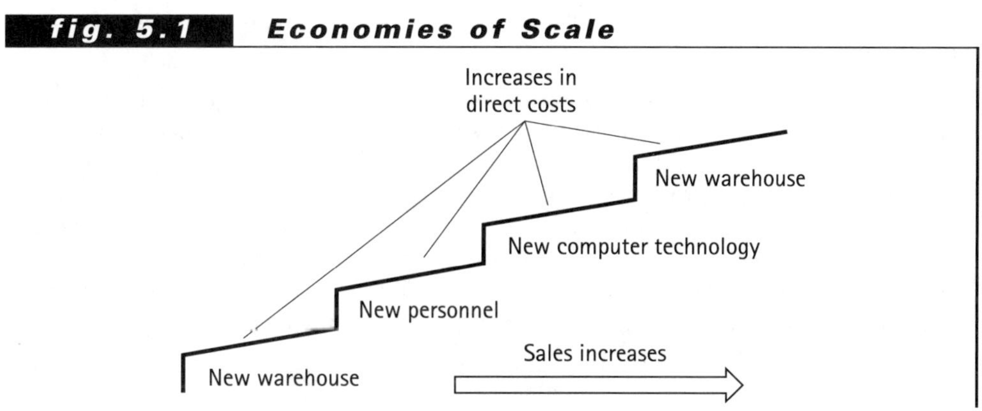

fig. 5.1 *Economies of Scale*

that exceeds the investment outflow. The assumption that costs do not increase at the same rate as sales comes from the fact that handling one hundred items does not cost as much on a per item basis as handling one. The firm does have increasing costs but not at the same rate of increase as sales, due to the fact that new facilities, people, and equipment do not need to be added in linear increases proportionate to the increase in sales. The effect is more piecewise, with some costs rising directly in proportion to sales (cost of goods sold, packaging, sales commissions) while others (adding a new person, opening a new warehouse, investing in new equipment) increase at critical trip points when new capacity is added. A new investment that increases capacity can theoretically provide an advantage for absorbing increased sales.

The problem with the economies of scale argument, however, is that most firms are operating next to a trip point. In other words, if capacity is available, it is likely to be put to use (although that use may not be optimal). Even though the use of capacity may be inefficient, processes that are already established are often hard to unseat. Another problem arises with environmental complexity. As an operation gets larger (higher sales), it frequently becomes more difficult to manage. The complexity of the operation can lead to sub-optimal processes that negate some economies of scale. Data integrity, damaged or lost materials, and ineffective utilization of equipment are just a few of the problems that can occur as an operation becomes more complex.

One firm held a strong belief that economies of scale had a major effect on their profitability. They believed that larger branches operated at a lower sales and administration cost (SG&A) than smaller branches. A regression analysis of their branches proved otherwise, however (see Figure 5.2). The regression indicated that, on average, SG&A cost increased linearly with sales.[3] The researchers concluded that the only differentiating factors were service complexity for customers in certain markets and managerial skill. Increased sales were not significant in cost reduction.

If sales increases cannot be relied upon to produce economies of scale, then additional margins from increased sales or the fear of lost margins when sales decrease are the only support for new innovations. An argument could be made, however, that information technology dispels confusion and may have a better chance at supporting economies of scale. Many firms have found this savings from decreased confusion difficult to achieve. The decrease in cost associated with a new technology is often absorbed by new costs associated with it (support people, facilities, equipment).

The difficulty in achieving economies of scale has caused many practitioners to limit themselves to increased profits on sales and decreased transaction costs in justifying e-business initiatives. Decreased transaction costs are actually an economy-of-scale issue, but the dramatic impact of literally replacing one process with another that costs a fraction of the original carries a lot of weight. Additional savings will be obtained from improved use of information. The use of information will be discussed in later chapters, but for now let's discuss the implications of transactions savings associated with sales force automation and increased sales associated with the proposed e-business marketing opportunities.

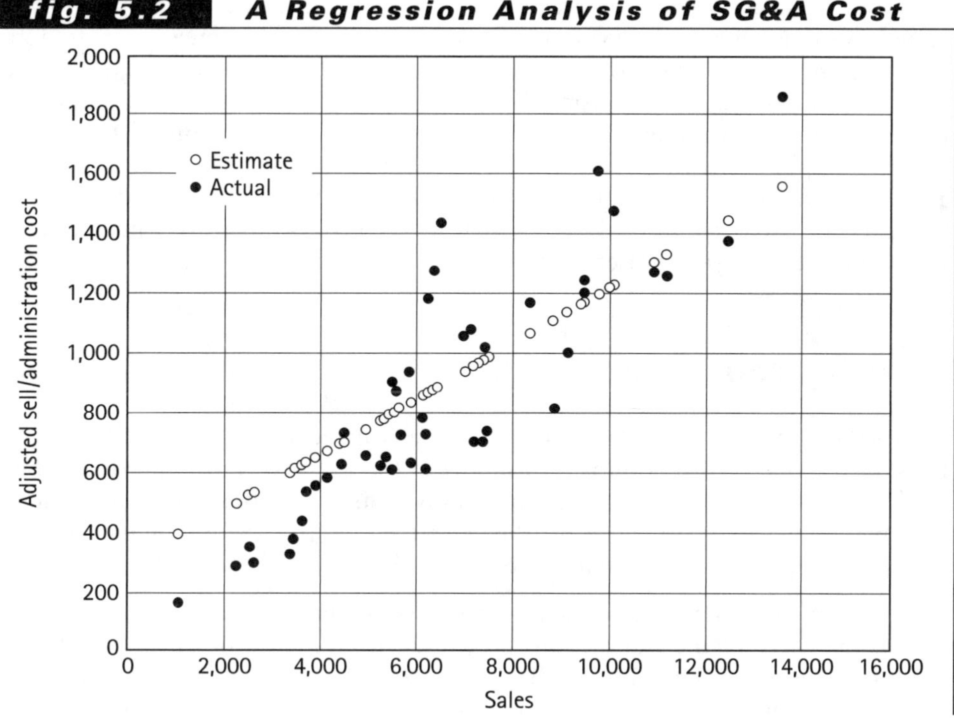

Source: E. Powell Robinson, F. Barry Lawrence, and Siddhartha Syam, unpublished logistics study, December 2000.

Sales Information

The transactional savings associated with e-business are typically mentioned first in any discussion on benefits. Transactional savings are the costs generated by activities associated with purchasing the item (not the actual price of the item). These costs consist of the time spent in the purchasing cycle: need recognition, forecasting, purchase order issue, and approval of purchase. The cost of this process differs across firms and industries, but a recent general industry estimate was $150 for the cost of issuing one purchase order.[4]

To evaluate the value-automated sales information, one must consider the savings associated with both the distributor and the customer's operations. From the customer's viewpoint, considerable savings can be achieved through a reduction in transaction costs. Assuming the customer allows instant access to point-of-sale (POS) information and has established a rule-based system for reorder, the savings in transaction costs alone could be substantial. The average cost of an electronic purchase order using a procurement card ranges from $5 to $25.[5] What would a seamless electronic buy look like?

Vendor Managed Inventory (VMI) can be used to illustrate what a totally automated customer management system would do. If the customer were to return information on usage (POS data), to the distribution firm in real time, the distribution firm could refill the customer's orders without waiting for a human-based purchasing system to intervene. VMI often frightens supply chain partners due to low-tech applications that required a tremendous investment by both the supplier and the customer. The applications were based on old technology that did not allow for real-time exchange of data or automation of processes. Before e-business, VMI was work-intensive and not effective at cost reduction.

Sales Automation

VMI as a form of sales automation will be discussed later. Automating the sales force means that information is returned with less expense, more speed, and better quality than under traditional systems. Many firms have considered sales automation but have tended to focus on the reduced activity expenses, which may not include the greatest savings that can be realized.

The other savings are more difficult to identify but may have a greater impact. First is the speed of the transaction: the great truism about information is that the older it is, the less reliable it becomes. The second potential saving is in accuracy. If a salesperson handwrites an order and then enters it later or, worse yet, has someone else enter the order, the rekeying of information is filled with opportunities for error. So the timeliness and quality of information are major drivers in the decision to automate the sales force. Many firms do not see or understand these costs and do not consider them in their cost/benefit analysis. Since these are potentially the biggest cost savers, the analysis is more likely to work against automation.

Other tools can be brought to bear. One large manufacturer/distributor developed a website for its sales force that could help a salesperson who was having problems closing a sale. The salesperson, during a break, could access the firm's website and describe the scenario. The system would ask a series of logical questions that should lead it to respond by providing some common purchasing procedure or technique with which the inexperienced salesperson might not be familiar. At the end of the queries, the website would present a video of a manager analyzing the situation. The manager might even have experience with the customer in question. The manager would tell the salesperson what was happening and suggest an appropriate response.

At first blush, this system only looks like a tremendous sales tool that principally benefits new hires, but look closer. Every time a salesperson accesses the website, the system gains intelligence on the customer in question. A major problem for distribution firms generally is that a salesperson may come to "own" the customer, and if the salesperson leaves the company, the customer may go with them. This way the firm has direct information on the customer's behavior that can be used to establish relationships between firms rather than between the salesperson and the customer. Thus, the information system owns the customer.

Marketing Information

Marketing information is used to determine how to approach the customer and position one's firm to increase sales. The methodologies currently employed by distributors include the prospecting sales force that offers services that suppliers do not choose to offer and thus understands the customer to a greater degree than the supplier. In essence, the supplier has outsourced the selling function to distribution firms.

The prospecting sales force is an expensive tool that distributors and manufacturers rely upon heavily, and it is unlikely to be replaced by any e-business tools. Services the supplier chooses not to offer include local inventory, financing for small customers, and consultative selling (technical support). Distributors position themselves to provide those things that suppliers cannot or do not wish to provide to such a diverse customer base. This positioning implies additional costs, which will likely be impacted by the e-business movement. Insights that can be gained about customers by the combination of the prospecting sales force, the customer maintenance associated with the inside sales force, and the services offered only through distribution could be very powerful if the information system can capture and manipulate the data.

E-catalogs

The sales force can be mirrored to some extent by e-business. The e-catalog can act as the distributor's connection to the outside world in much the same way that outside and inside salespeople have done in the past. To achieve this connection, however, the system must emulate the value-added services of a sales force. The first value, customer contact, has already proved problematic.

Customer contact value comes from knowing the customer and having access to decision makers in the organization. Outside salespeople generally know the customer and establish contacts throughout the firm that provide access for the inside sales force to continue maintaining the relationship. An e-catalog can emulate this procedure somewhat, but difficulties do arise. The system can make contact, as the outside sales force does, but the customer must seek out the site. This process becomes a major challenge when customers prove unwilling to "search" for distribution channels on the Web. In this situation, the customers are satisfied with existing channels and do not, apparently, believe the Web would provide the same level of services or a comparable discount that would offset the loss in service. Without the assurances of a credible outside or inside salesperson, the customer is unwilling to take the chance of using a website. A second problem stems from the accessibility of the websites. It is still difficult and time consuming for most purchasing professionals to use the Web. The problem may be equipment based (difficulty accessing the Web from a given location) or process based (customer processes requiring a written transaction that the Web does not provide). Even if these problems could be overcome, the Web machines are expensive to set up and maintain, so providers do not have the time to wait for customers to become comfortable with the idea.

The second value-added service is the provision of technical information and other support resources. Many customers are not willing to substitute the Web for inside/outside sales support due to standardization problems. Standardization of data and processes has not been ready when new sites were launched and so many distribution value adds have been lost in setting up a Web-based order system. We discuss standardization in Chapter 11.

Thus e-catalogs have faced considerable challenges. The idea, however, has appeal. If the customer could use the distributor's catalog and place the order by punching a few radial buttons in the catalog, the catalog could be much easier to use and would save the customer the time and effort associated with calling in the order. The distributor's cycle time in collecting customer information would be reduced as well. Faster processing of orders would also tend to reflect true usage and, therefore, be more accurate for forecasting purposes.

The preceding scenario assumes that the distributor's catalog is, in fact, a communication device that notifies the distributor as the customer punches buttons in the catalog. The tool would have to be wireless, with a broadband reach that could deliver information without the customer having to access anything. In addition, the information in the catalog would have to be rich enough to eliminate the need for a discussion with a salesperson regarding product attributes. Delivery requirements would also have to be standard and not require any special routing or documentation.

The combination of reach (broadband communications) and richness (depth of information) proved to be deadly for many e-catalogs. The broadband revolution created sufficient capacity for information exchange (called "bandwidth") in cellular and hardwired networks. The problem was the same as that consistently faced throughout the history of computer technology. Computer users have always needed to transfer more information than the technology would allow. Lack of capacity manifested itself in insufficient computer-processing chip speed (the rush to Pentium and faster chips was in response to the rapidly increasing need for faster processing caused by greater richness in information) and insufficient Random Access Memory, or RAM. We all learned quickly that maximizing chip speed and RAM gave us the ability to run programs that would lock up our computers if we tried them on lesser technology.

The same problem was even more pronounced with the bandwidths that would be necessary to transfer the technical information associated with industrial distribution firms. The information handled by inside/outside salespeople is personalized for the customer. In other words, customers have very specific needs and those needs differ from one customer to another. The system would have to capture all customer preferences, such as transportation needs, minimum purchase sizes, complementary products, customer's degree of technical sophistication, technology employed, time windows, and special handling needs. The number of permutations is tremendous when all possible product combinations and support processes are considered. Salespeople maintain a record of these needs in their files and mental notes. To do the same on a computer is certainly possible, and since the computer does not suffer from human shortcomings such as memory lapses and emotional swings, the computerized system may actually be more capable. The problem lies in creating a configurator that can handle all the possible permutations. The program would be very complex, take very long to create, and be firm specific and extremely difficult to code.

Assuming every firm was able to build such a configurator, the volume of information associated with driving the configurator would, in most cases, overwhelm the system's capability of transferring that information. This presupposes that the information to be exchanged would be in a format that allowed it to be transferred, a standardization issue that was yet to be fully resolved at the end of 2000. Even if the standardization problem could be conquered, the bandwidth issue still remained. At the turn of the twenty-first century, this technology was almost attainable; thus, the e-catalog appeared to be possible in the near future. Early attempts (especially by the dot-coms) had failed largely due to the standardization and bandwidth problems.

When these problems are conquered, the e-catalog could become a new weapon in the distributor's arsenal. It would complement the sales force's efforts and free them from the need to perform menial activities so they could pursue higher-level functions such as consultative selling. Logistics and product specialization are more in demand than ever before, and the distribution sales person could retool and pass off many easier functions to the e-catalog.

Conclusion

Assuming the customer can be connected, the e-business environment offers considerable benefits associated with automating mundane, low-skill processes for the sales force. This will free salespeople to add value in more complex arenas and continue to push technology providers to offer better tools to enhance customer service. The customer connection requires certain technological and process changes. In the next chapter, we explore some of the tools associated with connecting the customer to the distributor.

Distributor Retrospective

Marshall must realize what is involved in managing information. First, does Omega understand how to collect and utilize information? What specific information is required? How can this information be collected? What are the costs and benefits of obtaining the necessary information? What is Omega's return on the costs associated with obtaining the required information?

Issues to Consider

1. Discuss why suppliers are, or would likely be, reluctant to compensate distributors for sharing customer transactional information.

2. Discuss the changes that occurred during the early 1990s that affected distributor compensation.

3. Discuss the evaluation criteria a distributor should use for new products and services.

4. Discuss why, or why not, distributor economies of scale can be realized through increased sales.

5. Identify and describe the cost savings opportunities that sales automation may provide.

6. Discuss the challenges, and the potential value, in the use of e-catalogs by distributors. Include in your discussion the potential difficulties from a technical perspective and also from the customer's perspective.

Notes

1. "The Folly of Price Controls," *Investor's Business Daily,* January 19, 2001.

2. M. Clayton Christensen, "The Innovator's Dilemma" (Boston: Harvard Business School Press, 1997).

3. E. Powell Robinson, F. Barry Lawrence, and Siddhartha Syam, Unpublished logistics study, December 2000.

4. C. Cruz, "Purchasing Execs Take Shears to Corporate Costs," *Purchasing* 120 (8): 22–23 (May 23, 1996).

5. Robert J. Trent and Michael G. Kolchin, "Reducing the Transactions Costs of Purchasing Low Value Goods and Services." http://www.capsresearch.org/ReportPDFs/ReducingAll.pdf, pp. 83–86 (accessed April 9, 2001).

Using E-business Partners to Integrate the Customer into the Distributor's Operations

Distributor Perspective

David Mullins is president and CEO of Dalton Supply Company headquartered in Cleveland, Ohio. Dalton Supply, a heating, industrial piping, and air conditioning distributor with annual sales of $150 million, has five branches located in the Midwest. Recently, Clark Cassidy, Dalton's sales vice president, has requested that Dalton take the necessary steps to automate its customer-handling processes. However, Warren Stokes, Dalton's financial officer, has advised that the cost of automating these processes is greater than the possible benefits that might be realized from such an initiative. Cassidy has disagreed with Stokes's evaluation and has asked that Mullins employ an outside consultant to conduct an independent cost-benefit analysis. Mullins is concerned about the course of action to be followed. He believes that automating Dalton's customer-handling processes would provide some reduced expenses and should improve customer satisfaction. Mullins also believes such a course of action will be expensive and that in the final analysis, costs may well exceed benefits. However, Mullins realizes that he just doesn't understand all the ramifications of Cassidy's proposal.

Introduction

In the e-business arena, distribution sales and marketing takes on a new role, as described in the previous chapter. The marketing group develops a strategy and approach to draw the customer to the system-to-system connection. The outside sales force then seals the deal and builds the relationship. Relationship maintenance on the fulfillment side will then fall exclusively to the inside sales force with occasional assistance on new product design from the outside sales force. Under e-business the principal changes surround the use of new tools like sales automation for the outside sales force and e-catalogs for the marketing group. The inside sales force will also have many of its activities automated and its value equation redefined.

The new value equation for inside sales includes customer-handling processes too complex to automate and a greater emphasis on materials and logistics-handling activities in the firm. Many customers are going to require special services to meet their needs, which means a greater interaction with the sales force. The problems may be a function of the customer's technological sophistication or the complexity of their environment. Complex environments will typically result in logistical challenges like the inability to anticipate demand (rendering forecasting more challenging and making expert assistance necessary) or special product delivery/handling requirements. The inside sales force will find itself moving away from order taking (a mundane task, easy to automate) toward consultative selling.

The transition from traditional inside salesperson to e-business relationship manager mandates that the inside salesperson be equipped with tools that enable task automation and access to critical customer information. This chapter examines the e-business tools used to connect the customer

Market Makers and Application Service Providers

Market makers had a setback in the summer and fall of 2000. The market's slowness in accepting their services and the conflicting objectives of growing their market and not alienating potential customers (like distributors) who also served that market proved, for many, too much to handle even with the considerable start-up funds provided by Wall Street. Still the concept of market makers as technology outsource for distributors held merit. For the vast majority of distributors ERP (Enterprise Resource Planning) was more than they could afford and when e-business was added on top of that, they could not hope to put in the sorts of systems necessary to compete.

The market makers and, for ERP and its bolt-ons, ASPs (Application Service Providers) essentially offered the necessary infrastructure at a more affordable price. In the early 2000s, that price was still significant but considerably less than the costs for ownership of a Web-enabled information system. In addition to the cost of buying and implementing a system, the customer saved on continuing maintenance and upgrades. The downside was uncertainty over the stability of the market makers and ASPs. If the infrastructure provider was not viable, the customer data was at risk and an alternative provider would need to be identified. The implementation cost of the software was significant, so choosing a provider was an important decision.

Choosing an E-business Partner

Before choosing Channel Technology Providers (ASPs and market makers), the firm should complete an assessment of its internal and external goals. Those goals should then be reflected in its strategy regarding the four key e-business value drivers: Audience, Content, Commerce, and Collaboration.[1] The first step is to determine the audience, the customers to be served through the channel provider's systems.

E-business customers fall into different classes. The e-buyer is an individual who will purchase goods through the use of e-business tools. The e-researcher is one who uses the Internet to research product needs before contacting a typical channel provider. The e-wannabe wants to use the Internet in one of the two previous ways but does not have the capability due to lack of IT resources or business process constraints. The e-don't wannabes do not intend to use the Internet until forced to do so by business imperatives.

The size of each of these customer categories was a topic of considerable debate in the late 1990s and early 2000s. Ascertaining the composition of a firm's customer makeup enabled the company to formulate the appropriate e-business strategy to effectively address its target market. If the first class, the e-buyer, constituted a significant proportion of the company's customers, the firm needed a Web presence. On the other hand, if its customers fell into the second class, the e-researcher, who accounted for the majority of Internet users, then a Web presence was a necessary defensive move. If most, or all, of the firm's customers were in the wannabe or don't wannabe class, the firm could afford to wait until the market matured (if ever).

Many researchers and business analysts touted the "first mover" advantage as the reason to secure relationships with market makers in the late 1990s. Based on research demonstrating that early adopters frequently got an edge difficult to overtake, the common perception was that being first in the market was a tremendous advantage. After the ERP failures in the early '90s and the market maker collapse in 2000, however, the first-mover advantage lost some of its luster.

Assuming the firm needs a Web presence, the second step is to identify the content needs of the audience. Content is any information or service that will attract the customer to the site on a regular basis. The needs of those customers should help drive the Channel Technology Provider (CTP) choice. If the customer is principally an e-researcher, for example, then the choice should be driven by the CTP's ability to provide rich information. Graphics, searchability, and linkages to relevant public information sources are only a few of the capabilities the site should offer in addition to being able to serve as a host for the firm's information and assist the firm in putting its information on the Web. A CTP that does business as a research site has to be compensated differently from one that assesses transaction fees on every sale.

Typically, a CTP that operates primarily in a research mode will charge fees for advertising, visibility in the site (positioning), usage, and services related to setting up the information presented.

If the customer is an e-buyer, then the firm's Internet presence needs the ability to conduct transactions as well as provide information. This leads to the third step in choosing CTP's: customer need for commerce. The transaction dynamics that the audience prefers have to be determined (i.e., auction vs. exchange) as well as their preferences for a seller-driven, buyer-driven, or neutral e-marketplace.

A neutral market maker is industry independent, often supported by venture capital. These market makers serve as an exchange between buyers and sellers without favoring one over the other. Auction sites where buyers can list needs and sellers can post offerings are an example of neutral sites. Non-neutral market makers are typically supported through a firm or industry alliance to facilitate purchasing or sales efforts. An example of a non-neutral market maker would be a buyer-driven exclusive reverse auction site where the same customer or group of customers offers up business on a regular basis for suppliers to bid on. Another example would be a seller-driven site where the buyer gets information and can transact the sale with limited competition between sellers.[2]

Finally, collaboration is the development of e-partnerships to help serve the audience's needs as quickly and cost effectively as possible. Collaboration will require the formation of partnerships and alliances with other firms that have the audience, content, and commerce technology and business models that a company needs most. Market makers and ASPs have sprung up in most industrial segments. Important issues to consider include the following:[3]

○ Description of products and services—What products and services are offered? Does the offering match up well with the firm's customer needs?

○ Description of differentiating value proposition—What differentiates this CTP from its competition? Pricing? Visuals? Richness of information sources?

○ Financial position—Is the CTP financially stable? Will they be there for the long haul?

○ Business partners—Does the CTP have business alliances with complementary, noncompetitive firms?

○ Customer base—Does the CTP offer new customers your firm has been unable to reach before?

○ Fulfillment process—Does the CTP handle its own fulfillment or does it operate through existing channel providers? Does it compete with your current distribution channel?

Evaluating channel partners is complex and includes many factors. The firm should start with an assessment of customer needs and then advance to an assessment of its own capability to meet those needs. Once the position of the customer is understood and matched with the firm's capabilities, missing linkages can be identified and used to drive the Channel Technology Provider choice. First-mover advantage has not proven essential to this choice in industrial channels thus far, but the environment could change quickly if and when a new enabling technology becomes available that increases the number of e-buyers and e-researchers as opposed to the non-users. E-wannabes are the ones to watch, since an enabling technology will impact them first, and their movement into the e-channel will hasten the conversion of the final set, e-don't wannabes.

Justifying the Cost of the E-business Partner

Before, during, and after choosing its Channel Technology Providers (CTPs), the firm must provide financial justification for the cost. The initial costs will consist of setup and site development. ASPs will require a setup cost that consists of populating the distributor's data in the ASP's databases and connecting processes to the system. The connection process is the principal cost associated with the start-up, but afterwards the utilization fee will be an ongoing cost.

The cost structure is very similar for a market maker. The setup fee is associated with putting product and other information on the site and then connecting the firm's customer-facing processes to the site. The process is therefore very similar, but costs will vary widely based on the size of the distribution firm's catalog and number and complexity of processes to be connected.

Justifying the use of an ASP requires a look at how the automation of internal processes is facilitated by the use of the system. Automation reduces transaction costs that can be tracked through activity-based study. More significant, however, is the cost associated with data integrity and inventory imbalances driven through forecast error and supplier reliability. An effective ERP system can have a considerable impact on these costs, as we discuss in Part Three. Cost justification of an ASP-based ERP is similar to the methods we describe for in-house ERP with the exception of their magnitude and the risk associated with ASP failure.

The magnitude differences go to the heart of ERP functionality. Logic dictates that the greater the firm's need for special functionality the greater the potential magnitude differences. ASPs, with their limited flexibility, should be impacted more significantly by these special needs. While one might expect the ASP to be less expensive on installation (it should be) and more expensive in terms of maintenance and usage costs, the latter may not be true. For the ASP, the maintenance has been outsourced and is now charged for. For in-house ERP, the cost of maintaining an IT department is significant and can outweigh the cost of outsourcing. The maintenance cost from an ASP may still be less expensive than maintaining an IT department. The advantage to an in-house system is that it can be customized to the firm's business practices as driven by its customers' needs.

An ERP system that cannot be customized will push some transaction costs back on the firm. If the customer requires a process that cannot be performed in the ERP system, the company will incur the cost of custom development or business process changes, which bear an additional price tag. When evaluating which system to use, in-house or ASP, the analyst must place a cost on noncustomizable processes that will be weighed against the cost of an in-house team.

After weighing all activity and physical costs, the firm must take a look at risk. Unfortunately, at the beginning of the decade, Internet-based systems had not fared well. An ASP failure could result in lost data and system suspension, which could force the firm to establish a new ASP relationship or develop an in-house system. This risk could be minimized by agreements outlining data security issues that might preempt bankruptcy proceedings, allowing the firm to secure an alternative ASP while still maintaining the same ERP package. The risk was still considerable, but it could be mitigated though proper planning. Assuming risk minimization, the probability of ASP failure still had to be assessed and factored into the decision.

Justifying a market maker is very similar. Risk is still high and the cost of populating the firm's data in the market maker is not insignificant, but careful planning of data conversion could make it easier to transfer. The commitment to an ERP system is not applicable, so standardized data could be moved more easily. The most significant factor is ownership of the information. If customer information is generated through the use of the market maker and the market maker fails, the customer information might be at risk. Risk, again, becomes a factor in evaluating the investment in a market maker.

The cost justification for market makers is different, however. The transaction costs can be reduced for the distribution firm. A major promised benefit, however, is increased sales or protection from lost sales if customers choose to go to the Web for their purchases. The investment is, therefore, justified by both decreased costs and increased sales. Evaluating reduction in transaction costs is fairly easy, especially since we need only consider the reduction in sales processing costs, but evaluating new sales from the Web is very difficult. Forecasting from historical figures is challenging, but, as noted in Chapter 5, forecasting where there is little or no history, as in Web sales, is very problematic. Even more difficult, perhaps, is forecasting the risk of lost sales from nonparticipation in e-business. Justifying based on sales is, therefore, very difficult.

Web-based ERP (ASPs) is easier to justify than e-business (market makers), but the cost reduction associated with ERP is not much good if we lose the customer due to a lack of marketing prowess on the Web. The benefits of e-business cost reductions (transaction costs) are not likely to be achieved without a well-functioning ERP system, however, so the two decisions are inseparable.

E-business in High-Service Environments

Distributors faced great challenges at the end of the 1990s with the tremendous escalation of customer service expectations. The distributor was being asked to supply customers from the customer's site under Vendor Managed Inventory (VMI) or Integrated Supply (I/S), two programs that often required the distributor to "own" the inventory up until the customer actually consumed the product. These arrangements tested the inventory management skills of distributors. A shakeout of integrators started in the late 1990s, reducing the number of distributors involved in I/S, but VMI continued to grow. VMI can easily evolve into I/S, and if I/S is limited to the distributor's core-competency product offering, it becomes nothing more than VMI with sole sourcing. The two methodologies are very similar and share common technology needs.

Vendor Managed Inventory and E-business

VMI was first developed in retail channels and has seen significant growth since its inception. Retailers like Wal-Mart required suppliers like Procter and Gamble to own and maintain inventory on the shelf. Wal-Mart would not take ownership until the product was sold, which, in effect, might mean never. The distributor/supplier/vendor essentially used the shelf space at Wal-Mart to run its own mini-warehouse that sold almost directly to the public.[4] The advantage to Wal-Mart was a shift in inventory costs from Wal-Mart to its suppliers.

When VMI is conducted in distribution, the distributor may or may not own the inventory until such time as the customer actually uses (consumes) the material. Many distributors refer to all VMI as consignment, but important distinctions exist between the types of VMI. Under VMI, the distributor remains in control of the inventory. Consignment is the lowest level of a VMI alliance and typically results in the distributor losing control of the inventory while still owning it. This arrangement typically results in losses for both the customer and the distributor.

VMI is a service-intensive program. There are important distinctions to be made in the level of engagement in VMI, and any firm considering it should understand them well. The engagement rules will determine each party's responsibilities and the likelihood of success. The levels of engagement are:

1. Consignment without visibility: The distributor owns all inventories, but the customer determines what will be on the shelf. In addition, the distributor has no visibility into the inventory and relies on whatever counts the customer passes back or on visits from its outside sales force to know what has become of the merchandise. This arrangement is common in many channels and is usually driven by distributors anxious to get product out of their warehouse due to space constraints or to shorten lead times for end users.

2. Consignment with visibility: The distributor owns all inventories, and the customer determines what is stocked but now allows the distributor to "see," in real time, what is selling and what is not. This arrangement facilitates planning for distributors but still leaves them at the customer's mercy, since product changes and transfers can only be made with permission. If the distributor has an inventory imbalance (too much inventory at the customer's site), the approval process hampers redistribution of the slow movers, or excess inventory. This arrangement is less common, since firms employing "high-visibility" tools and systems-to-system connectivity usually have a more trusting relationship with distributors and, therefore, have moved to more automated, distributor-driven replenishment VMI.

3. Distributor-driven replenishment without visibility: The distributor owns all inventories and determines what will be on the shelf. The space is, in a sense, given to the distributor to stock. The advantages to this approach, for the distributor, are increased control, the ability to protect against lost sales due to customer stockouts, increased information flow, and the ability to introduce or withdraw products at will from the shelves. The disadvantages are increased inventory and the maintenance personnel required to check the customer's warehouse. The outside sales force typically carries out maintenance. Many times there is an in-house store set up where an inside salesperson at the customer's site maintains the inventory and interacts with the customer's employees. The cost of such an arrangement is high, but the additional information such an insider can gather and increased relationship status often outweigh the cost.

4. Distributor-driven replenishment with visibility: This relationship requires information automation where radio frequency (RF) technology or batch downloads directly transfer data from the customer's system to the supplier's. The distributor has the power to replenish as they see fit or through a "rule-based" replenishment policy, where the customer has instructed the distributor what the reorder point (ROP) is and how much to ship when an ROP trigger is hit.

5. Distributor-driven replenishment with the customer owning the inventory: The customer owns the inventory and the distributor manually or electronically manages the inventory on a regular schedule with the power to replenish as they see fit or through a rule-based customer replenishment policy.

The final level is best for the distributor, since it minimizes manual counts (reducing cost and human error) and minimizes inventory. The first is least desirable, since it requires the distributor to hold large inventories and lose visibility. The level of VMI engagement is a function of distributor objectives (desire to lock up the customer's business, use of real-time information), distributor and customer technological capability (manual counts versus automation), and distributor and customer channel power.

The distributor may be willing to endure higher service costs for the opportunity to achieve sole source status with the customer. VMI frequently carries with it a greater share of the customer's business so long as the supplier maintains a reliable fill rate and offers a sufficiently broad selection. This policy can demand higher inventory levels, however, as we discuss in later chapters. If the distributor does not intend to concentrate on efficient asset management methods, this policy could prove disastrous.

Inventory management must be technically enabled in order to efficiently execute VMI as a vehicle to secure stronger customer relationships. The highest level of VMI engagement requires a customer with real-time RF capability that will instantly notify the distributor's system at the point of use and either allow the supplier to fix reorder quantities or respond to pre-agreed amounts. Point of sale (POS) information, a capability typically only found in the most technologically developed channels like retail, should be captured. Even in most retail operations, however, there is still considerable batching, where the information is gathered together in batches rather than delivered in real time. The technology can ramp downwards through the batching process all the way to manual count, going to the supplier in a batch as the customer order is made when the customer gets to it. The further the distributor remains from real time, the more problematic (and expensive) the VMI process becomes.

Channel power is often a determinant in the level of VMI engagement. Although the supply chain can only sustain relationships where all the parties benefit, customers may believe they can benefit at the supplier's expense. Customers who mistakenly believe the only inventory cost is the cost of money often request consignment. As we shall explore later, the cost of money is only one (albeit significant) cost of inventory management. The customer, believing that the consignment inventory is free (in a sense), will neglect the inventory, leading to higher costs for the distributor.

Wiser customers will approach consignment differently, therefore, and insist on distributor involvement in inventory maintenance. The channel power relationship then becomes the determinant as to who will do what. If the customer wants close maintenance of the inventory but refuses to invest in the technology, the supplier will be faced with the decision of whether to bear the entire cost of technology or to manually maintain the inventory. For this reason, many distributors have feared approaching their most powerful customers with VMI solutions, since they may get additional business but also be asked to bear the larger portion of the cost burden.

Integrated Supply

Integrated Supply is an even more service-intensive model than VMI. In addition to the extensive tracking and system-to-system exchanges associated with VMI, I/S requires the lead distributor (integrator) to manage a second-tier group of distributors and manufacturers outside their typical channel. This poses even greater information challenges. Integrated Supply was one of the first applications considered by market makers in industrial channels due to its information exchange complexity. Market makers like Source Alliance.com and Supply Force.com started as a means for integrators to automate and extend their complex communication networks.

Many industry experts predicted in the 1990s that I/S would either go away or evolve into something else. The thinking was based on the number of distributor failures and amount of reported customer dissatisfaction with I/S. I/S has not died, although it may be changing. In 1999, a number of consulting firms assisted large manufacturers in setting a corporate strategy that would combine I/S with e-business. Essentially, the firms began requiring their integrator to use e-business tools to further improve fulfillment and reduce system costs.[5] Researchers have drawn the connection between Supply Chain Management (SCM) and programs like VMI and I/S. The advancement of SCM is driving and being driven by e-business initiatives. E-business is likely to drive I/S and VMI into more markets and increase the service offerings associated with SCM programs.

Integrated Supply was considered to be limited to MRO (Maintenance, Repair, and Operations) distribution at first, but recently retailers have asked distributors

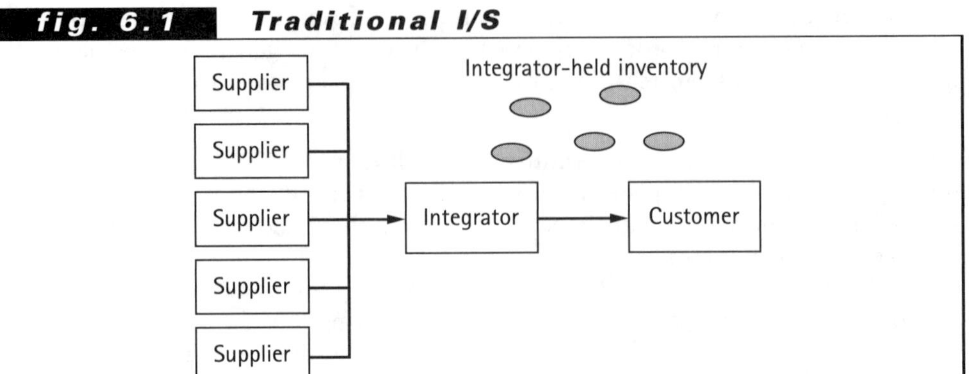

Source: Reprinted with permission of APICS—The Educational Society for Resource Management, Alexandria, VA, *Production and Inventory Management Journal,* Vol. 40, No. 2, Summer, 1999.

to handle entire product categories and manage all suppliers in that category. An example is a large retail distributor that manages major product categories for some major retailers. The distributor does not carry all the product lines and, therefore, relies on other distributors to handle fulfillment and offer technical support on those products. Retail is not the only new environment for I/S. Union Carbide and R. J. Gallagher have brought I/S into major construction projects.[6] MRO has seen tremendous growth in I/S, and other industries see it penetrating their markets as well under other names.

The early models for I/S set the integrator up as the single point of contact for the customer (see Figure 6.1). A consortium of manufacturers and distributors backed the integrator up with material outside of its product base. The integrator, or lead distributor, would manage all inventory classified as part of the agreement and handle all procurement and maintenance. This method held advantages and disadvantages for both the customer and integrator.

Customer advantages included decreases in holding costs, since the integrator held the inventory and reduced procurement costs due to the single point of contact. In addition, the integrator's expertise in inventory management led to less waste in the system. In many cases, the integrator's purchasing skills also led to enhanced pricing levels on supplies. The integrator was also asked to assist the customer in finding better uses for products or suggest new products that could improve manufacturing system performance. These were not new tasks for MRO distributors, but instead of an additional value, the process became an expectation that the distributor was now contractually bound to carry out. The improved access to the customer's operations and the sole sourcing relationship were helpful in achieving these objectives, but the lack of technical expertise in the second-tier distributor products still presented a challenge.

Customers faced potential disadvantages as well. The lack of competitive bidding could lead to complacency on the part of the integrator. An underfinanced integrator could fail and send the alliance back to square one. The integrator serves as an additional buffer between the customer and the technical expertise often needed on products. If the second-tier supplier is another distributor, technical expertise has to pass through two levels to reach the customer. Besides the time and difficulty associated with these layers, the distributors (integrator and second tier) may feel the need to shield the supplier and customer from each other.

The advantages for the integrator are long-term contracts, significantly higher volume, a more secure relationship with the customer, and increased information flow for forecasting. There are disadvantages for the integrator, however, which are a direct reflection of the advantages. The long-term contract and secure relationship are often viewed by the customer as "guaranteed business" that should lead to reductions in product or service pricing. It is difficult to explain to potential customers that not only are discounts unavailable under I/S, but that they must also compensate the integrator for services formerly regarded as free. Many distributors, in fact, have reported a drop from double- to single-digit margins in an I/S relationship.[7] This leaves little room for error in negotiating inventory management fees.

A key problem lay in the distributor value equation. Distributors have found it difficult to shift from traditional compensation models to "pay for performance" models required by service-intensive programs like I/S and VMI. Activity-based costing was used by some distributors to determine the cost and value of their services, but success was limited and the problem still loomed large in the early 2000s.[8]

To overcome the customer problem with technical support, a second model was introduced for I/S (Figure 6.2). This model allowed the second tier to ship to and interact directly with the customer. The integrator continued to act as the single point of contact in ordering and managing the customer's material needs, but the second tier was treated as a direct ship supplier. The trust implicit in I/S was elevated to a new level under this model. The customer had to demonstrate that the second-tier suppliers would not be used as potential replacements for the integrator. Although the second tier typically supplied product not carried by the integrator, the

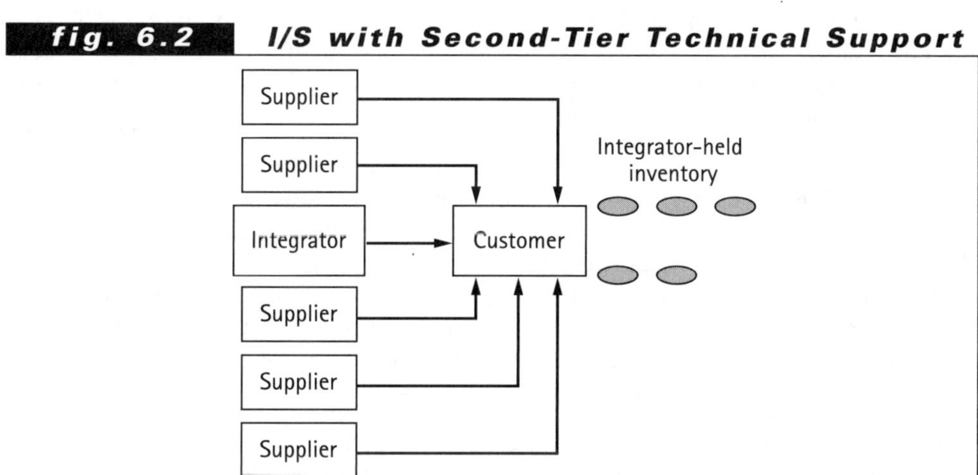

fig. 6.2   *I/S with Second-Tier Technical Support*

Source: Reprinted with permission of APICS—The Educational Society for Resource Management, Alexandria, VA, *Production and Inventory Management Journal,* Vol. 40, No. 2, Summer, 1999.

members of the second tier would undoubtedly contain firms who acted as integrators elsewhere.

The higher volume served as a dangerous "hook" for the integrator in the I/S relationship. The customer frequently used the promise of volume as a reason to cut the integrator's margins. An important requirement of I/S was, therefore, to develop a keen understanding of one's own cost structure and the customer's as well. Another equally important requirement of I/S is the need for a well-written Statement of Work (SOW). The integrator would write the SOW to specifically define the services and functions that they would be expected to provide under the terms of the contract. This document would provide both parties with a clear understanding of what was expected of the integrator. In many cases, the SOW would identify the fees to be paid to the integrator for each agreed-upon activity or service. This document would also protect the integrator from "activity creep," which happens when the customer asks the integrator to perform just a few more services than the contract specifies, but at no added cost.

With a clearly defined Statement of Work, the integrator can agree to perform new services, but only after the cost to provide these is included in a revised SOW. The revised SOW reflects the additional services that the integrator will provide and the resulting increase in fees that they will garner to offset the added cost. Understanding the customer's costs would make selling an I/S relationship easier, since the integrator could demonstrate customer savings to offset inventory management fees in the compensation negotiation. The potential for decreasing costs through direct ERP to ERP connection facilitated by e-business tools backing up an I/S implementation led to the development of sites created specifically for I/S.

Matching costs to customer savings is the key issue in successfully selling I/S and negotiating profitable contracts. Some costs could be identified with global information, some with customer specific data, and others would still be guesswork. In a successful negotiation, the customer-specific data is most powerful followed by global information. Guesswork should be limited as much as possible, since any unsubstantiated facts will become points of contention in the negotiation. The need for customer information to be integrated into the integrator's system is critical, therefore, and most I/S participants now recognize the significance to the process of e-business tools.

At the close of the 1990s, the key issue became not whether I/S would continue to grow (it did), but where distributors should position themselves. There were three options: integrator, second tier, and nonparticipant. To be a successful integrator, the distributor had to have certain characteristics, "table stakes" so to speak. These "table stakes" were product breadth, geographic scope, and technological capability. While an integrator could make up for weaknesses in one area with strengths in another, a distributor without a strong competence in any of the three would have a difficult time surviving as an I/S integrator.

Product breadth means the integrator has a major portion of the products called for in the I/S relationship. The wider the integrator's product offering, the less dependent on the second tier the relationship becomes. Since second-tier suppliers are a major challenge in an I/S relationship, the integrator would like to minimize the number necessary to meet the customer's needs. Note that this is also consistent with one of the I/S drivers, supplier reduction. If a manufacturer seeks supplier reduction and has the integrator work with the same number of suppliers as the manufacturer did prior to I/S, the supplier coordination problem has merely been pushed upstream.

Geographic scope deals with another major I/S driver. Customers were forming alliances, sometimes referred to as national or global accounts, in order to ensure consistent, reliable delivery at all their operations. Distributors, other than a few "super distributors," tended to be regional.

Distributors recognized the need for supplier consolidation, geographic reach, and technological capability and typically pursued one of two paths: become a consolidator or join industry alliances. A good example of an industry consolidator is W. W. Grainger. Grainger set out to bring as many product categories as possible under one umbrella. Grainger remains a powerful integrator and has interwoven its e-business initiatives into its I/S offering. The need to bring the customer's information directly into the integrator's operations has continued to drive home the connection between I/S and e-business.

Another strategy pursued by distribution channel members has been to develop industry alliance mechanisms that act as the integrator in the I/S relationship and factor out fulfillment to distributor members (the second tier). This strategy allows smaller distributors to maintain the integrity of their line card by limiting the engagement to products, which they are authorized to sell, and develop partnerships with other small regional players through the interface of the integrator mechanism to serve large customers. Affiliated Distributors (AD), an organization of distributors based on this strategy, set up an e-business mechanism, Supply Force.com, which would act as the e-business integrator. Supply Force would secure the contract (the same as AD did) and act as the integrator, using AD members for fulfillment.

A rival to Supply Force was Source Alliance.com, incubated at Rockwell Automation before being released into the channel. Manufacturers, Allen-Bradley distributors (a Rockwell product line), and other distributors were encouraged to take an equity position in Source Alliance and participate in the I/S arrangements it made. After some initial success, the dot-com integrators had difficulty sustaining critical mass. Source Alliance closed its doors in early 2001.

If the e-business consortiums were temporary, then the "super distributors" (such as Grainger) could eventually dominate the large I/S accounts. A remaining argument, however, was that the I/S movement would prove unsustainable and that integrators would be reduced to their core competency products. Instead of maintaining multiple product lines, integrators would retain their specializations and the customer would manage several integrators. While this appeared to be a step back for the customer, the increase in suppliers would be from one to maybe as many as ten. This is still a far cry from the dozens or hundreds prior to I/S.

This arrangement is not really I/S, however, but VMI with sole sourcing in a product category. The definition is mostly semantics, however, and the need for geographic reach and technological sophistication remains. The SCM movement would continue to drive the need for firms tied into their customer operations through system-to-system connections.

Regardless of the technique used to connect the customer—system-to-system, alliance, or both—SCM would push the e-business envelope. Distributors searched for ways to meet the SCM goals with new technologies and customer management methodologies but were hampered by the high costs and risks associated with e-business. E-business became less expensive with each new technological advance. Programs like Integrated Supply and Vendor Managed Inventory mandated better information handling. The distributor needed to lay out a strategy and justify, implement, and monitor it for continuous improvement. Chapter 7 will describe some of the tools used for e-business and Part Three will examine how to improve processes with those tools.

Distributor Retrospective

David Mullins must have an understanding of the e-business tools that can be used to connect Dalton's customers with Dalton's operation. Also, Mullins must have an awareness of the possible benefits and possible costs that will result from such an initiative. He also must understand the economic analysis that is used to conduct the cost-benefit study. Finally, Mullins needs to understand the strategic implications of the role of e-business within Dalton Supply.

Issues to Consider

1. Describe each of the four key e-business drivers and explain why each is important for success in e-business.

2. Discuss each of the levels of engagement regarding Vendor Managed Inventory (VMI), and why they are necessary to successful VMI. Include in your discussion the advantages and disadvantages of each.

3. Which levels of engagement in VMI are most and least desirable from the distributor's perspective and why?

4. What are the potential benefits of VMI for the customer and the distributor and why? Also discuss the technology enablers that facilitate this process.

5. What are the potential advantages and disadvantages of Integrated Supply to the customer?

6. Discuss the three primary drivers of a successful Integrated Supply alliance and why they are important.

Notes

1. F. Barry Lawrence, Ramesh Krishnamurthi, Nishet Dayal, Mona Raina, and Leigh Robinson, "Evaluation of E-Partnerships," Texas A&M University, 2001.

2. Gary Stading, F. Barry Lawrence, Bharani B. Nagarathnam, and Ram Narayan, "Neutral vs. Non-Neutral Marketmakers," Texas A&M University, 2001.

3. F. Barry Lawrence, Ramesh Krishnamurthi, Nishet Dayal, Mona Raina, and Leigh Robinson, "Evaluation of E-Partnerships," Texas A&M University, 2001.

4. "Discount Stores," *Chain Store Age,* improved inventory management supplement, December 1996,13A–15A.

5. "Streamlining Distribution," *Washington Technology* 14 (7): 28–32 (1999).

6. F. Barry Lawrence and Anoop Varma, "Integrated Supply for Projects," *Supply House Times* 43 (4): 41–42 (2000).

7. F. Barry Lawrence and Anoop Varma, "Integrated Supply: Supply Chain Management in Materials Management and Procurement," *Production and Inventory Management Journal* 40 (2): 1–5 (1999).

8. Pirttilä Timo and Hautaniemi Petri, "Activity-based costing and distribution logistics management," *International Journal of Production Economics* 41 October 1995, 327–333.

E-business Tools for Customer Relationship Management

Distributor Perspective

Henry Morgan, president of Associated Electrical Inc. (AEI), has been approached by AEI's vice president of sales, Richard Stanley, about automating the activities of AEI's sales force as well as automating certain customer relationships. AEI has annual sales of $200 million with sixteen branches located in the Midwest and is heavily involved in MRO sales for a variety of manufacturing processes. Stanley is interested in automating the sales force to enable AEI's inside-sales personnel to become effective in dealing with customer inquiries. Also, he believes that AEI can increase sales by interfacing its information technology systems with those of its customers. Stanley is somewhat hesitant to identify specific benefits that can be obtained from his recommendation and is unsure what the costs might be. Morgan is interested in Stanley's request but is unsure on how to develop an implementation plan.

Introduction

E-business tools reflect the nature of traditional distribution channels but are designed, for the most part, to facilitate information flow upstream and downstream as opposed to the strictly downstream flow that we associate with materials and services for the customer or end user. These tools are designed to connect the customer, automate transactions, offer a communication medium, develop catalogs, and integrate the back office into the supply chain.

Customer Relationship Management (CRM) tools are designed to automate an information-rich environment (distribution and its customers). As such, the rewards are tremendous, but the challenges are significant. Many firms and dot-coms made a tremendous investment in an effort to establish automated customer relationships in the late 1990s only to find it very difficult to get customers to utilize their services. One large distributor, for instance, established a website with the objective of automating the customer relationship, especially for obsolete products or special orders, but was unable to convince customers of the site's utility.[1] After extensive promotion, the company was forced to take a multimillion-dollar write-off due to lack of customer interest.[2]

A fundamental flaw in Internet CRM planning was the assumption that traditional relationships would bend to the new technology. Dell and Amazon.com seemed to demonstrate that the Internet would destroy traditional relationships rather than simply increase their efficiency. Relationships, however, are built on core competencies. The supplying firm demonstrates the value of its capabilities, and a relationship is developed based on the value generated for the customer and the reliability of the supplier to consistently deliver that service.

Core competencies are the skill sets that constitute a competitive advantage for a firm. For distribution, the key core competency is the facilitator role. The distributor facilitates the gaps between manufacturing capacity and market demand through inventory management, technical knowledge and support for the customer, and other channel-smoothing functions such as providing customer financing. Each of these functions is largely an information manipulation exercise that the distributor manages through its channel knowledge.

Defining CRM for Distribution

Distribution knowledge can be divided into explicit and tacit forms.[3] Explicit knowledge is information that can be explained in structured form and can, therefore, be programmed. Examples of explicit knowledge include the information necessary to match product descriptions to part numbers, converting an order by unit of measurement (a customer orders 100 items, which translates into one bag of parts for the distributor), and other such rote activities. These activities are consistent and can be handled by an automated system, although many of these systems are more difficult to automate than are others. Many sales activities fall under the category of explicit knowledge.

Tacit knowledge, on the other hand, is inconsistent, fuzzier to explain, and poorly understood. Customer behavior and the sales force response to such behavior is an example of tacit knowledge. Communication often carries hidden messages that an astute salesperson can discern and manipulate to both the customer's and the distribution firm's benefit. Some behaviors are simply so complex that explaining them explicitly appears impossible. Forecasting requirements from small customers who do not share information with their suppliers is often considered a difficult art form. Computers are not considered artistic, only capable of mimicking that which is well understood.

E-business focuses on the automation of explicit knowledge. Aggressive firms will seek to further define tacit knowledge and move it to the explicit realm where it can be automated. This procedure makes many distribution professionals uneasy, since it seems to threaten jobs and perhaps even corporate survival if applied incorrectly. For example, consider an inside sales force that works the phones for customer calls. Much of what the inside salesperson does can be automated or further facilitated by information automation. Sales transactions can be automated if a system-to-system connection exists and a rule-based system (see Chapter 9) for transactions is developed, removing the need for human decision-making. This sort of automated sales force was first envisioned in the early days of Electronic Data Interchange (EDI) in the 1970s.

Sales professionals are quick to point out that many of their activities are not so easily automated. Understanding the customer and his or her behavior can be a complex process. This is precisely, however, the purpose of data mining and customer profiling. Data mining is the process of examining data to determine if relationships exist that are not immediately apparent. When data mining is combined with customer profiling, in which the supplier tracks customer behavior and preferences, an automated system can develop an understanding (knowledge) of customer needs and behavior that may be hard for a salesperson to duplicate. Amazon.com and other database marketers have used customer profiling to suggest additional products of interest to a customer. This systematized relationship tool can be even more personal than dealing with a human being who cannot remember all of our preferences.

Many people are starting to expect systems to maintain a profile of their purchasing behavior and respond to predictable (repeated) needs instantaneously. Think how many times you have overheard the following or even said it to a salesperson yourself: "I've bought this item from you many times, doesn't your system show that?" Whether we know it or not, this process of automating explicit information has been under way for sometime. Customer expectations in this regard are not only continuing to grow but are growing at an accelerating rate. If a firm does not automate a function and thereby reduce its cost, then competitors may do so and render the process obsolete. Explicit knowledge, therefore, does not constitute a core competency, since it can be automated and replicated by many companies. Core competencies come from tacit knowledge.

If the inside sales force can have so many of its processes, including CRM, automated, is the inside salesperson destined to become extinct? Probably not— customer expectations have continued to grow at such a rate that IT systems will likely always

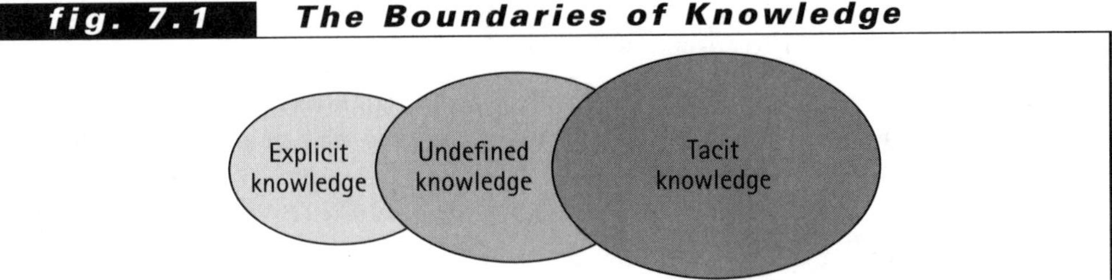

fig. 7.1   *The Boundaries of Knowledge*

Source: F. Barry Lawrence and William Christensen, "The Boundaries of Knowledge," adapted from course lectures at Texas A&M University, 2001.

lag behind what the customer desires. This implies the inside sales force will continue to grow into new areas of value add. As the inside sales force sees many of its functions become well defined, it will push the frontier of tacit knowledge and add new value that may not be currently envisioned but will be demanded as customers come to take the explicit knowledge that has been automated for granted and look for more. This implies that inside sales will be a moving target that keeps changing its nature.

If tacit knowledge is the key to competitiveness, the firm must seek to understand it as quickly as possible; as tacit knowledge becomes better understood, it will cross the line into explicit knowledge. The frontier between explicit and tacit knowledge is, therefore, where processes become well understood and then automated. The frontier on the other side of tacit knowledge is not clear, and its size is, for most organizations, impossible to define (see Figure 7.1). It may be, in fact, limitless, since a firm that has completely controlled a market and made the perfect offering does not exist, and if it did it would merely move into other markets and start the process all over again. The goal, therefore, is to simultaneously define explicit knowledge and automate it before your competition can, and continue to push the boundary of tacit knowledge outward to gain competitive advantage. This discussion has centered on the inside sales force but applies equally to other distribution processes, as we shall see in further chapters.

Hardware Needs

Getting connected has become very easy with the widespread availability of high-speed networks provided by Internet Service Providers (ISPs). Security has also come a long way with the introduction of firewalls and other security measures associated with Internet applications. No system is foolproof, and any firewall that can be built by one programmer can be breached by another. Every year many hackers penetrate the Department of Defense computers.[4] While due caution should be observed, Internet security tools have become quite robust, and most distribution operations will not attract the attention of the most dangerous hackers.

Viruses are a more serious threat and have had a significant impact but are usually designed to attack a system that has opened itself to random messages coming in. Setting up secure relationships with suppliers and customers can minimize this risk, but remaining alert to threats is still the best defense.

The main problems associated with connecting through the Web to suppliers and customers are the cost of catalog development and the risk of overwhelming your hardware and/or software. We will discuss catalogs later. The hardware issue revolves around database management. Software issues are what types of CRM software to use and to what effect.

The necessary hardware depends on whether the firm intends to employ a mainframe-based system or a client/server environment. Both methods can be used effectively; the issues to consider are cost, control, and legacy systems. Large firms with many locations might favor a mainframe system with inexpensive dummy terminals, whereas a smaller firm might employ a client/server approach in which each client has more power relative to the information system server so that analysis can be performed on the local computer. On the other hand, some firms favor a centralized approach to information management and prefer to have all information centralized. While client/server systems can achieve centralization, mainframe systems tend to bring information into one central location, which may give management a greater sense of control.

The most common determining factor, however, is past practice. Whatever system the company has utilized in the past is likely to be utilized in the future. Once the IT system has been integrated into the company, it maybe easier to upgrade that technology than to change to another technology. The transition does not just involve hardware, but also how sales and logistics processes interact with the system. Changing how sales and logistics operations draw critical information and then feed it back into the system is a major redesign that many firms are unwilling to undertake. Given the capability of both system types to carry out distribution operations, most firms have not found it necessary to switch.

The most important issue is capacity. Underpowered systems have to be upgraded if sufficient space or computing speed does not exist. The computing needs associated with data mining and customer profiling are immense, and distributors that are interested in better understanding their customers should not underestimate the impact on their system. While it may appear logical to buy a less powerful system and upgrade as needs dictate, this process will likely cause IT and process specialists to be conservative in initiating critical competitive marketing and operations programs. At the very least, it will slow the process because initiatives that run up against system constraints will have to be shelved while the system is upgraded. The loss of time could have an effect on the firm's competitive position.

Software Needs

Choosing which CRM software to employ is also a difficult decision. Communication standards hampered the process of connecting the customer throughout the 1990s and have troubled firms into the 2000s. If the customer could not easily be directly connected, the question remained as to what analysis could and should be performed based on the limited information that could be exchanged. Standardiza-

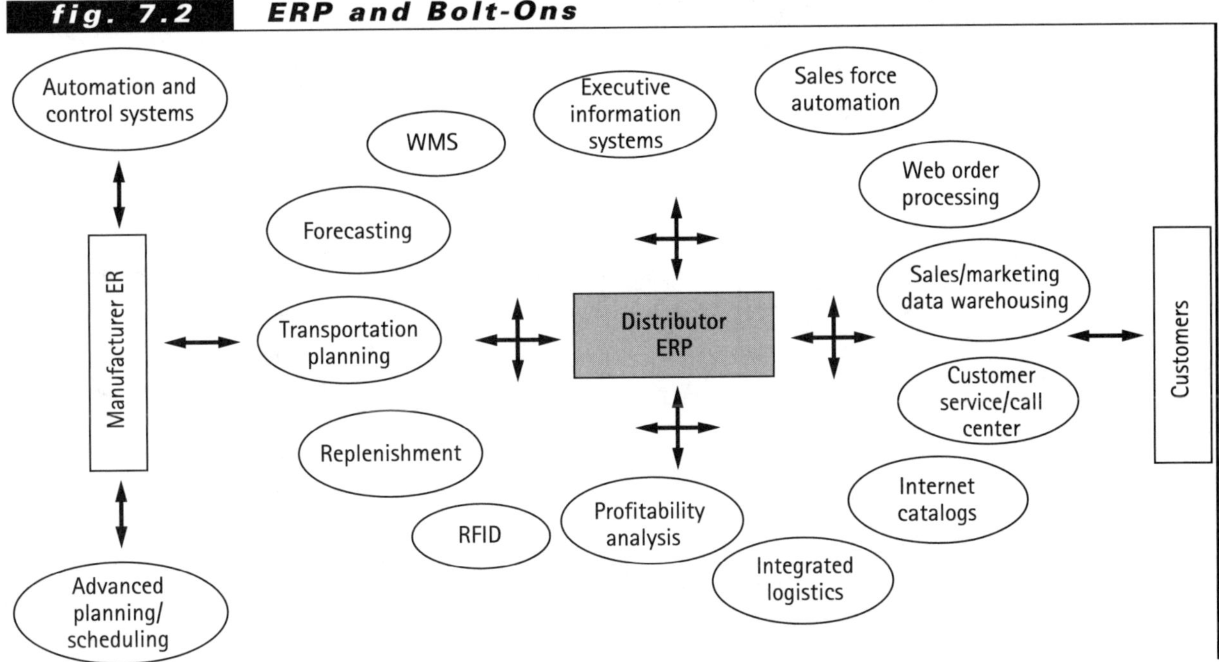

Source: F. Barry Lawrence and Ramesh Krishnamurthi, "Supply Chain Systems Laboratory: Simulation of Supply Chain Systems," proposal submitted to National Science Foundation, 2001.

tion is discussed in greater detail in Chapter 11. At this point, we consider what type of analysis is possible at any level of customer data collection.

Types of Analysis

Customer data is collected on a regular basis by all firms. The data is also entered into whatever information system is employed at the firm. What sort of software analysis tools can be applied to this data? The mission of customer data management is to anticipate and meet customer needs, minimize system costs, and develop new opportunities. Figure 7.2 lists some of the potential software solutions that surround the distributor's ERP or back office systems.

Anticipating and Meeting Customer Needs

Anticipation of customer needs falls into two categories: predicting with historical information and predicting with little or no history. Meeting these needs involves all of the customer contact mechanisms often referred to as Customer Relationship Management (CRM). When CRM is programmed and systematized, it becomes CRM software (see Figure 7.3).

The front-end CRM tools collect information to drive the ERP customer and sales force support tools. Sales force automation automates rote tasks and collects data

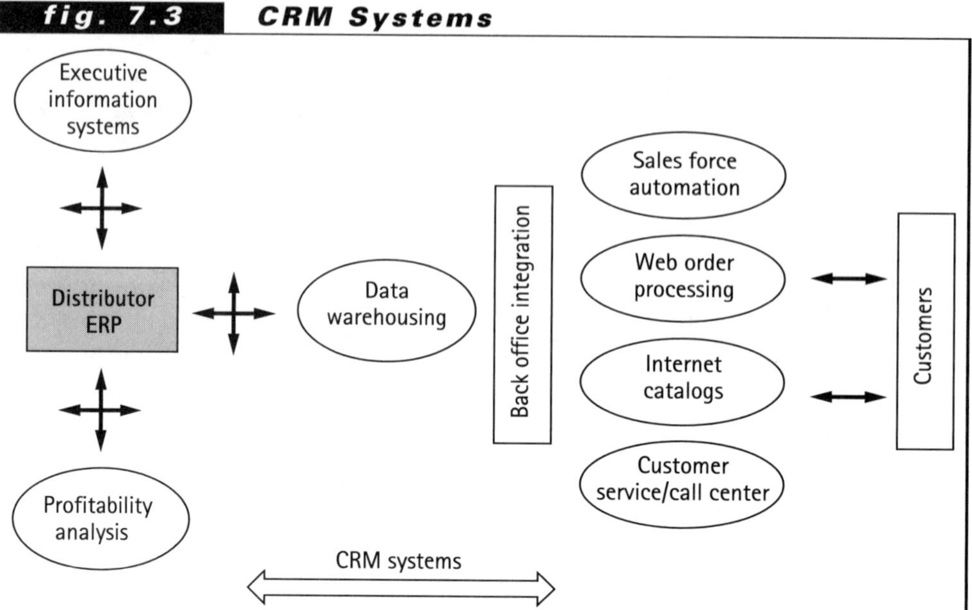

from the sales force for rapid transferal to the ERP system. The same is true for Web order processing, Internet catalogs, and customer call center software except that the information is typically being collected directly from the customer.

ERP support tools include systems for forecasting, executive information, profitability analysis, transportation, data mining, warehouse management, and various other analysis tools. The information collected by these programs is stored in data warehouses after being put in understandable formats by back-office integration techniques. Once in place, executive information systems create reports that give management an understanding of the firm's performance.

Forecasting Tools

Data collection activity is the base of forecasting. If the underlying data is inaccurate, the forecast will be inaccurate. Garbage In/Garbage Out (GIGO) is the rule. The system must be guarded against activities that will cause the data to be false next year. To do so requires processes that are well understood, documented, and automated to the greatest extent possible. Human beings are variable, and the greater the human interaction with the data collection process, the more error will be introduced into the data. There are limitless examples of how human interaction interferes with the accuracy of the data collection process.

Let's examine some examples from the customer, the distribution operation, and suppliers. Forecast data problems generated by customer activity are many. The customer may, for example, buy from multiple suppliers either (1) to diversify the risk that any one of the suppliers will stockout or (2) to drive prices down. This means that the distributor may obtain the sale one year and not the next year or vice versa.

The customer actually needs the product. Thus the demand is real, but the sale is lost due to pricing or some other service issue. This means the distributor's system does not have a clear picture of actual customer needs.

Customers may also order at irregular intervals if their counts are not systematic. If ordering takes place when it is convenient for the customer to do so, and if the customer carries a significant inventory, the orders may not take place in the periods in which the need really existed. Next year the inventory status or timing of counts may push the same demand into another period. The customer's product utilization may follow a regular pattern, but the data in the distributor's system will not reflect the "true" pattern.

Solutions to customer data problems typically combine strategic alliances with software/hardware solutions. The strategic alliance—VMI, I/S, or some other agreement—provides the distributor access to the customer's data. Once access is gained, hardware and software solutions can be implemented. On the hardware side, the customer's operations and "real-time" utilization are delivered to the distributor through Point of Sale devices such as radio frequency (RF) scanners that connect to the customer's information system and are then connected to the distributor's system. In the past, the technology associated with these types of connections was prohibitively expensive for most firms, but the cost is dropping quickly and adoption is spreading.

If the customer's system does not utilize "real-time" tools, then the process—for distribution—becomes one of understanding the impact of batching. Information batching means that blocks of information are gathered and acted upon at differing time intervals rather than instantaneously. The issue is one of time and control. On the time side, the length and regularity of the batching process will influence the reliability of the information for forecasting. The distributor also needs control to ensure that the information is of sufficient quality (data integrity) and to understand its weaknesses (timeliness, accuracy) so that appropriate analysis takes place. Batching periods are a function of how the customer's ordering process is carried out.

If RF technology is employed, the system is immediately notified as an item is scanned, and the distributor's system is instantly notified of the movement. The next level is scanning and batching in short intervals. The customer may scan the item with a device that stores the data and then put the device in a "cradle" that transfers the information from the device to the information system that communicates with the distributor's system. In this case the batch period is the length of time between updates from the scanning device and the customer's system (usually measured in hours).

If, on the other hand, no technology is employed, the customer's system update might be measured in days or longer periods. If no connection exists between the customer's system and the distributor's system, the combination of batching information for loading into the customer's system and batching information when the customer places orders will lead to gaps of weeks or months in information timing for the distributor. The longer the information-batching period and less system-to-system control of information handling, the more opportunity there is for error to be introduced through human interaction or the fact that the batch combines activity into buckets that do not reflect the exact time that demand occurred.

Beyond the hardware and software associated with bringing the customer's operations to real time, the connection between systems is another challenge. Throughout its history, EDI has been plagued by cost and standardization issues, and in spite of the efforts on the part of professional associations such as Rosetta.net, the same issue remained a problem in the early 2000s. Commerce One and Ariba were attempting to overcome the problems by providing communication standards and infrastructure that would allow companies to communicate seamlessly, but the difficult hurdles remained. One problem was uncertainty as to whether the industry would be forced to adopt standards or the standards would be forced to reflect the industry and allow firms to continue customizing their relationships. If the latter occurred, the introduction of e-business would be a more intense programming and design process and would proceed much slower than originally predicted.

The best scenario is real-time entry and capture, which is growing in adoption, but in the meantime, the software solutions must deal with the time gaps associated with batching. This means CRM software tools must be robust (capable of providing good analysis with flawed data). Forecasting software typically comes in two forms: embedded in ERP software or as a bolt-on. Bolt-ons can be used with many different systems and operate essentially the same as those embedded in ERP software. The principal difference lies where each gets its data and functionality.

ERP forecasting will draw its data from the system's database(s) and use it in its forecasting process. Problems frequently arise because the database is also storing data for multiple other functions of the ERP system. The other functions may require data storage that limits the space for forecasting data. One response is to limit the number of periods of historical sales data stored. The most powerful forecasting techniques require three years of data, which requires considerable space.

Standard forecasting methodologies employed by many ERP systems are statistical forecasting and simulation. Statistical forecasting techniques include moving averages, exponential smoothing (a special form of moving average), and linear regression. These techniques are discussed in detail in the next chapter. The ERP versus bolt-on decision will typically be based on the quality of these systems offered as part of the package. Some ERP systems, for instance, do not have exponential smoothing, regression, or simulation. Exponential smoothing has proven to be a highly effective mathematical method that minimizes system utilization. Regression allows the user to add other impacting variables besides last year's sales, such as new building permits issued (important for building materials distribution planning), customer forecasts, and stock market performance. Simulation will typically take a variety of techniques and determine which has been most effective in forecasting a product, and will use that one for the next forecast. The strengths and weaknesses of each as well as how they are calculated will be addressed in the next chapter.

Besides functionality, deciding whether to use your system's forecasting capability or use a bolt-on involves process issues. If the base data is filled with integrity problems, your ERP package may be preferable to a bolt-on with greater functionality. One firm was investigating its forecasting problems when it discovered (through testing) that methods considered to be superior to the ones in their ERP system would not work as well due to the firm's data integrity problems. More sophisticated algorithms could not handle the wild, seemingly unpredictable swings in the data. The data was flawed for many reasons, and the firm's ERP forecasting model over-smoothed the data (typically a bad thing). However, over-smoothing was effective in this example because it removed a great many false patterns in the data. If the data had been sound, however, the method would have removed true demand patterns and underperformed the more sophisticated methods that are present in a bolt-on.

Bolt-ons are comparable to specialists in any field. The specialist will have a greater degree of capability but may not be justified if the firm is unable to react to the specialist's skills or recommendations. An investment banker could offer good advice and services for selling your firm, but if you do not have sufficient volume and profits, the cost outweighs the benefit. If a firm cannot provide good data to an expensive bolt-on, then the firm may be better off without it. The firm should also not assume that the methods employed by the bolt-on are superior just because the software is specialized. Many programs were developed years ago and are sold as modules to software providers. The bolt-on may, in fact, be using the same basic code and logic as your system does, but may offer other features your firm does not need or cannot use because of system or data constraints.

One feature offered by some forecasting bolt-ons is inventory decision-making capability. The system will take the forecast and translate it into safety stock recommendations (discussed in Chapter 10) and then give the buyer a recommended order size. This communication between the forecasting system and the inventory decision modules is essential. If a firm uses a bolt-on that communicates with its ERP or back office inventory decision-making modules, then proper transfer of forecast error metrics and estimates of demand must be transmitted to the ERP system. If the firm uses the bolt-on's inventory decision module, the inventory levels (regular and safety stock) and purchase amounts will have to be communicated back to the firm's system. Where and when to use a bolt-on and at what point in the process to return data and analysis to your system are important tactical decisions in bolt-on selection and implementation.

Software decisions also deal with cost minimization. An accurate forecast goes a long way toward cost minimization, but there are other possibilities as well. Software available on ERP or bolt-ons includes packages that will allow for transportation management, profitability analysis, facility location, warehouse management, and other potential savings.

Customer Transportation Needs

Transportation management is critical for the success of distribution firms. Most distributors go from the few to the many, meaning that distributors take product from a few suppliers and deliver it to many customers. The number of suppliers can be quite large but is usually well below the number of customers. The inbound transportation management issue is important and can be merged with outbound issues. However, outbound transportation issues typically involve greater expense items than do inbound transportation issues. Outbound transportation is usually considered more important because of the number of shipments, the customer service implications, the fact that freight is paid by the distributor, the involvement of private fleets, and the auditing of freight bills.

The transportation function for most distributors is closest to the customer and therefore highly critical. Distributors struggle with scheduling outbound trips to meet customer demands that vary from day to day or even hour to hour. The distribution firm will either manage the process through common carriers, a private fleet, or some combination of the two. Common carriers do not require the distributor to handle the routing of trucks, but the carriers will frequently give discounts if the customer provides a back haul (a load on the return trip) or at least places the truck into an area where other business can be found. Transportation to or near a major logistics hub such as Chicago, Dallas, or Los Angeles, for example, may be less expensive than to a destination where the opportunity to take advantage of the back haul is less likely. Florida, for instance, tends to take in more freight than it ships out; therefore it is typically cheaper to ship out of rather than into Florida.

Anyone who has scheduled airline tickets from different cities and seen how the fares vary with the time of day and from airport to airport knows that scheduling transportation involves complex decisions. Deciding what route to take and when can make a significant financial difference. Distributors continuously dispatch freight to customers. Thus not only are the savings opportunities immense, the complexity of scheduling can be overwhelming.

The scheduling decision is not the only problem, however. Freight classification and contract negotiations are also quite complex. If an item is shipped under the wrong classification, a nonbreakable commodity versus a fragile special item, for example, the freight cost can vary tremendously. Contractual agreements are established in advance to set freight rates and costs with preferred carriers to simplify the shipping decision. Even so, the freight commonly gets misclassified by either the firm or the carrier, or the contractual agreed-upon price is not recognized by the carrier and the firm is overcharged. Freight bill auditing is an important function that can lead to substantial savings for a distribution operation.

If the firm maintains a private fleet, the effects of these decisions are magnified. Poor routing decisions have a direct impact on fleet utilization. The company must directly attempt to limit empty back hauls and trucks that are not fully loaded whenever possible. Poor utilization leads to increased need for capacity (more trucks). With a private fleet, the firm must deal with labor issues involving drivers in addition to environmental and safety issues. Also, many of the issues involved with a private fleet are subject to governmental regulations, as opposed to the classification and contractual arrangements involved in the use of common carriers. Thus, with a private fleet, the proper loading and routing of trucks becomes both an efficiency and legal issue.

Transportation software solutions for distribution typically come in the form of ERP bolt-ons, complementary packages, or external providers. ERP bolt-ons include specialized software for vehicle routing that can minimize back hauls and optimize utilization. The complexity issue does get in the way, however, and the firm should closely examine the software, especially the basic assumptions of the distributor's transportation process. For example, one such assumption is that the distributor will provide the system with a preloaded truck. The loading process, however, is dependent on the route (we do not know what to put on the truck until we know its route and vice versa), so loading and routing have to be handled in an iterative fashion in which loads are established, routes set up, loads are reevaluated, and routes are reset, until a good solution is determined. Many software packages cannot handle such a complex problem. The bolt-on will also be challenged by the "hand-off" of information from the distributor's information system.

Packages complementary to ERP will establish an environment that combines transportation software with warehouse management systems and other logistics software. Commonly called channel software or logistics packages, these programs provide for a more all-inclusive solution but carry a price tag frequently comparable to that of ERP providers. In firms in which the transportation issue is huge, however, these packages can make a significant impact.

Another option, popular in recent years, has been to outsource transportation decisions. A third-party logistics company (3PL) will manage all freight through its own software and the use of common carriers, the distributor's fleet, and the 3PL's own fleet if it has one. This strategy puts the transportation function in the hands of a specialist with its own tools (software). The decision to go in this direction is based on the 3PL's capability, distributor freight volume, and customer relationships. Capability means that the 3PL can minimize freight expenses to such an extent that it pays for itself and returns additional savings to the distributor. However, without sufficient distributor freight volume, this is unlikely because of the implementation and operational costs of the 3PL. Customer relationships refer to the attachment the customer has to the distributor's transportation service. If the driver is viewed as part of the service (a problem solver for the customer), special provisions must be made to ensure the 3PL driver functions as an employee and representative of the distributor.

Application Service Providers (ASPs) have also become involved in the transportation activity. The ASP cannot engage in in-house activity, but the interaction with the common carriers and possibly routing and freight bill auditing can be handled over the Net. A major complication in managing common carriers is knowing, up to the minute, what the common carrier rates are and what configurations can be formed to minimize freight costs. This requires a database with complete common carrier scheduling and rates at any point in time. No distributor system can maintain such a relationship, so ASPs are springing up that provide access to this type of information, usually in conjunction with other bolt-ons such as freight bill auditing and routing software. A 3PL can also use these sites, but many firms are forming their own relationships with these new ASPs that have been created, in many cases, by 3PL's.

Profitability Analysis

Profitability analysis software uses Activity Based Management (ABM) techniques to identify the value provided by an action. An example is sales analysis, when a customer service representative (CSR) is in the process of negotiating a sale. Many activities are involved that will determine the profitability or nonprofitability of the transaction. Direct cost factors such as the amount the customer is willing to pay, the cost of the item, logistics costs, after-sale support, and credit have to be compared with the magnitude of the sale, the amount of inventory in stock, the value of the customer (long-term versus one-time transaction), and so forth before deciding whether to make the sale, modify the terms, or refuse the sale. The CSR typically makes this challenging decision on the fly without much guidance. This decision, in effect, determines the profitability of the distributor.

Profitability analysis software considers the cost of support activities (from an ABM analysis) and combines them with the margin, inventory levels, and other factors to determine whether a sale is profitable. The softer issues of customer value can be handled by the CSR, or the ABM analysis can also perform a customer value analysis and use it as input as well. To be successful, this type of software will be very dependent on the quality of the ABM analysis.

Facility Planning

Facility location software can be used to analyze the functioning of a distribution network. The firm may use the software to determine whether and where a new site should be opened or whether others should be closed. The decision-making process will consider inventory requirements, transportation costs, facility fixed and variable costs, labor availability and cost, and customer allocation, among other factors. The software will typically be loaded with current levels for each of the variables and then will "run." It can then be rerun repeatedly with differing levels for the variables that are in dispute among the management team until a decision is made. This type of software can be used to make a one-time decision, such as where to open a new facility, or for ongoing evaluation of when and where customers should be allocated and how the facility network should respond to customer demand.

Warehouse Management Systems (WMS) govern inventory storage activity and make the connection between demand (from the sales systems) and logistics response (shipping and delivery) while maintaining as efficient a configuration and as productive a movement as possible in the warehouse. The logic is similar to facility location in that there are locations, and material is moved as in transportation networks. The connection to the ERP or other information systems is critical to fulfillment performance for a WMS.

There are other packages that can optimize distribution operations and respond to the customer, and more are being developed on an ongoing basis. Any adoption or use of specialized software already on a firm's system requires an understanding of the information needed for effective decision-making, and awareness of its availability and reliability. If the information is not available or not reliable, the firm should give serious consideration to its data collection and storage techniques and the impact of less than perfect information on the quality of the solutions provided by the software.

Developing New Opportunities

If anticipating customer needs, maintaining customer relationships, and minimizing costs are essential to corporate survival, a further consideration in software selection is the ability to open up new opportunities (markets) for the firm. Dot-coms promised to offer new markets, but many did not succeed. Data mining techniques, discussed earlier, promise to identify marketing opportunities such as trends, new product/service offerings, and other customer relationship issues that may not be detected through standard means. The key to using these tools is developing an understanding of how the tools are used, integrating them into other processes, and developing ways to respond to identified opportunities.

Database marketing refers to both data mining and the storage of useful data for mining. Data warehousing is becoming increasingly important to make available information that can be used to transform businesses. The key to database design is maintaining the right data, in the right form, in an easy-to-access fashion.

The right data simply means the data that can be used for the desired analysis. An example would be forecast data. Sales data stored in dollars may be useful for financial planning, but is not useful for forecasting purposes. To forecast demand, we need unit sales data. The data also needs to be in the right format. If the firm is designing a warehouse and using the cube dimension of product to determine its shelving needs, the data needs to be in a Unit of Measure (UOM) and dimension that the product would typically be stored in. If the product typically gets stored and sold in bags of one hundred, the cube space should apply to the bag. In WMS systems that use random put away to minimize space utilization, dimensional data must be in the proper format to succeed. Finally, the analysis software must be able to access the information easily. If data mining requires extensive manual efforts to access data and to manipulate, the opportunity to use it will be reduced.

The key software components for uncovering new opportunities, therefore, are proper data analysis tools that can predict trends or unsatisfied customer demand and data warehousing tools that offer storage for large amounts of data in easily accessible formats. There are many data storage packages available. Analysis software is less common and much of it is still experimental. Firms should use caution and retain experts for analysis in this area. The chance to uncover new opportunities has never been greater, however, and will likely improve as new solutions are developed.

Catalog Development

A great deal of attention was paid to catalog development during the late 1990s, when the expectation was that distributors would maintain their own catalogs. The costs associated with standardization gave birth to many attempts to standardize data that were still unrealized at the beginning of the twenty-first century. In 2001 thoughts on catalog development began to shift from a defensive posture with catalogs viewed as a way of preventing disintermediation by selling on the Web to a focus on exploring the value created by offering an online presence.

The lackluster performance of e-catalogs and the cost of their development have slowed the movement somewhat. However, with more IT companies offering catalog development, catalog costs were beginning to decline in the early 2000s. In addition, the value proposition was changing. Some distributors began to see catalogs as a method for generating product inquiries. If their customers directed end users to the distributor's site, the distributor could redirect them back to the customer after the inquiry had been generated. Take, for example, a building materials distributor whose customers (installers) send their customers (homeowners) to the distributor's website to select product. The distributor would assist customers, then return them to the installer for final delivery. If the site attracted homeowners on its own, the distributor could reward its best customers with these leads. The site would tie customers to the distributor with a mutually beneficial offering.

Slowly, catalog development and configurators began appearing as firms recognized the opportunity to share costs and benefits; hence, they have become more significant. Configurators, as explained earlier, were very difficult to build because of the number of different configurations in any sale, especially one in which building or maintenance of complex systems was at stake. As more IT companies worked on the problem, however, and distributor IT groups grew to understand e-business and its potential benefits, the slow but controlled move toward stronger customer interfaces through websites grew as well.

Back-Office Integration

Back-office integration refers to the tools that connect channel partners to the distributor's or manufacturer's system. As discussed in earlier chapters, this function is extremely complex, and tools for back-office integration were still in development at the beginning of the twenty-first century. Solutions fell into two categories: point-to-point integration and enterprise application integration software. The point-to-point method was commonly used in EDI applications in which the more powerful channel partner forced less powerful ones to adhere to its communication standards. This led to fragmentation in EDI communication and limited its adoption. Where it was adopted, the relationship typically favored one supply chain partner over another. The less powerful member bore the greater cost through having to adopt the more powerful partner's standards.

The other option was enterprise application integration (EAI), which took disparate systems and acted as a translator helping the two to communicate. While not a universal translator by any means, the EAI software absorbed more common standards of communication and made it possible for many systems to communicate. Any prior customization of software by supply chain partners might not be covered by the EAI system, however.

The dot-coms adopted EAI, and professional associations drove standards development to encourage easier data exchange and development of EAI software. The role of supply chain facilitator could have been a good role for the dot-coms, but after the shakeout in the summer and fall of 2000, it was not clear whether any dot-coms would remain to meet the need. The standards movement met resistance from firms that did not want to change, either for competitive reasons or because they could force the cost on their supply chain partners. We discuss the standards issue in greater detail in Chapter 11.

Conclusion

Most firms regard the CRM equation as the one most important to their survival. Systems failure in this area could prove fatal, so a great deal of thought is directed toward developing systems that will not lead to customer problems. The success of these systems depends on many logistical/operational functions, however, that will have to be connected to the entire system.

Distributor Retrospective

The material presented in Chapter 7 provides an understanding of the issues involved in Henry Morgan's implementation of Richard Stanley's recommendation to automate AEI's sales force as well as automating certain customer relationships. The automation of these relationships will depend on AEI's assessment of the importance and magnitude of their CRM relationships compared to the capability of their ERP system. Where either the ERP system or the currently utilized processes are sufficient, AEI should avoid the use of bolt-ons. In cases where the processes require a better solution than the ERP or current processes offer, the firm must investigate the true needs of the process and find a qualified solution, be it bolt-on, Internet provider (ASP), or a third-party logistics firm.

Issues to Consider

1. Discuss how the use of radio frequency (RF) technology improves the distributor's ability to meet customer needs. Include in your discussion why real-time RF data transfer would be preferable to a batch system.

2. Discuss the standard forecasting techniques used in ERP systems.

3. What is/are the primary difference(s) between a distributor's explicit and tacit customer knowledge, and why is each important in deciding whether or not to implement Customer Relationship Management (CRM) software?

4. What are the principal differences between ERP-based forecasting and "bolt-on" software forecasting methods?

5. What are the primary elements that create complexity for distributors concerning transportation?

Notes

1. "Hughes Supply Acquires Remaining Share of bestroute.com; Added Fuel for Hughes' Technology-Thrust and Growth Strategy," *PR Newswire,* September 27, 2000.

2. "Hughes Supply, Inc. Reports Fourth Quarter Operating Results," *PR Newswire,* March 21, 2001.

3. F. Barry Lawrence and William Christensen, "The Boundaries of Knowledge," adapted from course lectures at Texas A&M University, 2001.

4. "U.S. Government Computers Widely Hacked in 2000," *News Factor Network,* April 6, 2001. http://www.newsfactor.com/perl/story/8758.html (accessed May 31, 2001).

Forecasting, Purchasing, and Planning with E-business Tools

chapter

Forecasting in an Information-Rich Environment

Distributor Perspective

Harlan Davis, president and chief executive officer of Hastings, Inc., couldn't believe his firm's most recent financial statement. Last month, inventories had been $50 million, and the top management team at Hastings had expected this month's inventory to be reduced by $10 million to a total of $40 million. Instead, inventory for this month was reported as $62 million, an increase of $12 million. Also, the branch sales managers at Hastings's fourteen branches were reporting that the wrong items were in inventory and that the branches lacked the proper product to fill sales orders. Rolf Means, Hastings's chief financial officer, had been on his soap box complaining about Hastings's inability to forecast sales properly. Davis began to wonder, was Means correct? Was forecasting a problem at Hastings?

Introduction

At the close of 2000, forecasting ranked high in the expectations for e-business opportunities. For distributors, forecast error is a leading cause of inventory. Inventory is carried to protect against unexpected demand (forecast error) brought on by foreseeable and unforeseeable events, lead-time variability, and transportation costs. Foreseeable events cause error that could have been prevented if the correct forecasting procedure had been applied. With unforeseeable events there was no way to forecast the demand with the tools currently available.

Improper forecasting of foreseeable demand is caused by poor data collection techniques, inappropriate or no use of mathematical techniques, and lack of a solid methodology for involving other experts who hold key information impacting the forecast. These are information systems issues that can be addressed with a combination of technology, knowledge of how to use that technology, consistent procedures for data collection and handling, and a few common mathematical tools.

Unforeseeable demand that is not captured in the forecast is caused by events that are at this point considered unpredictable. Examples include certain weather patterns, accidents, and other "acts of God." To label these events as unpredictable is not entirely fair, however. They are, in fact, only more difficult to forecast. Consider hurricanes, for example. A hurricane is definitely outside the control of the channel, but it is not entirely impossible to forecast. The National Weather Service (NWS) predicts the number of hurricanes for the coming year.[1] Statistically speaking, looking at past hurricane seasons, a certain number of those hurricanes will hit Florida, North and South Carolina, and eight or ten other states.

A building materials distributor trying to prepare for surges in demand caused by hurricanes could use the NWS prediction and statistical estimates for the states most likely to be affected to plan how much inventory to carry and where. The exact landfall is not necessary as long as the inventory is staged close enough to respond. The strength of the hurricane might still be a mystery, but out of so many hurricanes, a certain number on average will be very powerful, others of moderate strength, and some will be less dangerous. Combining the foregoing gives a better, if not perfect, forecast of a natural disaster than no attempt to forecast at all. To make no attempt at forecasting will result in "just in case" inventory that is typically larger than necessary and concentrated at the wrong locations.

Very few events cannot be at least partially predicted and prepared for. Whether attempting to shed additional light on difficult-to-forecast events or trying to perfect the forecast for items that follow a consistent (easy to predict) pattern, forecasting is a 100% information-based exercise that generates the largest part of a distributor's inventory. As forecasting becomes more scientific and less a "fly by the seat of the pants" exercise, the process will absorb more and more difficult to predict events by applying greater amounts of information and more sophisticated tools. It may seem that supplier performance could be an equal contributor to inventory. Supplier lead times, as we shall see, however, are merely a function of distributor forecasting problems.

Cycle Times and Forecasting

Lead times are a form of cycle time. As cycle times lengthen, the forecasting process becomes longer. Longer-term forecasts must reach further into the future than do near-term forecasts, thus the accuracy of long-term forecasts is reduced as a function of time. Intuition tells us that the longer time period we have to forecast, the more unexpected events can occur. Customer demand is less likely to change in the near term for a number of reasons: the merchandise may already be paid for, the customer's customer has already committed to take delivery, the financial status of the customer may be less likely to change in the immediate future than it might in the long term. Long supplier lead times, therefore, will force the distributor to forecast customer needs further into the future and cause the distributor to carry more inventory for lead-time demand and for the decreased accuracy associated with the longer-term forecast.

What causes supplier lead times to expand? First, let's define the components of supplier lead times. The first component is production cycle time, the amount of time it takes to actually manufacture a product. For manufacturers operating in an environment in which product is produced to stock and is manufactured to meet forecasted demand and stored in inventory, this is typically very short compared to the total lead time. For manufacturers that produce to order—for whom production does not begin until the customer places an order—this is the largest component of lead time. Produce-to-order environments are not as common in channels that use distributors, since the customer is typically waiting for the order when it is finished and it can be immediately shipped direct.

In produce-to-stock firms, products that have a stated lead time of two weeks might have a production time of only a few hours or minutes. The second and largest contributor to lead times for these environments is the scheduling function. A manufacturer has limited capacity with which to make its product lines, and to switch from one product to another with each order is often impractical. Manufacturers typically have a setup time and cost associated with changing existing manufacturing lines to a new product line. Most manufacturers try to limit this setup to reduce cost and increase flexibility (ability to change lines), but once the limit is reached, the supplier must use fixed schedules to manage incoming orders or increase capacity to respond. Increasing capacity is, in effect, moving to a produce-to-order environment, which may be prohibitively expensive due to the higher cost associated with production capacity as compared to the cost of stored capacity (inventory).

The effectiveness of the scheduling function, therefore, becomes the key to lead-time control. As explained in previous chapters, the manufacturer uses the schedule to plan setups to minimize cost and maximize capacity. This strategy leads to fixed time windows from the manufacturer as a product is scheduled on a rolling horizon schedule. A product may be scheduled, for example, for production at the beginning of a four-week schedule that cycles through each of the associated products. The manufacturer will indicate a stated lead time of four weeks.

If the distributor orders at the beginning of the cycle and all operate as expected, delivery will take place in four weeks. If, on the other hand, the distributor orders in the second week of the schedule, the delivery will take place in three weeks (earlier than expected) due to the cycle being completed sooner. This will result in unexpected inventory for the distributor. Another possibility would be for a major customer to place an order and to purchase the entire product that is scheduled to be produced. This is a problem for distributors, since they are often small customers and will not be a priority customer in times of shortage. If a distributor orders at the beginning of the cycle and gets bumped by a larger customer, the lead time will go to eight weeks. Consider the situation of a certain fishing distributor. A large number of fishhooks are purchased from the distributor's largest supplier. Spring comes early and Wal-Mart increases its order by an amount that just happens to wipe out the manufacturer's inventory. The distributor is forced to wait until the next production cycle or until the supplier decides to schedule additional production runs to make up for the shortages. This type of situation leads many distributors to believe some supplier lead times are completely unreliable.

While suppliers are fixing schedules and thereby creating wide, variable time windows, the customer has moved in the opposite direction. Starting in the 1980s, customers began demanding faster delivery with narrower delivery windows. In addition, many customers were unable or unwilling to assist the distributor by providing more accurate forecast information. This narrow time window on the front end and wide window on the back end is referred to as the "Distributor's Dilemma" (see Figure 8.1) and contributes to increases in distributor inventories.

The supply chain was transitioning from a "push" to a "pull" environment. A push environment is the traditional environment in which the manufacturer produces to a schedule that makes economic sense and entices other members of the supply chain to buy through discounts or other means (see Figure 8.2). The push model assumes that customer demand outstrips capacity and can be manipulated to optimize equipment utilization. That changed in the 1970s, and the move to a pull environment (such as Just in Time) has been accelerating ever since.

The pull environment (Figure 8.3) is a situation in which the customer places the order and the entire supply chain responds immediately. Commonly called Just In Time (JIT), the system is dependent on flawless communication delivered in real time and without any system failures (machines, trucks, communication networks, etc.). This expectation was nearly impossible to achieve with the technology of the 1990s. However, many firms believed that JIT could be approached with e-business. Such a belief was a major contributor to the dot-com craze in the late 1990s. After the dot-com crash, the next phase involved distributors as well as other members of the supply chain pursuing the objective of JIT.

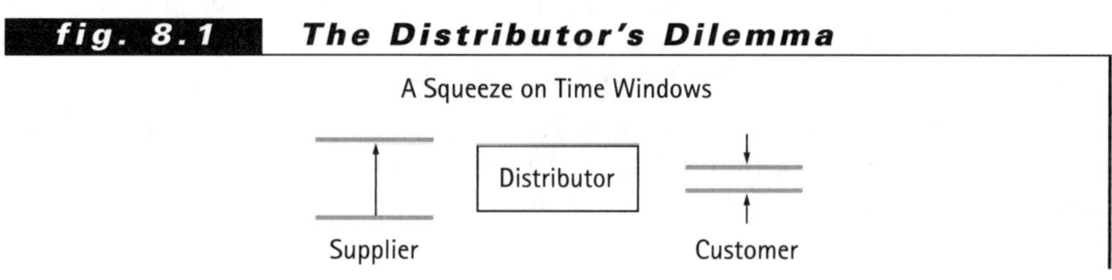

fig. 8.1　**The Distributor's Dilemma**

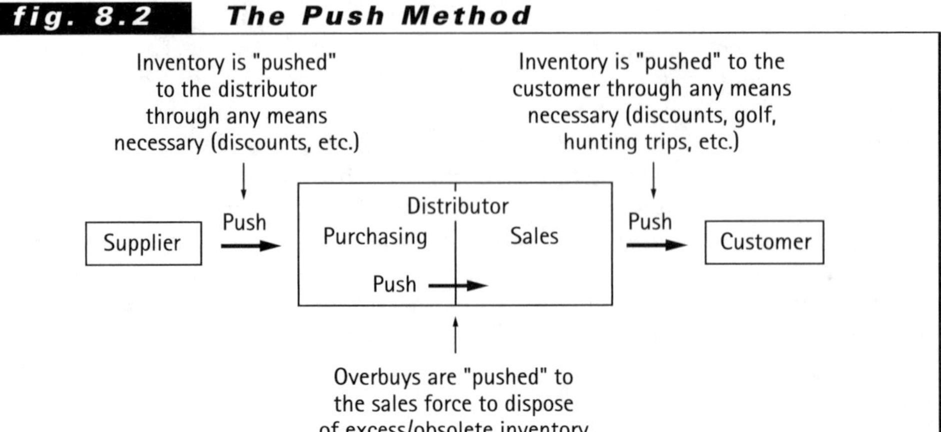

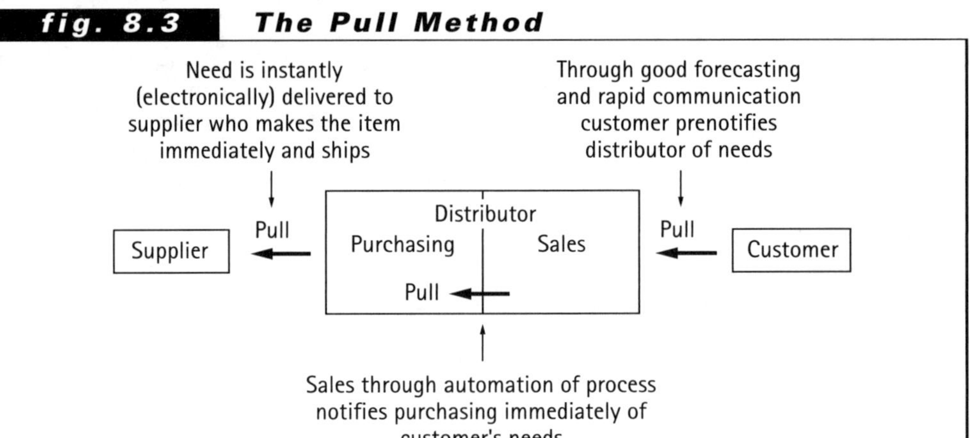

Unfortunately, the challenges at the beginning of the 2000s were daunting. Customers increased their expectations for JIT delivery, but the forecasting, sales automation, and communication tools needed were either not in place for most distributors or not even invented yet. This led to manufacturers protecting their scheduling from unreliable distribution forecasts and distributor inventories rising to meet increasing customer expectations in a supply chain that could not adjust to meet them through any means other than inventory. The distributor was caught in between manufacturer push and customer pull strategies (see Figure 8.4). The resulting inventory increases led to margin compression and forced distributors to seek other solutions to the lead time/forecasting dilemma.

Other lead-time components are more controllable for distributors but frequently get caught up in the general confusion and are not separately addressed and minimized. Lead times associated with transportation are controllable through tracking

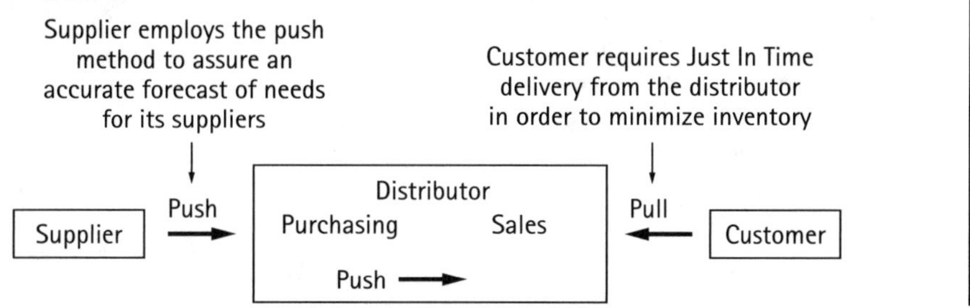

systems offered by many providers and by choosing providers with the most stable systems. Another area is those lead times that fall directly under the distributor's control. Receiving and quality control are internal processes that often get caught up in overall lead times. If the item is not available for sale, the planning group must assume that the product is somewhere in the delivery pipeline and treat it as additional lead time. This forces the planners to buy more to cover the additional lead time associated with these internal processes.

The e-business movement offers great promise of improving forecast error and thereby, alleviating lead-time problems. If the distributor achieves a better forecast and uses it to improve supplier planning, both problems will be reduced simultaneously. The lead-time problem necessitates that a great many distributors achieve the same forecast accuracy improvements at the same time, which is unlikely, but an improvement on the part of a lone distributor will enable that distributor to improve activities under its control and negotiate with the suppliers for favored treatment in exchange for better forecasting information.

The Cost of Forecast Error

Improving the forecast function is difficult, so what are the benefits? The cost of forecast error can be measured using the Total Relevant Cost Equation (TRCE) for inventory (see Ballou for an advanced treatment of this subject).[2] The components of the TRCE are:

1. Procurement cost

2. Holding cost of regular inventory

3. Holding cost of safety stocks

4. Stockout costs

The TRCE has the word "relevant" in its title because the costs that are considered are only those costs that are relevant to inventory decision-making. The actual purchase price of the inventory is not directly considered, since it will be passed through to the customer. Note also that this equation involves not just the cost of carrying an item in inventory but also the cost of not carrying the item (stockout cost). When stockout costs and additional procurement costs of treating an item as a special rather than the larger buys associated with inventoried items exceed the cost of holding regular inventory and safety stock, the item should become a stocked item.

Procurement cost is the activity cost associated with issuing and maintaining a purchase order (PO). Some industry associations have estimated the cost at $150 per PO.[3] This is a useful total figure but the cost of issuing a PO for each firm differs with the cost of personnel involved, the level of automation employed, and the number of items on a typical order, to name just a few impacting factors. Every distributor should conduct an activity-based analysis of the cost of a PO. The total cost equation takes into account the total number of all POs for a product and multiplies that number by the cost of issuing a PO on the item to get a yearly procurement cost for the equation.

Regular inventory holding cost is the cost of holding in inventory an item that is moving. If an item does not move, it is safety stock. This means safety stock is much larger than many believe. Regular inventory costs, on average, are half as much as safety stock. If we assume inventory is consumed at a steady rate, then the average amount of inventory on hand is half the total. This means the average inventory for regular inventory is half its highest amount. Safety stock, on the other hand, is not predicted to ever leave inventory and therefore is taken at its full value in computing its cost. Safety stock does leave, of course, but just as often as it leaves, it does not and regular inventory above it also stays. So, on average, safety stock never leaves.

While procurement and regular inventory holding costs are significant, for most firms they are minor costs compared to safety stock and stockout costs.[4] Safety stock not only costs twice as much as regular inventory but also constitutes the largest portion of the inventory. To continue this discussion, however, it is necessary to demonstrate how to calculate holding costs.

Holding Costs

An important question to ask is "What is your firm's inventory holding cost?" Such a question will generate a discussion with many viewpoints and can generate many arguments. Some individuals believe that the inventory holding cost for their firm is 6% because this may be the amount of interest their supplier charges them. Gordon Graham, the distribution inventory specialist, has advocated using an inventory holding cost of 30%.[5] The difference between 30% and 6% is significant. This leaves quite a gap and leads to a great deal of confusion. Graham's number was based on years of observation in distribution firms but did not capture the variation in different environments. It also does not capture the rising expectations for investment capital (Return on Investment). Graham had a difficult time convincing distributors that their inventory holding costs were more than single digits (6–9%), so the number he proposed had to be conservative. For most distributors, holding costs are even higher than Graham's suggested number. Holding costs fall into four major categories:

1. Cost of capital

2. Storage costs

3. Obsolescence cost

4. Insurance and taxes

The cost of capital is typically the greatest of the four. The interest rate charged by the supplier is frequently, and incorrectly, considered the cost of capital. Others say it is the opportunity cost, the amount one can obtain from other investments such as the stock market. If this were true, then the company should sell all assets and invest the cash in the stock market, which might be much easier than running a distribution firm. The true cost of capital is the value of money to ownership. Holding companies make this easy to compute: the cost of capital is the required return on assets for the company. A 20% to 25% return is not uncommon. The number can become even larger if there are products that cannot be carried in inventory due to financial constraints. An "A"-item inventory is often understocked. If the money invested in the wrong inventory were invested in "A" items, then the return might go to 30% or higher. The minimum number is whatever the owner requires. However, a management team that returns a lower ROI than the owners should expect will eventually see their firm sold out from under them.

Storage costs are easier to determine. Whatever it costs to store inventory, in terms of personnel, equipment, space (rent), energy usage, etc., is the storage cost. Taken as a percentage of the inventory's value, the storage cost can usually be computed in a straightforward fashion. Many argue that rental costs cannot always be included. One owner has stated that rent was not relevant to him, since he had no intention of selling his warehouse if he achieved an inventory reduction. While that may be fine from the owner's point of view, one day he may decide to sell the company when another investor sees a possible value in the land and offers a premium price.

Asset management is one of the major responsibilities for management, and facilities (storage) are big assets. One firm had previously purchased land and built distribution warehouses on three sites in Northern California. These three sites had since increased from a book value of a few hundred thousand dollars each to over a million dollars for each site. If management continued to manage that property at book value instead of its real value, when the company was sold the new owner could sell the property to help pay for the firm. Continuing to manage at the current valuation was not an effective use of assets for current ownership. The company instead sold the property and consolidated the three branches into a new one on reasonably priced land. The windfall on the sale was returned to the ownership (a holding company). Inventory reduction was another benefit, which we will discuss later.

A common storage cost is 15% to 20% of inventory valuation. The calculation can be developed from the company's books, but actual value of property should be calculated. The analysis may lead to other managerial decisions, such as the one described above, but should be as complete as possible in the current environment.

Obsolescence cost can be divided into two categories: functional and physical. Functional obsolescence refers to outdated material that cannot be sold at its original price. Physical obsolescence is product that was damaged while in the distributor's operations or transportation system. Obsolescence costs include any markdowns or scrap associated with disposing of the material. The cost should reflect not only what was written off but also what should have been written off. Sometimes meeting profitability goals causes firms to write off material on a schedule that doesn't reflect when the product actually became obsolete.

Obsolescence costs differ dramatically from one industry to the next. Some examples from different channels include 5–7% in building materials, 10–25% in high tech, and 20–40% in some fashion retail sectors. The variation within channels is extreme and heavily dependent on each firm's management skill and market constraints. Some operations may be located in highly competitive markets that force them to carry larger inventories. The larger the inventory and the lower its rate of turnover, the higher the obsolescence cost since inactive inventory is a higher obsolescence risk.

The final category, insurance and taxes, is also industry dependent. In some channels, this category is only 1% or 2%, but in channels with hazardous products or warehouses that carry flammable products it can be as high as 5% to 10% or even higher. This number is also easily accessed from accounting records.

Even if we take the lowest possible numbers from this analysis (20% cost of capital, 15% storage cost, 5% obsolescence, and 1% insurance and taxes), we get an overall holding cost for the firm of 41%. In simple terms, this means a distribution operation with $10 million of inventory pays about $4.1 million a year just to carry that inventory.

At Texas A&M, several experiments were conducted with distribution experts from multiple channels to determine holding costs. Some interesting results came out of these discussions. Salespeople and manufacturers do not like to see the cost of capital above 10%, operations and branch managers usually go for 20–25%, and distribution owners do not like to see it below 30%. Facility costs are rarely argued about and typically fall in the range given above. Branch management, sales, and manufacturers usually have a poor understanding of obsolescence costs, but distribution owners will usually place them in the 5% to 15% range. Distribution owners usually put insurance and taxes at 5% to 10%. In the group exercises, holding costs ranged between 30% and 70%, with the average being about 45%. The major differentiator was the cost of capital.

Stockout Cost

The other major contributor besides safety stock cost is stockout cost. Ask a salesperson how much it costs the company to stockout and you will get one number, ask a purchaser/planner and you will get another; ask the owner and you will likely receive yet another number. Such an exercise suggests that many firms do not have policies in place to evaluate how much it costs to stockout. A stockout occurs when, during the time it takes to get a product from a supplier, customer demand exceeds available inventory. This is a serious cost because customer relationships are at risk. However, very few companies have studied stockout cost.

If your firm has not defined a stockout cost for critical products, then your stockout costs are many, as many as the number of people involved in the purchasing decision. Every different planner, branch manager, and influential salesperson will have his or her own stockout cost. The differences will depend on personal experience and risk aversion. Risk averse individuals will buy products or encourage buys that will minimize stockouts and maximize inventory. This implies a high stockout cost. Whether the company can compete at that level of perceived stockout cost is difficult to determine.

Many people can influence the purchasing decision through their influence on stockout cost. An influential salesperson or branch manager can impact stockout cost by applying pressure when stockout costs occur. Customers can do the same, as can executives who get involved with the process when a favored customer suffers a stockout. This process leads to an embattled purchasing/planning group that becomes increasingly risk averse. Unwritten stockout costs increase, and inventory (safety stock, to be exact) grows with them.

So how do you determine your stockout cost? The Texas A&M study used a matrix to first determine what the firm currently believes, then used the results to realign the policy. One case involved a group of roofing supply distributors (See Table 8.1). The following matrix was used:

table 8.1   *A Stockout Matrix*

Percentage				
	Lost Sale	*Expediting*	*Buyout*	*Trade Up*
Lost profit margin				
Expediting				
Goodwill				
Employee reaction				
Total				

Listed horizontally across the table are the potential reactions to a stockout. If a stockout occurs, the following four actions are possible: a firm will lose the sale, expedite the product from the supplier, buy it from a competitor (buyout), or trade up to a better product at no cost to the customer.

The top row is used to depict the percentage of time the firm takes each action. The cost of the stockout actions are presented vertically. Some of the stockout costs are hard costs such as lost profit margin and expediting, while other stockout costs are soft costs such as goodwill and employee reaction. Each action along the horizontal axis may or may not include one of the stockout costs. Expediting costs, for instance, are only associated with expediting an order and refer to the charge that the manufacturer and logistics provider assesses for expediting. For example, the manufacturer's charge is based on expediting at the plant, while the logistics provider's charge is based on shipping at a premium cost. Lost profit is associated with lost sales, buyouts (margin is given to a competitor), and trading up to a better item at no additional cost to the customer.

Goodwill and employee reaction are much more difficult to determine. Goodwill is the reaction of the customer to stockouts. While this may seem nearly impossible to define, there are ways to define goodwill. If a customer calls in and a stockout occurs, the customer's buying habits could be analyzed afterwards by tracking sales before and after the stockout. The same procedure could be performed for each stockout that a customer experiences after the first one. Some customers will react somewhat to the first stockout, more to the second, and even more to the third stockout. Customers' reaction will range from diversifying their purchases to competitors, reducing their total sales with the firm that stocked out, or ceasing all business. The probability of regaining the customer's business can also be assessed by tracking who returns to buy what product and over what time period.

After determining the probabilities of different customer reactions, the firm needs to determine the lifetime value of a customer. Many firms have done so, and the results often prove alarming. The value of a customer can be determined by tracking the average amount purchased during the life of the relationship and computing the profitability associated with those purchases. The probability of various customer reactions can then be combined with the value of the customer to determine the cost of the stockout. For example, a first stockout with a particular customer type on a particular product type might typically cause the customer to buy 25% of that product from competitors. Resulting lost profit can then be applied to the particular action.

Employee reaction is the behavior that a firm's employees exhibit when a stockout occurs. Possible reactions include hiding inventory for a rainy day, pressuring planners to overstock, looking for another job if the pressure becomes too great, pirating inventory from important customers to quiet a vocal but unimportant customer, and additional expediting activity in shepherding the order. These activities are very expensive and are insidiously hard to root out.

Sound like a lot of analysis? It is, but remember the basic premise of this book: the distributor is the supply chain information manager. If the distributor does not perform this type of analysis, who should? Will someone else (disintermediation)? E-business tools will enable this type of analysis. Most of the analyses will be automated, tracking customer behavior at each contact point. Much of this discussion was envisioned by the dot-coms. The simple fact is this: unless the distributor knows its stockout cost by customer type, inventory classification, and product type at the very least, making the proper inventory decision and deciding on the appropriate customer service level (fill rate) is pure guesswork. For most products, the reaction will be far too much inventory, while for others there will be far too little.

Continuing with our example: the distributors were asked to estimate these costs (as opposed to an empirical study as suggested above). An estimate does not take long to carry out with a few executives and can be used for comparison with empirical data as the system collects it. The distributors' responses to each category are included in Table 8.2:

	Lost Sale	Expediting	Buyout	Trade Up	Total Stockout Cost
table 8.2					
Lost profit margin	20	0	18.6	33	
Expediting	0	79	12	0	
Goodwill	30	9.6	1.6	0	
Employee reaction	9	14.6	4.6	6	
Total	59	103.2	36.8	39	**71.57%**
Percentage	4.2	50.4	28.4	17	

The distributors believed that lost sales would occur 4.2% of the time, resulting in a lost profit margin of 20%, a loss in goodwill of 30% (of transaction value), and a negative employee reaction of 9%. The distributors also believed that expediting would occur 50.4% of the time, resulting in 0% lost margin, expediting costs of 79%, goodwill at 9.6% (some felt that customer service might suffer from the scramble to get product), and a negative employee reaction of 14.6%.

Buyout was thought to happen 28.4% of the time with nearly a complete loss in margin (18.6%). Some reciprocal trade relationships were possible in which a competitor might be willing to give a trade discount, but this was considered rare. Expediting costs (12%) were lower than those for freight from a manufacturer, since the only cost was sending someone to pick up the product. Goodwill (1.6%) was minimally affected, since customers would get what they wanted on time, but some risk was associated with the action since competitors might let customers know what was happening. Negative employee reaction (4.6%) was considered low, since the stress of not meeting customer needs was reduced.

Finally, trading up was considered to affect only profit (33%) and employee reaction (6%). Trading up was estimated as happening on about 17% of all stockouts. These estimates were associated with an "A" product costing $100. Differences in product type, customer type, sales volume, and product cost would all affect the analysis.

Once you complete such an analysis, what do you do with it? One starting point is to judge whether your firm is behaving rationally. The executives in the study do not seem to be rational at all. The lowest-cost options, buyout and trade up at 36.8% and 39% respectively, were used a total of 45.4% of the time, while the most costly, expediting (103.2%), was used 50.4% of the time. This does not seem logical. If buyout were used 50% of the time and trade up 50%, the stockout cost would drop to 37.9% (almost cut in half)!

This analysis, however, is easier to explain than most of these exercises. Buyouts are limited to how much the distributor can get away with before competitors inform customers or suppliers. The number of opportunities to move up to a better product also limits trade ups. Not all products have such an opportunity, or the upgrade product may be out of stock as well. Lost sales are also listed as less expensive than expediting, but that applies to customers who are not valued. A lost sale to stockout ratio of more than 4.6% may lead to a higher per-customer lost sale cost. So this policy may be best, but many such policies are not and policy changes on how the sales force should react under a stockout may be appropriate.

One building materials distributor, for example, had a policy against trading up. After looking at stockout costs, it was discovered that lost sales had a 200% cost and was used in 50% of all cases. Trading up was never used but would only cost the company about 20% on their top-selling products. They changed their policy on trade ups immediately and made them the first choice for all stockouts. In another example, a fluid power distributor discouraged the use of buyouts and allowed a lost sale in 55% of all stockouts. Buyouts, they discovered, cost about 15% due to reciprocal trade agreements that their branch managers had established with their competitors. Even more surprising, the branches were more rational than the executive staff and were already using buyouts whenever they could get away with it. The executive staff was unaware of this action but changed policy and began to encourage it.

The next chapter will examine how to use stockout and holding costs to determine how much inventory to carry. The first line of defense against stockouts is inventory, but since resources are limited in most distribution environments, hard decisions have to be made about what to carry and how much. This decision determines the competitive position of the firm and its customer relationships. Stockout and holding cost are the key to this decision. For now let's examine the opportunities to increase forecast accuracy and use the inventory holding and stockout costs to justify the expense of process improvements.

Forecasting Methods

One of the first efforts firms make to improve forecasting is to buy an information system that has a powerful forecasting module or buy a stand-alone module and link it to their operations. To understand the impact that a forecasting package can have, we need to understand what methods are typically offered and how they are affected by the firm's data and sales environment. ERP systems typically have a forecasting module embedded in them that may or may not be the best option. Before we consider the strength of the mathematical models, however, we must first deal with the old garbage in, garbage out (GIGO) problem.

Most distributors are trying to forecast from data that does not represent true demand. This can be caused by lost sales that were not recorded so that next year the demand that we missed this year is not missed again. Recording lost sales is difficult, since the sales force is required to make an estimate of why a sale was lost at the moment the transaction terminates. The first problem is generally a lack of real-time system utilization. If the customer contacts the customer service representative (CSR) and makes a request, unless the CSR can check pricing and stock status in the system with the customer on the phone, the CSR may be required to call back. This forces the CSR to handle the process offline and discourages recording lost sales. If the system is interacting with the CSR, when the query is ended the system can ask what caused the termination of the transaction.

Another problem occurs when the capture of the lost sale is too complicated. One firm had ten different "reason codes" for termination of a sale. The number one response by a large margin was lack of inventory. While this may have been the biggest reason, it was interesting to note that it is also the first option of the reason codes and may have been selected just to get the process done quickly. If the CSR chooses this code just to be able to move on, the system no longer has an accurate estimate of lost sales.

Back orders are another forecasting challenge. Back orders occur in one period and are recorded as sales when the merchandise comes in. Merely having the information system put back orders in the order period in which they occurred easily solves this problem. The data series that is used for forecasting will collect back orders and put them in the appropriate time bucket. While this sounds elementary, many systems do not have the capability to capture back orders that are negotiated by the sales force.

A back order in which an agreed delivery date gets pushed back due to supplier inability to deliver on time is easy to capture. On the other hand, many times the customer requested delivery by a certain date and the item was out of stock. If the CSR can convince the customer to wait for the product, the negotiation may lead to a new delivery date that the system assumes met original customer desires. Next year the customer will likely want the product on the same schedule they originally requested. If the forecasting system does not capture the demand in the correct period, the customer may be disappointed again. In addition, the company may overbuy for the later period in which the back order actually occurred.

Assuming we have eliminated as many problems in the forecast series as possible, we are now ready for mathematical forecasting using either the ERP system or a bolt-on. Chapter 7 discussed the strategy in the choices between different bolt-ons versus the ERP or back-office system. Now let's address some of the mathematical models in these systems.

Moving Averages

The best-known mathematical model is the moving average. Moving averages simply take a certain number of periods and add them together, then divide by the number of periods. If sales in January were 500 units, February 600 units, and March 400 units, then a three-month moving average forecast for April would be 500 units (500 + 600 + 400 = 1,500 units divided by 3). The method is very simple and can be adapted for seasonality and trend.

The strength of moving averages is they are understandable by most individuals and so we avoid the "black box" syndrome. Planners understand the process and can manipulate it fairly easily. The weaknesses of moving averages are their data requirements, limited information capacity, and inflexibility. Moving averages need data manipulated for as many periods as are considered in the analysis, and number of periods for the divisor must be kept track of. For a six-month moving average, this requires the system to manipulate seven numbers as opposed to as few as three for other methods. While this may seem inconsequential, when multiplied by 5,000 to 40,000 SKUs in many distribution firms, it can become a system strain. Even though moving averages can be a data hog, they actually use less information in their analysis than most other systems, so their accuracy is reduced. Finally, the moving average is difficult to manipulate in terms of weighting the importance of data.

Exponential Smoothing

Perhaps the most successful mathematical technique is exponential smoothing.[6] Exponential smoothing is parsimonious in its data usage, uses more information, and is more flexible than moving averages. Exponential smoothing is, in fact, a special form of moving average created to overcome some of the moving average forecasting problems.

The exponential smoothing formula is:

$$F_{t+1} = F_t + \alpha(A_t - F_t)$$

F_t: Forecast for current time period

A_t: Actual value for current time period

$A_t - F_t$: Forecast error for current time period

α: A constant between 0 and 1

The new forecast is simply the old forecast plus an adjustment for the error that occurred in the last forecast. The effect of a large or small α is analogous to the effect of including a small or large number of observations when computing a moving average. These forecasts will always trail any trend in the data. Simple exponential smoothing can also be written as

$$F_{t+1} = \alpha A_t + (1 - \alpha)F_t$$

The forecast is based on weighing the most recent demand data, A_t, with weight α and weighing the most recent forecast with weight $1 - \alpha$. The exponential smoothing model requires less storage than the moving average method since it uses only three numbers (α, A_t, and F_t). It is important to understand how this forecast works in order to avoid treating it as a "black box." When a computational program is a "black box," planners will either distrust it or they will depend on it even when it is likely to be wrong, or both. Both scenarios are undesirable—planners should have a complete understanding of how a forecast works inside the program so they can react appropriately when the forecast is at risk or leave it alone when it is operating efficiently.

A good way to understand how exponential smoothing works is to compare it with moving averages. A moving average puts the same weight on each period or follows a structured weighting system for a limited number of periods. If performed in the standard way, a moving average will equally weight the periods for the length of the forecast data series. In our example, the three-month moving average weighted each period as one-third of the total. Dividing by three has the same effect as multiplying each period by one-third. This method assumes that each period is of equal importance in determining the future. For most scenarios, however, recent data is more representative of the future.

A structured weighting system can overcome this problem by giving the most recent period the greatest weight and then having the weight decline as we go backwards in time. In our example we might choose to weight the most recent period (March) at 50%, the next (February) at 30%, and January at 20%. If we had six periods the weights could go 25%, 20%, 15%, 15%, 10%, 10%, and 5%. While this may better represent the reality of recent data being better, it is cumbersome and difficult to program.

Exponential smoothing is just such a structured weighting system. The most recent actual (A_t) is given the weight α. The previous period's forecast is given the weight $1 - \alpha$ and is equal to:

$$F_t = \alpha A_{t-1} + (1 - \alpha) F_{t-1}$$

Simply put, this means that the same equation was used but the actual demand came from the previous period (A_{t-1}) as did the forecast (F_{t-1}). The same is true for the forecast two periods back (F_{t-1}) and so forth back in time:

$$F_{t-1} = \alpha A_{t-2} + (1 - \alpha) F_{t-2}$$

As it turns out, the exponential smoothing model contains as much past periods demand data $(A_{t-1}, A_{t-2}, A_{t-3}, A_{t-4},$ etc.) as has been captured since the system started collecting forecasts $(F_{t-1}, F_{t-2}, F_{t-3}, F_{t-4},$ etc.). This means exponential smoothing uses a structured system that goes back indefinitely and contains a great deal more information than moving averages typically can maintain. The weighting system is exponential (hence the name) in the sense that it applies a steadily decreasing rate of weight on previous actual demand data. The current period is multiplied by α, and each period back is multiplied by α and $1 - \alpha$ times the previous forecast in the equation. The constant α is usually set between 0 and 1, so the effect is to decrease the amount of significance of previous periods at a steady rate as we go back in time. To set α at 0.2 is common and means that the period just finished (A_t) is given a weight of 0.2. The previous period (A_{t-1}) is weighted as 0.16 (0.2×0.8). The next previous (A_{t-2}) is weighted 0.128 ($0.2 \times 0.8 \times 0.8$) and so forth.

How α is set is an important decision and depends on how important more recent data is and how reactive the company wants the forecast to be. If α is set low (0.1 to 0.2), unusual, nonrepeatable incidents are smoothed out. As an example, suppose a competitor runs into supply problems for some reason and many of its customers begin to buy from our inventory. If we do not believe we will be able to hang onto that business, then we would prefer the forecast to downplay the significance of the occurrence (see Figure 8.5) rather than predict the pattern continuing into the future. A high α (0.3 to 0.4) would cause the forecast to react quickly and lead to increased buys even after the pattern ended.

As the figure demonstrates, a higher α will miss the mark on a false data pattern and increase the magnitude of the error. On the other hand, if sudden sustained surges in demand are common, the higher α may be appropriate (see Figure 8.6). The higher α catches up to the demand pattern more quickly. This is known as the

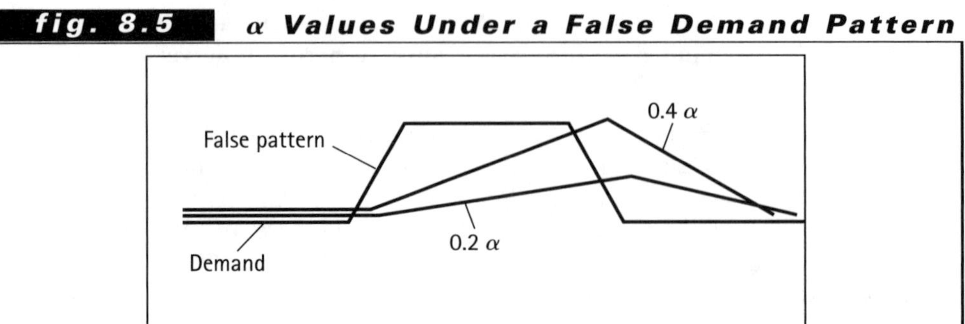

fig. 8.5 α *Values Under a False Demand Pattern*

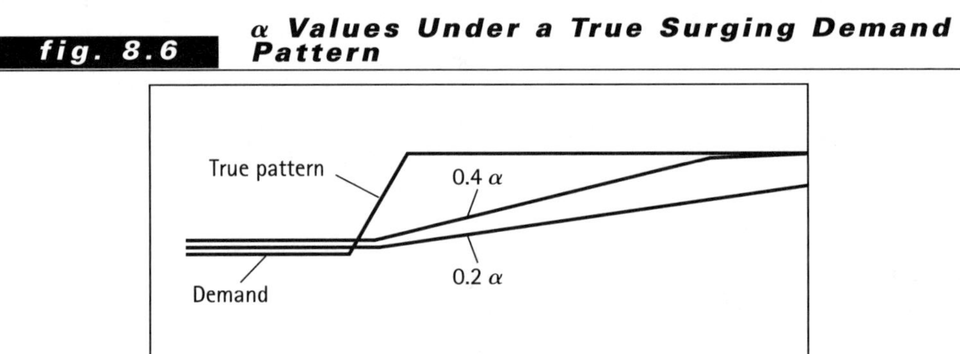

fig. 8.6 α *Values Under a True Surging Demand Pattern*

responsiveness versus stability tradeoff in forecasting: the more responsive a forecast, the more likely it is to capture sudden changes in demand if they are sustained. On the other hand, a more stable forecast is more likely to be appropriate if demand surges are often false (spikes in the data, promotions, etc.) or the data itself is flawed (poor data integrity). If demand surges are false but unavoidable, the firm is better off with a low α, but if surges are common and predictable, the most appropriate response is to clean up the data instead of expecting the mathematical forecast to smooth out the problems. If a nonrecurring promotion is the issue, for instance, its effect should be removed from the data used for forecasting.

To initialize or start exponential smoothing, the first actual demand value can be used as the initial forecast and the model can be run from that point onward. If a data history is available, it is possible to "go back" in time, start the forecast with the first period available, and run the forecasting model on all periods up to the present. This will give the firm a forecasted series that eliminates any start-up period. The forecast can also be tested for accuracy (error metrics, introduced in Chapter 10) and how it would perform under different α values. This process allows the company to study ways to optimize the forecast before actually using it.

Exponential smoothing can be modified for trend and seasonality. The formulas go beyond the scope of this text but can be found in many forecasting textbooks (see

Makridakis[7] for some examples). Trend and seasonality formulas may look intimidating, but they are easily manipulated by information systems and can be found on many ERP systems and in many more forecasting bolt-on packages.

Other Mathematical Techniques

Other techniques include regression techniques, simulation, and combination forecasting. We address combination forecasting in the next section. The mathematics behind regression goes beyond the scope of this text, but a simple explanation of how it works should suffice. Regression allows the company to combine any data that can be reduced to numbers in the forecast. The mathematical forecast generated by the system would be a likely input to the regression model. The sales force's estimate of demand is another. City demographics, the stock market, and the number of building permits issued in the past few months are all variables that can give the company an idea of what might happen.

All these variables are entered into the regression equation along with the past data, and the regression will find which variables contribute to the best "fit" of the data (predict what will happen from period to period most accurately). If an input does not improve the prediction ability of the system, the system will recommend it not be entered anymore (saves on system resources). The strength of regression is its ability to consider what may be forward-looking variables (sales force estimates, city growth trends) as opposed to relying strictly on historical data (last year's sales).

The power of regression suggests it will soon be offered on many ERP or bolt-on packages. For the time being, however, few offer it and when they do it typically only handles one or two variables. When offered, regression will require an analyst with stronger skills in forecasting and data manipulation. Since the trend in distribution seems to be toward information management, it seems likely that by the time regression is offered, there will be distribution experts capable of using it.

Simulation consists of modeling real world activities. A computer program is written that duplicates what happens in the business environment. Once written, the simulation can be run and rerun as many times and under as many different assumptions as necessary, to give the analyst a picture of what will happen. An example would be modeling the customer's behavior under different economic conditions and then running the simulation under each to see what will happen in each scenario. Since the scenarios are virtually endless, simulation can become quite expensive and time consuming to develop. Simulation software has been created to ease the burden, but these packages have been applied mostly to problems other than forecasting. The firm could code its own simulation using these tools, but considerable internal expertise may be necessary.

Some ERP packages are using a simulation technique that requires some explanation. The method uses multiple mathematical forecasting techniques like exponential smoothing (simple, trend, and seasonal models), moving averages (same group), simple linear regression (not as powerful as the regression models explained earlier), and a simple comparison that takes last year's sales plus a growth factor (a.k.a. the naive method, for its simple assumption that what happened last period will happen again with little change). The simulation then runs each model and selects the one that has done the best job on this product for a specified period. This simulation method has been used with other advanced forecasting techniques but has not been proven to be statistically superior to exponential smoothing.[8] If the data is flawed, the model could "overfit" the data (see a pattern that does not actually exist) and switch to an inappropriate model.

Simulation is powerful but should be carefully applied with the understanding that if the firm plans to use only historical mathematical models the improvement over a solid methodology like exponential smoothing may be marginal at best. A solid understanding of how mathematical models work, combined with expert input, is far more effective, as explained in the next section.

Combination Forecasting: The Information Edge

Assuming the firm is running from as clean a historical sales data set as possible and that mathematical forecasting is properly understood and applied, the next step is to include the intangible but critical information that only the keepers of the company processes can provide. The sales force has information about the customer to which no one else has access. If planning is centralized, the planners may have a view of branch activities that will not be detected by a pure mathematical forecasting technique. Marketing may be aware of promotions that have not occurred before. Management may know things about the competition that are new and will impact the forecast.

The sales force operates in an information-rich environment. One firm had a sales force that handled "two-step" and regular distribution. Two-step distribution has the distributor selling to retailers who sell to the end user. Most of these retail customers were quite large. A recurring problem was that branches did not prenotify the purchasing/planning group when new retailers were coming into a territory. A large, new retailer could literally wipe out the branch's inventory and force the regional distribution center (RDC) to ship direct to the retailer and wipe out its inventory as well. When an RDC stocks out, many other branches will be affected, causing a regional problem to become a national one. The account manager at the branch could have eliminated this problem by warning the planning group in advance and offering an estimate of the store's needs. Retail store openings are not well-kept secrets, and a savvy account manager would know that the store would be opening well in advance and could make a good estimate of the impact.

Planners have opportunities to influence the forecast as experts, too. For instance, planners in a centralized planning department know what new products are going to be introduced and can speculate on what impact those products are going to have on existing product lines. New products frequently make older ones obsolete or at least cut into their market in some way. Predicting the effect and reducing the established product's forecast will be critical to prevent overbuilding inventory. Other opportunities exist based on planner understanding of the strategic direction of branches and the company as a whole, market conditions, weather, and other factors. If there is a long winter, for instance, the planners will need to adjust for the different demand patterns that will emerge. The primary employer in a branch area might close its doors, throwing many customers out of work, and so on. Planners have many variables to consider and must react in the short term. If planning is not centralized, forecasting these activities may fall to branch managers with little forecasting training.

Marketing plays a major role as well, but typically marketing activities drives demand rather than follows it. Marketing promotions and new product introductions are among the most difficult forecasting exercises. Forecasting becomes more complicated as historical data become scarce. New product introductions are especially difficult in this regard. Marketing must examine how introduction of similar products was accepted under similar circumstances. After matching as many similarities as possible, marketing specialists must extrapolate outwards the growth rate of the firm, current strategic initiatives, changing customer demographics, and so forth. Forecasting new product introductions, new branch or territory demands, and promotional activity requires very sophisticated procedures.

Finally, managerial decision-making has a big impact on the forecasting decision. Management sets policies that determine what inventory turns the company must meet, what return on investment new product introductions or other initiatives must produce, what the competition is up to, and how the sales force and branch management will be compensated, along with many other critical decisions. Take, for example, one small distribution firm that had new competition coming into its territory. The competition was a nationwide powerhouse with deep pockets. The regional manager dropped in on the small firm and promised to take the market by storm. The management team got together and decided that the best strategy was to fight fire with fire. The distributor would increase its inventory to match the large firm and not let them grab any customers due to stockouts. While the strategy seems foolish (David and Goliath, if you will), the small distributor knew that the large firm was publicly owned and required to report losses to its stockholders on a quarterly basis.

The plan was to take losses in profitability while losing some, albeit minimal, sales. The minimal loss in sales brought about by inventory-driven sales would eventually frustrate the larger firm, forcing it to give up. The strategy worked. After two quarters of losses, the larger firm pulled out the majority of the inventory and transferred their manager to a more successful operation, replacing him with a local salesperson with lesser skills. The smaller firm was able to relax its posture to some degree, but the pressure was continued for two years, and the large competitor pulled out. The normal process for forecasting demand and matching it with inventory needs was suspended under this scenario, so management had to become part of the forecasting decision. Predicting competitors' actions and deciding the corresponding company strategy is top management's responsibility.

The forecasting decision is, therefore, the responsibility of many individuals within the firm. The most important part of forecasting, however, is the day-to-day activity that predicts what is needed to meet the customer's requirements. This is the purview of planners and the sales force. The process of including the sales force together with the planners in the combination forecast must be consistent and reliable to be successful.

Integrating the Sales Force

The purchasing/planning group has regular access to forecasting information and can use Online Analytical Processing (OLAP) to select forecasting techniques and error measures for determining what changes need to be made to a mathematical forecast. OLAP is a real-time analysis that allows the planner to view visual and numerical information pertinent to decision-making as the decision is taking place. While not limited to forecasting decisions, OLAP is very useful for forecasting analysis.

Most planning departments routinely carry out combination forecasting. Planners, in fact, are less guilty of overreliance on mathematical forecasts than of overreliance on their own expert forecast. The problem typically stems from distrust of the forecasting system due to a perceived lack of accuracy, or not understanding how the system arrives at its forecast ("black box" syndrome). The latter problem is best addressed with education. Planners should receive training on the use of mathematical forecasting techniques and what takes place inside the system. The system will still do the calculation, but the planner will derive a greater degree of comfort from knowing how it works and will know how and when to intercede if the environment throws the system a curve.

A perceived lack of accuracy comes from the planner not trusting the system to calculate correctly. This problem is best addressed with measures of forecast accuracy (described in Chapter 10) that will tell the planner what the level of accuracy of the forecast has been over the past few periods. The planner may still choose to alter the forecast, but the system can then be prompted to measure forecast accuracy before and after modification. If the mathematical forecast outperforms the planner-altered forecast (or at least gets close), the planner will likely come to trust it and leave it alone as long as accuracy measures indicate it is performing well.

The sales force does have extensive information that can assist the planners in putting together the combination forecast. The biggest challenge is moving that information from salespeople into the hands of inventory decision-makers in a timely fashion with minimal impact on sales force productivity. Sales force automation (SFA), discussed in Chapter 7, is a fast-growing technology that uses hardware and software to connect the salesperson to the information system in a way that is as close to real time as possible.

The growth of wireless technology has enabled many companies to offer hardware solutions that allow a salesperson to connect to the information system from anywhere at anytime. IBM, for instance, offers wireless technology that allows the sales force to transmit orders, truck drivers to transmit invoice status, and plant machinery to communicate with manufacturer information systems, all in real time. As the hardware develops, the software will follow or possibly even push hardware solutions as "killer apps"—what the software industry calls applications that extend beyond hardware capability, forcing upgrades in hardware technology—are developed.

The sales force will use the hardware, together with Customer Relationship Management (CRM) software, also discussed in Chapter 7, to communicate not only customer transactions in real time but also opinions on future activity from the salesperson or the customer. CRM software is easily customized for mining of existing data, but it will be challenging for firms to adapt it for integrating opinions and other "soft" estimates.

The problem with soft estimates is their dependence on the skill of the person making the estimate and standardizing the estimate into a category that can be measured. This requires a scalable estimate that the estimator understands and can use in a consistent fashion. Likert scales are used in survey work and have been proven to be reliable.[9] A respondent is asked to answer a question and is given a scale of answers from 1 to 5 or 7 or 9. An average is taken and used to evaluate the views of respondents on topics varying from food preferences to expectations of a competitor's actions.

The sales force could be trained to use this type of reliable process that could evaluate—as they are interacting with customers—the customer's satisfaction level with service, the areas that need improvement, and so on. The information could be transmitted in real time, allowing the operations division to respond before the next order goes out. Forecasting could be improved through opinions or facts captured at the site of the customer's operations and transmitted to planners before they can be forgotten or filtered through memory to mean something else. This type of analysis requires the planner and the sales force to have a process in place that evaluates the information as it comes in. The planners may discover, over time, that a particular customer increases purchases by 10% every time manufacturing capacity is increased 5% through the acquisition of new equipment. If the salesperson can report these actions in real time, forecasts can be altered and long lead-time products ordered in time.

Distributor Retrospective

Harlen asked Rolf for advice. Rolf felt that the first step would be to examine the mathematical techniques available on the system. He had been reading up on the various techniques offered by Hastings's ERP system and was sure that the data collection process was flawed and that the methods being used were sub-optimal. Rolf suggested that the math models be tested for accuracy and the best methodology be selected.

Rolf then sugggested that the sales force, marketing, and management team be introduced into the process. Harlan thought that including so much expert information would be extremely difficult. Rolf agreed but said that forecasting at Hastings had too much variability to leave solely to a math model.

> *Harlan sighed slowly. "Is this really necessary? I can hear the sales force screaming already, and you know marketing is going to claim they didn't know!"*
>
> *Rolf nodded. "Look at the inventory. If we can't forecast, we get the wrong inventory overloaded and still can't meet customer expectations!"*
>
> *Harlan knew Rolf was right. Investigating the math models would not stir up too much trouble, but soon he would have to involve others. The present course would bankrupt the company. He looked hard at Rolf and said, "Let's get started."*

Issues to Consider

1. Discuss why forecast error is a leading cause of inventory.

2. What are the factors affecting supplier lead times and what are the typical supplier responses to these components?

3. Describe the difference between the "push" and "pull" inventory management environments, including the advantages and disadvantages of each.

4. Discuss the four principal components of the cost of forecast error included in the Total Relevant Cost Equation (TRCE).

5. Describe the four major categories of inventory holding costs, including which is the largest and why.

6. Discuss the components of stockout costs and the typical organizational measures taken to overcome stockouts.

7. What are the primary forecasting methods? Which is most advantageous, and why?

8. In utilizing exponential smoothing as a forecasting tool, discuss under what circumstances a large or small forecast error α would be most appropriate and why.

Notes

1. National Hurricane Center. http://www.nhc.noaa.gov/aboutmodels.html (accessed May 31, 2001).

2. Roland H. Ballou, *Business Logistics Management,* 3rd ed. (Englewood Cliffs, NJ: Prentice Hall, 1992).

3. National Association of Purchasing Management. http://www.napm.org/NAPMReport/index.cfm (accessed May 31, 2001).

4. F. Barry Lawrence, "Closing the Logistics Loop: A Tutorial," *Production and Inventory Management Journal* (spring 1999): 43–51.

5. J. Gordon Graham, "How to Revitalize Dead Stock," *Industrial Distribution* 71 (4): 153 (1981).

    ———, *Distribution and Inventory Management for the 1990s* (Texas: Inventory Management Press, 1987).

6. Spyros Makridakis, Steven C. Wheelwright, and Rob J. Hyndman, *Forecasting: Methods and Applications,* 3rd ed. (New York: John Wiley & Sons, 1997).

7. Ibid.

8. Ibid.

9. Bill Trochim's Center for Social Research Methods. http://trochim.human.cornell.edu/kb/scallik.htm (accessed May 31, 2001).

Scientific Purchasing Enabled by Improved Information

Distributor Perspective

Malcolm Davis is a regional manager for Integrated Distributors (ID), a large general line distributor. Davis has profit responsibility for nine branches. Recently, because of declining profits, the president of ID has mandated that inventories in the branches supervised by Davis be reduced by 20%, and Davis has ordered his branch managers to respond. However, several branch managers have advised Davis that they have the following problems associated with their inventories: (1) the overstocking of a large part of their inventories with safety stocks that cannot be quickly removed from inventory and (2) large quantities of slow-moving items in inventory. Thus, in order to meet the 20% inventory reduction, the branch managers will be forced to avoid placing some fast-moving items in inventory. Such a reduction of fast-moving items in inventory will have a negative impact on their ability to service certain accounts. If the branch managers don't purchase the fast-moving items for their inventories, they will lose sales and alienate several customers. Also, the branch managers purchase some items in truckload shipments in order to receive quantity discounts from their suppliers. In order to adhere to Davis's order to reduce inventory levels, they will be forced to forgo the purchase of some truckload shipments. Thus, they will lose their quantity discounts.

Davis senses that he is in a difficult situation. What should he do?

Introduction

The forecast is a form of need recognition. Need recognition occurs either when the forecast prenotifies a planner of upcoming shortages and a count is taken that sends a message for replenishment (a reorder point trigger), or a stockout occurs. Prenotification of need is best since it allows inventory planners to avoid a stockout without an overdependence on inventory. If a count is conducted that identifies a need for replenishment, as in Min/Max programs, the company must maintain inventory for the time period required to get the merchandise that will cover for forecast error and supplier failure. An accurate forecast will identify need before it occurs and allow for reduced inventory. Stockouts are the least desirable form of need recognition, but, as we shall see, they are commonly used for items that do not justify inventory.

This chapter reviews the purchasing and planning functions—the impact of the forecast, supplier actions, and technology on customer service and inventory balances. Each section will begin by reviewing classic procedures for effective inventory planning and close with suggested technological solutions that can improve on existing procedures or implement better ones. The chapter will end with a step-by-step procedure for improving the purchasing/planning function using e-business and other tools.

Planning and Replenishment

Once a need is recognized, the forecast is used together with other important factors to determine the order quantity. For most companies, these factors include balancing manufacturing capacity, ordering in truckload quantities, the length and variability of supplier lead times, and production processing times. A typical nonautomated replenishment process is outlined in Figure 9.1.

In nonautomated environments, planning and receiving are work intensive. Most inventory movement will require manual checks of availability and planner estimates on supplier lead-time performance. Suppliers are contacted via phone or e-mail and respond based on their capacity and the desirability of the sale. After selecting the supplier, the planner will develop a purchase order, manually key it into the information system, and then fax the purchase order. The order will then be tracked by phone if necessary. Finally, the items will be received and placed into stock.

The manual portion of the process is its greatest weakness. Data gathered manually in haphazard fashion will inevitably have data integrity problems. Processes for data collection and interpretation will always be slowed and thereby made irregular when they are performed manually. This irregularity has more to do with the erratic nature of business demands on people than the speed of data transfer. People are frequently called away for other duties or emergencies when carrying out seemingly less important data collection procedures (checking in merchandise, cycle counting, picking, etc.).

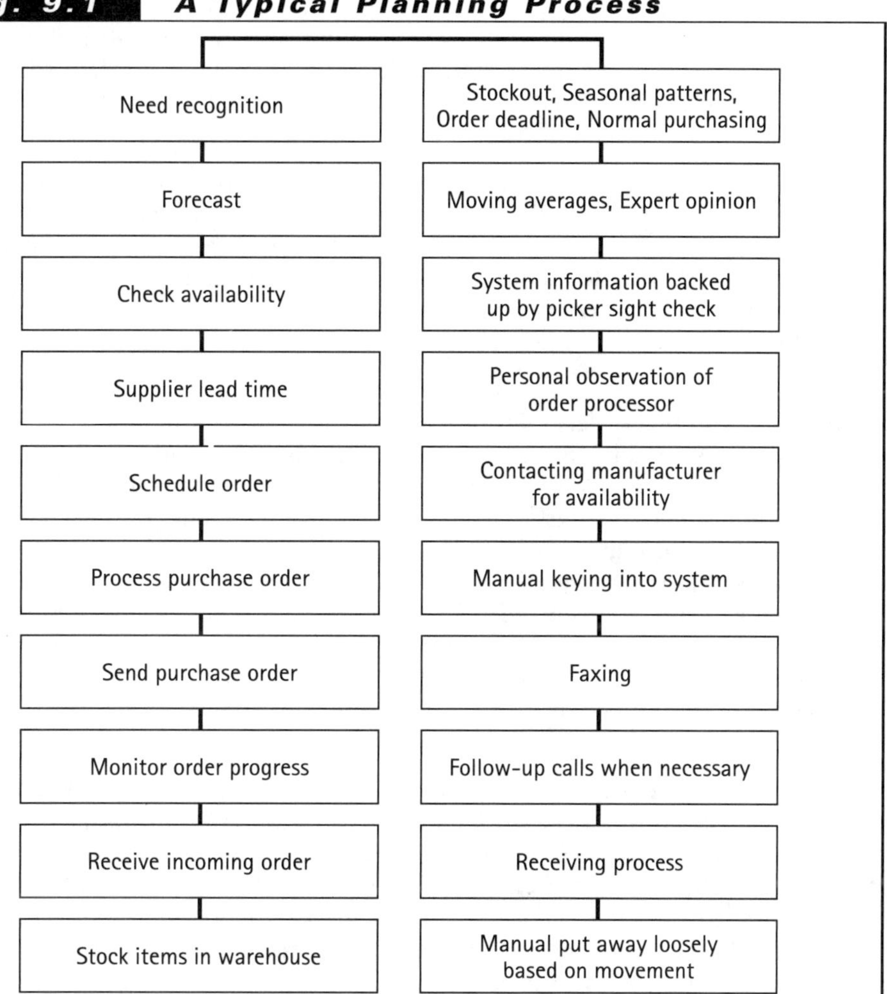

fig. 9.1 **A Typical Planning Process**

The replenishment decision is typically driven by several factors:

1. Demand as determined in the forecast.

2. Forecast error.

3. Lead time.

4. Lead-time variability.

5. Transportation economies of scale.

6. Supplier discounts or other forms of encouragement.

Either the planner or the information system (in an automated environment) considers each factor in the purchasing process to determine the lot size. As the next step after forecasting, the planner determines the expected lead time and adds the forecasted lead-time demand to the reorder point so that inventory will not deplete while new orders are coming in. Next the planner calculates safety stock. Safety stock is used to cover supplier failures (lead-time variability) and forecast errors.

Safety stock should be determined dynamically. The system should have the capability to examine how supplier lead times are changing over time and to then adjust the safety stock as required. For example, the quantity of safety stock may be either increased or decreased based on the number and length of supplier missed order dates. The system should also have the capability to examine forecast error measures to determine how reliable the forecast is and to then adjust safety stock based on performance.

This process is confused at many firms because the planners do not separate the components of the reorder point but instead make an educated guess at what these reorder points should be. Reorder points (ROP) should include demand during lead time (DDLT) and safety stock. These separate issues are lumped together to get one number, often referred to as the Min in a Min/Max system. Supplier evaluation is limited, and global figures (as opposed to more specific, and hence more accurate, ones) are used in setting reorder points. The reorder point is then established as a global figure. This problem gets further confused in many information systems where the reorder point is simply referred to as "safety stock." This method forces the company to "set" the reorder point based on a mixed number without any true calculation of its components (in other words, to guess).

This safety stock number is established based on an intuitive estimate of lead times, minimum order quantities, and forecast error. If surprises (stockouts) happen, the reaction is to raise safety stock to cover the size of the surprise. The sales force and branch managers will tend to be very proactive at this point and will frequently call planners requesting an increase in safety stock. The surprise, however, may have been generated through an episode that is unlikely to be repeated. Once a safety stock is established or changed, it may become static and not be examined for a considerable time period. The problem with a static Min is that it lumps together dynamic aspects. For example, demand during lead time, forecast error, and lead-time variability may change.

Customer demand is obviously dynamic, especially for seasonal products, and thus establishing a static Min will not capture changes in customer demand. Because the estimate for necessary inventory to cover supplier shipping time is dependent on the volume of demand during that time, a seasonal product should have a higher Min at high season and a lower one during slack demand. Many firms do have a "summer" and "winter" Min, but since demand rises and falls along a continuum, the inventory will only be correct twice a year. The Min should rise and fall in lock-step with demand.

Customer demand is not the only dynamic component of the ROP (Min), however. The typical supplier's lead time will increase when demand rises and decrease when demand falls. If the summer is the busy season, the supplier will likely ship at the outer limit of its estimated lead time then, and during the winter the supplier will likely ship ahead of schedule since capacity is slack at that time. This means that in addition to being adjusted during lead time based on forecasts, demand must also be adjusted for varying lead times. A static Min will not capture the variability.

Safety stock will also be affected because the level of forecast error, which will typically increase when sales increase, must be considered. In addition, safety stock takes into account the accuracy of the lead time and not just the length. When the supplier's lead time increases, the variability of that lead time will also increase because the longer average lead time frequently carries larger swings between high and low delivery times. The process of setting safety stock must also take into account that longer lead times will lead to more opportunity for forecast error. A static Min, therefore, will be very high during slow periods and possibly too low during high-volume periods. The reality, however, is that an ROP that is set too low will result in stockouts, causing immediate reaction from the sales force. Branch managers will contact planners in a stockout and push for increased safety stock. Once set higher, the safety stock may not be reviewed, and the inventory will be set for a "worst case" scenario during the highest-demand periods. When demand slackens and/or suppliers improve their performance, the Min will continue to carry excessive inventories. The static Min in a Min/Max policy is depicted in Figure 9.2.

Many IT systems have an automatic calculator for safety stock and the Min. The problem with such systems is that they often set the Min based on a calculation that smoothes out the seasonality and other factors. These automated "static" systems will generate an average Min that risks both stockout and overstock although they may not be quite as extreme as the previously described human-set system. The system will establish a constant safety stock that "splits the difference" as depicted in Figure 9.3. The human-based estimated Min is the top line.

Proper calculation of the ROP (Min) requires tracking of forecast error to determine how much safety stock is needed to cover demand surprises, and tracking of supplier performance to determine how much inventory is needed to cover supplier delivery failures. The ROP will also require an estimate of demand during lead time (DDLT). DDLT is calculated by totaling the forecasted demand for the time it takes to get a supplier order delivered. When applied statistically, the variables are determined mathematically and the reorder point is calculated. When human intervention is present, some or all of these variables are determined on the fly and remain unchanged for long periods of time (static). Period demand may be determined using a guess for the forecast. Lead time is determined based on the distributor's purchasing person's best guess of the manufacturer's response time. Fill rate is determined based on the planner's experience with the company's reaction to a

fig. 9.2   *Min/Max Policies*

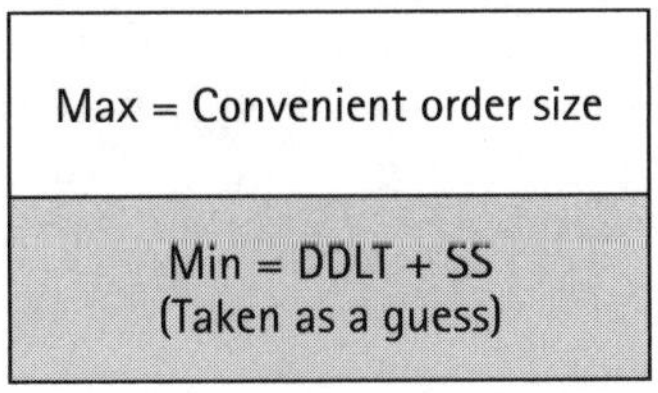

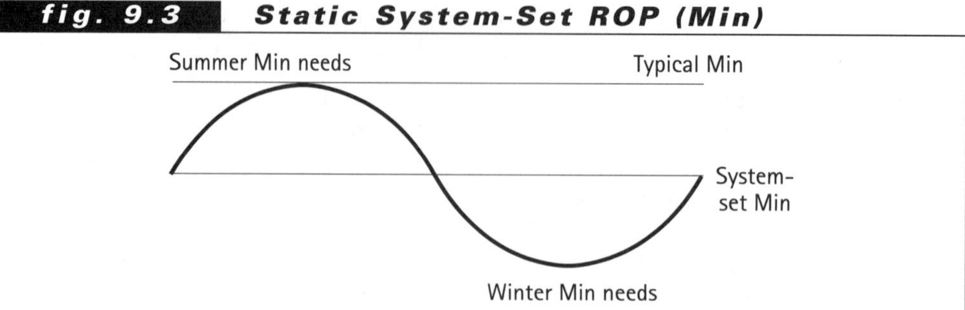

Source: F. Barry Lawrence et al., *Master Halco: A Logistics Software Implementation Study* (Texas A&M University, 2001): 38.

stockout. Variability will probably be handled by some sort of "fudge factor" to represent a "Just in Case" mentality.

The more guesswork is employed, the greater the possibility for errors. This is especially true when one considers that most human beings are risk averse and fear a stockout more than they fear a surplus inventory. We see evidence of this in the large amount of dead inventory carried by many companies. If the ROP is calculated statistically, we can remove emotional response, adjust for real problems rather than perceived ones, set improvement objectives by focusing on the safety stock drivers, and measure the effectiveness of policies for reducing inventory. An additional benefit is that while the equations associated with dynamic statistical safety stock may look intimidating, it only requires a few lines of computer code and can be calculated instantly from data automatically collected as part of normal operations. By comparison, a purchasing person could spend much more time collecting information and utilizing his or her own experience, only to obtain a far inferior result.

Some of the foregoing terms require explanation. Period demand is merely the demand that occurs in one period as measured by the company (day, week, month). Lead time needs to be measured in the same units as demand so that a straightforward multiplication gives us the DDLT. The most important measure, however, is the target fill rate for the product. The fill rate raises some issues:

○ What should the fill rate be?

○ How much does it cost to change fill rates?

○ How should the fill rate be calculated?

The fill rate should be based on the profitability of the product, its volume of sales, and criticality to important customers. If a product carries high margins or turns extremely fast (higher turns can make a low margin product very profitable), then the company would most likely seek a higher fill rate to protect profitability. If a product has high sales but low margins, even if the profit is still not significant, the sheer volume may impact cash flow such that the company needs the sales. This is especially important for small firms that may not be able to pay their bills in the short term if some high volume products stockout.

The final consideration, criticality to customers, often gets abused. If an important customer requires that an item always be in stock in spite of slow sales, the company may support the product at a loss. The loss becomes even riskier if only one customer uses the product. If that customer goes away, the product could become a 100% loss. In spite of the risk, however, it may be necessary to give some products a higher fill rate than makes sense for profits or cash flow simply because a larger, more profitable volume of business may be lost if the product is not in stock when needed.

The problem with this reasoning is that it is often taken to apply not only to critical products or critical customers but to others as well. If any customer might turn away any sale because of the lack of the unprofitable product, the sales force might push for its promotion to higher fill rate "just in case." This type of thinking leads to unprofitable inventories. Where the sales force is compensated based on sales revenue rather than profitability, the problem becomes especially acute.

Thus, setting the fill rate takes considerable thought. Fill rates can be directly determined mathematically for profitability and cash flow, as we will demonstrate, but the managerial decision-making associated with "promoting" fill rates for customer reasons other than profit or cash flow must be closely controlled. The fill rates are set through managerial decision-making but can also be simulated to find the most economical fill rate. All things remaining equal, however, fill rates can only be manipulated to find the lowest-cost policy based on the environment. The fill rate is a target the firm seeks to achieve and should be manipulated to determine the best rate at the lowest economic cost. Once the optimum fill rate is achieved, other tools may be used to improve system costs with no reduction in fill rates. Thus, such a fill rate has value as a continuous improvement tool.

For example, a fluid power distributor was asked for the stockout cost and holding cost for a product. After determining supplier performance and forecast accuracy, the company's total cost of the current fill rate policy was simulated for that product (see Figure 9.4).

The diagram demonstrates that costs decrease as the fill rate or service level increases. When the fill rate hits about 93%, though, the costs begin to rise again. The decrease in costs as the fill rate increases is due to the decrease in stockouts resulting in a lower total cost, even after adding in the higher inventory holding costs. Completely eliminating stockouts requires more and more inventory, however, and eventually the few remaining sales associated with stockout cost reduction do not counteract the rapidly increasing inventory holding costs.

To simulate the best fill rate, a company needs to use the total relevant cost equation (TRCE) discussed in Chapter 8. The TRCE is a sum of procurement costs, regular inventory holding costs, safety stock holding costs, and stockout costs. The formula is as follows:

Total Cost = Procurement + Regular Inventory Holding + Safety Stock Holding + Stockout Costs

The Economic Order Quantity (EOQ) balances procurement costs and regular inventory holding costs to find the best order quantity. As the order quantity

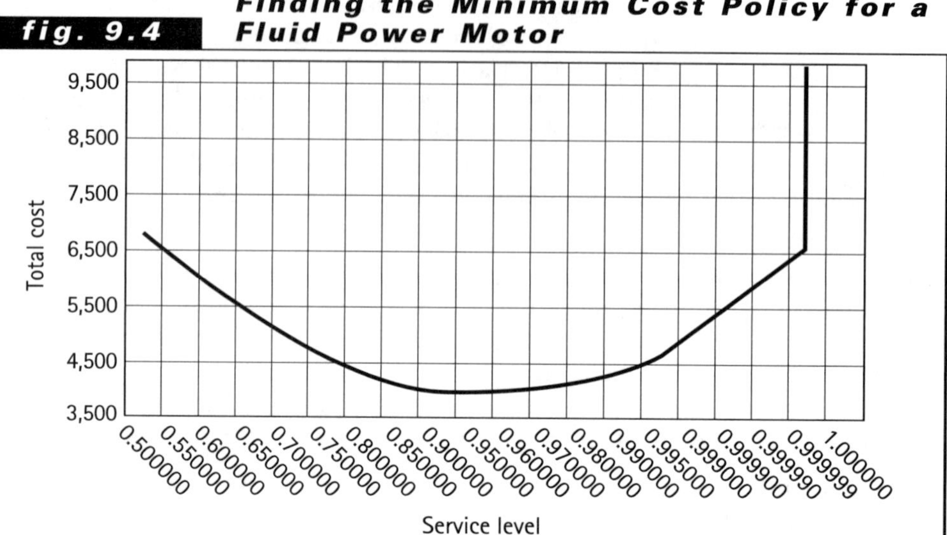

fig. 9.4   *Finding the Minimum Cost Policy for a Fluid Power Motor*

Source: F. Barry Lawrence, *Berendsen Fluid Power: A Logistics Study,* Texas A&M University, 1999.

increases, procurement costs decrease. Larger orders mean fewer orders and hence lower procurement costs. On the other hand, larger order sizes mean more inventories because the firm has to carry those larger orders until they are depleted. Inventory carrying costs, therefore, increase as the order size increases.

The minimum cost is found where the procurement costs are equal to the cost of holding regular inventory.[1] An important note: this classic result does not include the safety stock and stockout cost portions of the total cost of ownership. The relationship is similar, however, since increases in safety stock will lead to decreases in stockout costs. Since safety stock and stockout costs have an inverse relationship, seeking the minimum total between the two functions minimizes the safety stock and stockout costs.

Stockout costs, however, are difficult to determine. If the concept of stockout cost is not well understood within the company, then different individuals within the company will attempt to "guess" the actual stockout costs. The sales force can significantly influence the level of safety stock that is maintained because of its power within the firm and its relationship with the customer. Essentially, purchasing is left without any guidance and will frequently overbuy if it is believed that stockout costs are higher than they actually are. If the stockout cost in the preceding formula is perceived to be extremely high, safety stock will explode.

This means that the balance between safety stock costs and stockout costs is determined by one factor, the fill rate. So if we know the stockout cost for a product, we can determine the minimum cost fill rate (based on safety stock and stockout costs) for a product. We call this the Economic Fill Rate (EFR). The EFR on an "A" item may be 93%, 95%, 98%, or even higher, rather than the commonly used 95%.

The EFR gives us better information for minimizing costs. A bigger bonus may be that it allows the system to determine the fill rate automatically rather than forcing decision-makers to guess with inadequate information. Since the computer will have all necessary information, the entire process, from forecasting to customer service and back, can be automated. The system calls for assistance with items on an exception basis only and relieves purchasing and inventory control specialists of many trivial tasks so that they can focus on important tasks.

This methodology suggests that the information system could determine and use the EFR. An iterative procedure would be used wherein the total cost of operation for a specified period of demand (one year, perhaps) is determined for different fill rates. The different variables that are used in the system are estimated beforehand from studying procurement, holding, and stockout costs. The EFR is determined through simulation by iteratively resetting the fill rate until a minimum total cost is achieved.

Whether the firm chooses to calculate or estimate its fill rate, the end result will be a safety stock that, in turn, determines customer service. There are several levels and outcomes to fill rate estimation:

1. Make no attempt to track or estimate fill rates, stockout costs, or holding costs; allow planners to make the determination as they see fit. Outcome: Planners will be at the mercy of powerful customers and the sales force. Fill rates will be understated as each stockout is highlighted more than the successful order fills. Items that do not get the attention of vocal customers and salespeople may experience stockouts. Items that get too much attention will build large inventories that become obsolete quickly when critical customers lose interest. The result will likely be large inventories together with a seemingly inexplicable inability to satisfy customers.

2. Track fill rates on critical customers; do not estimate stockout or holding costs. Outcome: Critical customers will likely have their service objectives met, but inventories will expand even more than those under the first scenario, and noncritical customers will be treated even worse, leading to a complete reliance on today's critical customer and poor development of new opportunities.

3. Track fill rates on all customers; do not estimate stockout or holding costs. Outcome: Across-the-board higher fill rates for all customers, improved customer service, increasing inventories, and declining margins.

4. Track fill rates on all customers, estimate and apply holding costs, and do not estimate stockout costs. Outcome: Improved customer service, an awareness of the cost of the policy in inventory terms, difficulty making the tradeoffs that minimize cost and maximize profitability.

5. Track fill rates on all customers; estimate and apply stockout and holding costs to determine the best fill rate. Outcome: Improved customer service on most profitable sectors, decreased inventory, company wide understanding of profitability and inventory.

Option five is most desirable, and the technology necessary to obtain this option is e-business related. The information system is required to track the fill rate at certain junctures in the fulfillment process. The most common point at which to check fill rates is at "ship-confirm," or when the product goes out the door. This fill rate is what the customer sees and is, therefore, critical to improvement processes. The ship-confirm fill rate does not, however, tell the company where the failure occurred. Other fill rates can help with this dilemma.

Ship-confirm comes at the back end of the transaction. Another interesting fill rate is the "order initiation" fill rate. This fill rate occurs when the customer places the order. When the customer contacted the company, were there sufficient items available to meet the order or was expediting or some other method necessary to meet the customer's demand? This fill rate is more complicated, since a lower fill rate at order initiation may be a good thing. If a customer typically calls and gives three days' notice on a product that can be delivered by suppliers in one day (leaving two for shipping to the customer), the planning group would want to keep inventory low, since a stockout is unlikely at ship-confirm and costs can be minimized. The same is true if the product is made in house or can be transferred from one location to another.

The company may need to maintain a 99% fill rate at ship-confirm for competitive reasons but only need a 85% fill rate (far less on-hand inventory) at order initiation to achieve the desired ship-confirm fill rate. If the order initiation fill rate falls to 70% or below, it may indicate a risk the supplier could stockout, lead times might lengthen, expediting might be necessary at a higher cost, and so on. The company may need to manipulate these fill rates to seek a proper relationship between the two.

Once the fill rate is determined and applied mathematically to the safety stock, the firm should be able to calculate the cost of the policy and know whether to increase or decrease the safety stock. Continuous improvement does not stop here, however. The firm should now consider the other variables that make up the safety stock and stockout cost (supplier and forecast performance). E-business can have a major impact there as well.

ABC Classification of Inventory

ABC classification of inventory refers to the process of ranking items based on activity, profitability, or other measures and then using that ranking for purchasing decisions and/or warehouse layout. Common methodologies employed in ERP systems include ranking inventory based on sales volume (units or dollars), total dollars invested in the product, and the number of times the item gets picked (hits).

The first method is straightforward: that which sells the best is ranked the highest. A's, B's, and C's are typically generated entirely on an 80/15/5 sales rule. With this approach, A's are those products that generate 80% of sales, B's are the next

15%, and C's are the last 5%. The rule has some complications in application. First is the problem of slow movement versus customer criticality. An item may move slowly but be very important to a large number of customers or to a single large customer. A second problem arises in using sales dollars rather than units as the measure for low-price items. Expensive products will rank higher even if their movement is not significant. Even if the unit-based method is used, it is still not clear what this classification scheme tells the planner. Low-margin products may have a high velocity but little profitability. A product may also have a high turn but only go to one large customer. If that customer goes away, the firm could get stuck with a large dead inventory.

Another problem arises with transfers. If an item is frequently transferred between branches it is debatable as to what this means. On the one hand, frequent transfers could demonstrate a high demand or an inventory shortage, signaling a product that needs attention. On the other hand, counting transfers may lead to double counting a product's significance to profitability, since the firm will only sell it once.

The second method, total dollars invested in inventory, suggests that increased attention should be given to those products that absorb the most resources. The inventory policy for this method is to keep planners aware of the risk associated with this inventory. It places emphasis on high-volume products but may also focus a great deal of attention on items that do not move well and that generate large inventories as a result. Planners require a clear policy in responding to this metric. Other items—normal to slow sales or low total-inventory items with high turnover—do not get emphasized, and the planners may not know how to manage them as a result. The profitability of items gets lost as well as the risk of stockout.

A third method, number of picks, is very useful for warehouse layout. Such a method allows management to determine where product should be placed to minimize travel time for pickers. High pick-frequency items should be placed near the shipping area or at the ends of rows to decrease congestion and speed warehouse operations. For safety purposes, a warehouse layout plan often places heavy items on lower shelves or high-pick items in the "golden zone," the area between an individual's shoulders and knees, to avoid bending and lifting pressure on the individual's back.[2]

Warehouses are dynamic environments. "A" pick items migrate down to B and C, and new products start slow and move toward an A classification. This constant migration of products means that a paper-based warehouse layout arranged for efficiency will quickly become inefficient. Paper-based systems are simply too cumbersome to keep up with dynamic environments. A major equipment manufacturer introduced carousels into its warehouse to increase their picking efficiency. A carousel has small bins that will revolve horizontally or vertically (depending on the type of carousel) to the picker when an item is requested. Carousels can pack inventory more densely because of the narrower aisles that are utilized. For example, in a carousel system, humans or forklifts are not required to move in the aisles between the carousels. Carousels can reduce the warehouse floor space required for inventory by as much as 60% and can reduce picking time by bringing product to the picker.[3]

In one particular warehouse, however, the manufacturer's information system was not connected to the carousels and did not have an effective method to transfer inventory in and out of them. The original plan was for the fastest-moving items to be on the carousels, but the result was that OSMI (Obsolete and Slow Moving Inventory) took over the carousels because the system did not regularly remove items as they slipped out of the "A" category.

To be successful as an optimal warehouse layout, the warehouse management system (WMS) needs to be connected to the sales order process. Many ERP systems do not have a WMS, or they have a WMS that is not designed for distribution purposes. A WMS that is not designed for distribution is based on manufacturing scheduling packages such as Material Requirement Planning (MRP) systems.

Most ERP systems have an ABC classification that can be used in the warehouse or for purchasing decisions. The purchasing decision is better served, however, by information on item profitability. Developing a Gross Margin Return on Investment (GMROI) for inventory is straightforward, and even though most ERP systems do not have a direct method to calculate GMROI, such a measure can be easily developed. Some distributors have calculated GMROI, which is total margin for the period divided by average inventory, and have used such a measure to rank their inventory. This type of calculation lets the planners know not only what is selling but also which items support the company's profits. A stockout on a fast-moving product is bad—a stockout on a profitable fast-moving product is even worse.

A common problem occurs, however, when inventory either builds up for unneeded products, or rapid demand outpaces the system's ability to respond to these new demands. The problem is one of comprehension, in that the sheer number of SKUs overwhelms the ability of the system (IT, planner, branch manager, etc.) to track all the items. The purchasing decision requires guidance in eliminating dead inventory and managing fast movers.

The problem is that many firms have not properly defined inventory. Defining inventory based on volume (particularly dollars) does not reflect profitability and stakeholder return on investment. ROI should be the key performance indicator for planning. An example of an ROI calculation would be to stratify the ABC classification based on margin return versus inventory investment. One firm used the following classification:

A items = 200% or greater ROI

B items = 0 to 200% ROI and significant cash flow

C items = low to negative ROI and/or insignificant cash flow

The first classification line (200%) should be adjusted to reflect no more than 10% of total inventory. B items will likely constitute no more than 20% of inventory. This will leave 70% or more of inventory classified as C. Determining ROI is not as simple as it may seem. Some items will have dating (payment occurs after a certain time period), while other items will be on consignment. For many items, however, the problem is not as complicated because the difficulty in maintaining the inventory often outweighs the financial benefit of consignment or dating. In other words, a return on inventory asset value with no regard for the actual money invested in that asset may be appropriate.

Once the ROI limits are established and products are classified, the next step is to define an appropriate response to the classification scheme. The firm mentioned previously used the following:

A items = order as needed to a reorder point trigger (ROP) of demand during lead time plus safety stock.

B items = order as needed to an ROP of demand during lead time (no safety stock).

C items = do not reorder.

Since this classification scheme is very simple, it might cause some concern. Its strength, however, is in its simplicity. A planner has more than enough issues without dealing with a complicated buying decision. The objective, however, is not to reduce human thinking, just the number of things that humans have to think about. Most firms do not have the human resources to deal with the number of issues the environment throws at them, so automation is needed on the rote tasks. High-criticality items are not a rote task. The planners need to identify them and move them up (manually) from B or C status to A or B status (whichever is most appropriate). Fortunately, high-criticality items that do not sell well are not numerous. In the interest of keeping these items from becoming dead inventory because of changes in market dynamics, this list should be reviewed frequently.

The obvious solution to inventory problems is to attack C items with the objective of reducing them to desired levels. The problem is that the nature of financial management does not allow enough time to eliminate C items in an organized fashion. The company is left with two choices: suffer with excess inventory reports or dump C inventory. Such dumping of obsolete inventory affects profitability because these "dumped" items have to be written off. A typical inventory scenario is depicted in Figure 9.5:

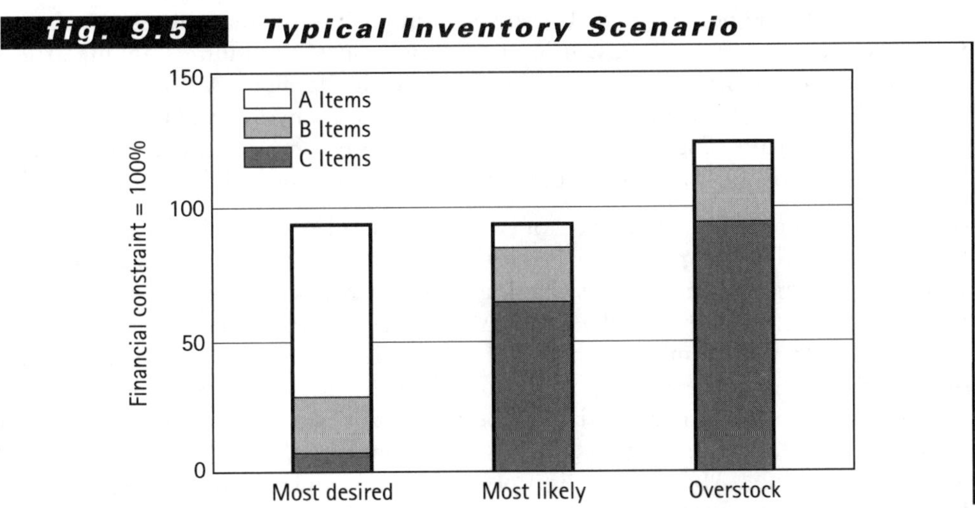

fig. 9.5　*Typical Inventory Scenario*

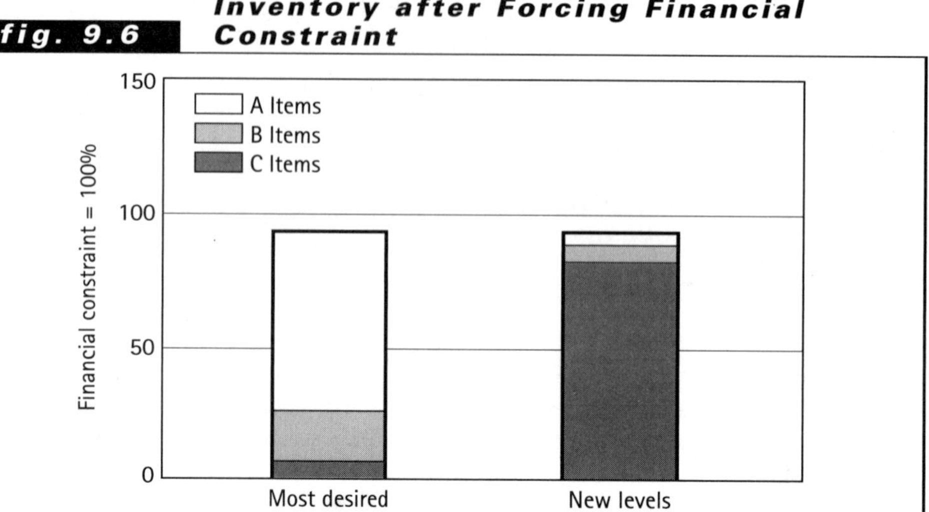

fig. 9.6 **Inventory after Forcing Financial Constraint**

Figure 9.5 demonstrates that for profitability and customer service reasons, the most desired arrangement is to have about 70% of the inventory in A items, 20% in B items, and only 10% in C items. Unfortunately, most firms usually have 10% of their inventory in A, 20% in B, and 70% in C. Things get worse when the company finds itself in an overstock position, as depicted in Figure 9.5. A and B items remain the same, but C items typically expand. Every firm has a constraint on how much inventory it can carry. Some have physical constraints such as warehouse size, but most have financial constraints. If the financial constraint on how much inventory a firm can carry is penetrated, planners may be forced to stop all buying until the financial constraint is not binding again. A (and to a lesser extent, B) items will liquidate quickly, but C items (due to slow movement) will not (see Figure 9.6).

The result is a decrease in customer service and increasing system costs. The firm will be forced to expedite A and B items to minimize the damage to customer service. The increased expediting will increase freight costs (premium shipping at less than truckload quantities) and expediting fees from suppliers. A decreased service level on A and B items is prohibitively expensive, but many firms play this scenario out again and again. The only way to prevent the problem is to track item activity, identify slow movers, and remove them before they dominate the inventory.

The majority of ERP systems do not currently provide direct calculation of inventory based on ROI. The procedure is not that difficult to create as a special program within your system in most cases. Failing that, the firm can always download the data quarterly or even biannually and analyze it with spreadsheets if necessary. The other ABC criteria—number of hits and sales volume—are usually available and only need trained employees and solid procedures to be implemented. In the information age, information can and must be traded for inventory to be successful at distribution. Since rightsizing inventory is a constant battle and information is the manager's best tool, ABC analysis is a powerful way to plan and control inventory. Information systems already enable much of the analysis.

Order Quantity

The ABC analysis determines what should be bought and where it should be stored. The ROP determines when it should be bought and how much safety stock and demand during lead-time inventory is necessary. The only remaining criterion is the order quantity. The order quantity is the amount that should be bought once the reorder point is triggered. The order quantity must take into account forecasted demand, capacity restrictions at the supplier and distribution firms, and any applicable discounts.

The capacity restriction may come from space problems but will more likely be financial constraints of the distribution operation or production constraints (inability to meet demand) at the supplier. For the order quantity decision, however, the more difficult problem comes from the economies of scale associated with quantity discounts, line-buys, or handling and freight.

Quantity discounts consist of price reductions when buying in bulk. Many manufacturers will offer a discount when bulk buys are made. The purchasing decision becomes more complicated when the logical amount to buy is less than the minimum buy for a quantity discount. Sometimes the decision is simple: the firm needs 90 but gets a 10% discount for buying 100. That means the next 10 are actually free. Other times the decision is more difficult, however. What does one do if the needed amount is 60 and the 10% discount is at 100 units?

The same problem exists for freight discounts. On a per unit basis, it costs less to ship 100 units than it does to ship 10. This is particularly true when the shipment approaches a truckload. Truckload shipments are typically much less expensive on a per unit basis than Less Than Truckload (LTL). Many firms make this a requirement: planners are instructed to buy and transfer only in truckload quantities. As was stated earlier, however, the larger the order size, the longer it takes to liquidate that inventory. This means that, on average, a much larger inventory is carried when larger buys are made.

Consider this simple example: If we assume that customers buy at a fairly steady rate, then the average inventory between buys is half the order size. When the order comes in, the inventory hits its maximum, then depletes at a steady rate. The average inventory is, therefore, half of the order size (not counting safety stock). If a firm orders in increments of 100, the average inventory is 50 units. If, on the other hand, the firm orders in increments of 1,000, the average inventory is 500 units. The firm will place fewer orders (one-tenth as much), but the amount of inventory typically on hand will be ten times as large. The trick is to determine whether the discounts (freight and quantity) associated with larger order sizes and the reduction in purchasing effort (purchase orders) more than offset the additional inventory holding costs.

The problem becomes even more difficult when one considers other products that a supplier might carry. Most buys involve multiple products from a single supplier. That means freight costs must be split over multiple products. Splitting freight costs to determine when to order more makes it more difficult to determine which, if any, of the products should be ordered in larger amounts to reach freight or quantity discount hurdles. Another possibility is to buy fast movers that have not yet reached their ROP in order to fill out a truckload. Still another complication is the line-buy where suppliers require the distribution operation to buy a "line" of products in order to get favored products they desire.

Some ERP packages have line-buy algorithms built into them, but beware: this is computationally a very complex problem and the algorithms will be forced to make some very restrictive assumptions for their recommendations. Line-buys, freight/ quantity discounts, and capacity restrictions go beyond the scope of this book (see Ballou for an in-depth treatment of these issues).[4] For the purposes of this text, we recommend that such programs be evaluated and their shortcomings understood before making them part of the purchasing procedure.

Many ERP packages use the Economic Order Quantity as an algorithm to determine order size. The EOQ has its limitations but is widely used as a purchasing tool. The theory was first advanced in 1914, and many extensions (quantity discounts, line-buying, etc.) have been developed.[5] Its original form, however, is the one most commonly used in ERP systems. It is fairly easy to understand and, within limits, can provide good results if the planner understands its underlying assumptions and knows when those assumptions are violated to such a degree as to necessitate intervention.

The basic EOQ formula is developed from a total cost equation involving procurement cost and inventory carrying cost. It is expressed as:

Total Cost = Procurement Cost + Carrying Cost

$$TC = (D/Q) \times S + (ICQ)/2$$

Where:

TC = total period relevant inventory cost, dollars

Q = size of each order to replenish inventory, units

D = total demand for the item for the requisite period of time, units

S = procurement cost, dollars per order (cost of a purchase order)

C = value of the item carried in inventory, dollars per unit

I = carrying cost as a percent of item value, % per period

The formula for the EOQ is:

$$Q^* = \sqrt{2DS/IC}$$

The basic assumptions of this lot-sizing model are:

1. Known, continuous demand.

2. Known, constant lead times.

3. Linear holding costs.

4. No quantity discounts.

To use the EOQ, the planner should understand its assumptions and what the likely outcome will be if those assumptions are violated. Demand that is known and continuous means no forecast error. Lead times that are known and constant mean the supplier will always deliver on time with no missed time windows or shortages on products. These assumptions are not likely to be accurate in most environments. Safety stock is maintained to protect against forecast error and supplier failures. The planner needs to understand the limitations of the safety stock and watch for situations where violations of the foregoing assumptions might cause disruption. A well-designed system, therefore, will include monitoring of forecast error and supplier lead times (as discussed in Chapter 10).

Linear holding costs and quantity discounts refer to the economies of scale discussed earlier. It costs less to move 100 items on a per unit basis than 10, whether we are moving them through trucks or a warehouse. Manufacturers face the same issue: it costs less to make 100 items than 10, on a per unit basis. Manufacturers offer quantity discounts in order to make larger production runs while avoiding carrying the additional inventory. Economies of scale are a valid reason to order larger amounts and thereby create additional inventory. The planner must either use more sophisticated tools or develop greater estimation skills to determine when to trade more inventory for economies of scale. The EOQ is a good advisor for order quantities but not a substitute for planner skills and training.

In essence, the order quantity is a difficult decision that has many uncertainties associated with it. The good news is that when combined with an effective safety stock procedure, good forecasting, and supplier evaluation, the EOQ and other order quantity procedures tend to have a "flat bottom effect." This means that missing the optimal order size (too high or too low) does not cause a major increase in costs as long as the difference is not too large.

Step-by-Step Planning and Replenishment

Under an information-driven planning and replenishment system (see Figure 9.7), the process would become more automated, and accuracy would be addressed through mathematical forecasting combined with expert opinion and statistical estimation of significant variables. The ERP system and any necessary bolt-ons would handle as many processes as possible. Processes designated ** in Figure 9-7 would be highly automated; *** indicates a need for other technology to be in place (at the supplier, for instance). The following steps describe such a system:

1. The system continuously updates forecasts and lead times (on an ABC classification-based order rule system) as information becomes available (e.g. sales, supplier lead times) and uses them to calculate the ROP.

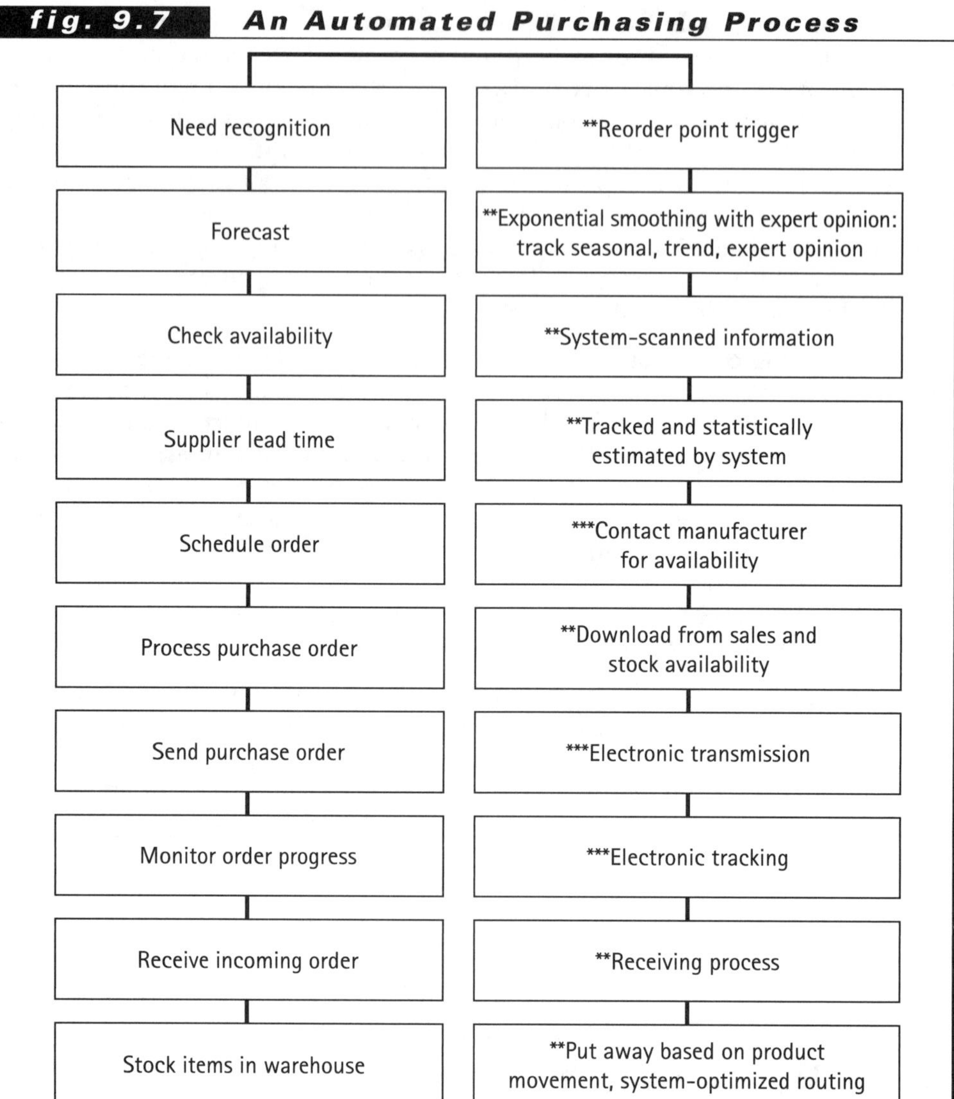

fig. 9.7 **An Automated Purchasing Process**

2. The ROP, once triggered, uses the EOQ with expert assistance or specialized programs (line-buys, etc.) to make a recommended purchase size. Planners, once notified of an ROP trigger, may:

a. accept the recommended buy, at which point the purchase order is generated automatically.

b. query the system to determine if the forecast and lead-time data seem reasonable and decide to accept or override the suggested buy.

3. If the manufacturer has e-business capability, the order is transmitted electronically.

4. If the logistics provider and manufacturer have e-business capability, the order is tracked by the system through the logistics provider's software and the Internet.

5. The receiving and put-away process is automated through the Warehouse Management System (WMS).

6. Order picking is routed (by ABC hit-based warehouse layout maintained by WMS) for maximum use of picker's time and minimized risk of injury.

Specials and New Product Introductions

A major issue arises for most firms regarding how to handle special orders and new product introductions. New product introductions have always been a challenge for forecasting. For distribution, the supplier catalog usually includes much more than the amount of inventory that can reasonably be carried. The result is a great many special orders. These specials create two problems: The first is the dead inventory created when customers refuse to take delivery on the special when it arrives. The second is the decision as to when to add a special to regular inventory (i.e. make it a stock item).

The e-business logic introduced in this chapter and the previous one deals with both issues. Specials that come into inventory and are not taken by customers need to be eliminated as quickly as possible. Unfortunately, they often escape notice, and the opportunity to eliminate them before 100% obsolescence gets lost. The ABC classification procedure will identify these items as "C" or "D" and set them up to be purged from inventory.

Deciding when an item should be made a stock item is more difficult and is analogous to the new product-forecasting dilemma. The e-business relationship can improve the decision, however, by examining information that was not available before. The decision to add or not add an item to inventory can be supported by taking the number of special orders generated on it over a year and, the margin generated from those orders, determining what its reorder point would be if it were stocked, calculating the stockout costs for every attempted order (every time a non-stock item gets a call it is a stockout), and adding up the costs of not stocking versus stocking the item. If putting the item in stock is less expensive than the current non-stock policy, it is time to put the item in inventory.

Conclusion

The technology associated with scientific purchasing is now available. While many systems lack specific capability, most can be modified to work with an information-automated planning procedure. The opportunities for cost savings are immense, but an understanding of basic theory and the implementation of your system are essential to success.

> ### *Distributor Retrospective*
>
> *Davis realized he must come to understand how safety stocks and stockouts can impact a distributor's inventory, and how a distributor utilizes information to manage purchasing decisions as well as maintaining inventory control. His firm should consider employing dynamic safety stocks, ABC classification, and more information in the purchasing decisions. A general refocus should be put on inventory management and customer service that properly emphasizes truckload shipping versus inventory and other issues faced by the firm. Most importantly, an information-based analysis should be substituted for the current educated guesses of employees.*

Issue to Consider

1. Discuss the advantages and disadvantages of using Min/Max as an inventory management technique.

2. How does safety stock add to unnecessary inventory? What are the sources that lead to larger than necessary safety stock?

3. Discuss the elements used to determine an effective fill rate.

4. How and why are safety stock and stockout costs inversely related?

5. What are the advantages of using Economic Fill Rate (EFR) for determining fill rate?

6. Discuss the five levels of fill rate estimation, and explain which is most desirable and why.

7. How and why can a profitability-based inventory classification system yield improved purchasing decisions?

Notes

1.   Ronald H. Ballou, *Business Logistics Management* (Englewood Cliffs, N.J.: Prentice Hall, 1992), 420.

2.   John J. Bartholdi and Steven T. Hackman, "Design of Fast Pick Area," *Warehouse and Distribution Science,* Release 0.08 (2000): 65–85.

3.   John J. Bartholdi and Steven T. Hackman, "Storage and Handling Equipment," *Warehouse and Distribution Science,* Release 0.08 (2000): 19–29.

4.   Ronald H. Ballou, *Business Logistics Management* (Englewood Cliffs, N.J.: Prentice Hall, 1992).

5.   F. W. Harris, "Operations and Cost," *Factory Management Series* (Chicago: A. W. Shaw, 1915), chap. 4.

10

System Visibility: Measuring and Improving Distribution Channel Management

Distributor Perspective

Clark Rogers has just been promoted to distribution manager of United Industries (UI), a firm that custom designs and manufacturers earth-moving equipment. An important part of UI's sales revenue is the aftermarket for parts sold to independent distributors who provide a variety of services for UI's customers. Rogers has embarked on a tour of two major UI manufacturing facilities that inventory and ship parts for their independent distributors. Rogers is very concerned about the manner in which the shipping, receiving, and warehouse functions are currently being managed in these two facilities. The same products are stored in a variety of locations within the warehouse. Products received from vendors are inefficiently staged in a variety of locations. Heavy products are stored too high, creating a safety hazard, pick slips are inaccurate, incorrect freight rates are assigned to shipments, inventory records are inaccurate, and many products are shipped late. Three of UI's largest independent distributors have just complained to Rogers about the poor customer service they are currently receiving. Rogers has scheduled a meeting with the manager of each manufacturing facility to review his concerns.

Introduction

Albert Einstein said: "If you can't measure it, it isn't science." At an academic conference on information systems technology in the early 1990s, a less eloquent college professor engaged in a heated public argument with a speaker on inventory control said: "If you ain't got data, you ain't got [censored]!" In another discussion on the future of distribution information systems, Don Webb of Prelude Systems, Inc., said: "Whoever builds the network first wins." The preceding statements, listed in chronological order, reflect both the underlying theory of the value of information and the way technology and business practice are converging to make that theory a reality.

A common business tenet is that you get results only on what you measure. In other words, if it is not measured it does not receive attention and therefore does not lead to improvement activity. When a problem exists but is not measured, executives will complain and ask questions that cannot be answered, branch and operations managers will shrug, and line personnel will disregard the issue. Line personnel believe (rightly so) that if management really cared about the issue, they would measure it. Branch and operations managers do not believe they can be held responsible if they do not have the means to understand the problem (also correct). Executives are, therefore, isolated with little information and no means to resolve the problem. Einstein's observation reflects the fact that nothing can be truly believed if it is not accurately measured. In business, nothing can be acted upon unless we know what is happening and have concrete metrics to show us what to change and how to monitor the success of our actions. In situations in which critical processes that support customer service are at stake, acting on speculation and innuendo is not acceptable.

Until the expansion of information system technology in the 1990s, however, the ability to measure many critical processes was dependent on a tremendous manual effort or expensive technologies like Electronic Data Interchange (EDI), which most firms could not afford. If a firm could afford manual processes, they often gave up the effort when the irregular data collection associated with human-based systems caused data integrity problems that negated much of the benefit. The new technology introduced in the 1990s reduced the cost of EDI and other e-business tools, increasing the pressure to improve information handling. The excuse that data collection was too expensive and doomed to failure anyway began to lose credibility. Meanwhile, Deming and others were continuing to push for Statistical Process Control (SPC) as a way to test an ongoing manufacturing process without shutting down lines.[1] Many executives became fond of the phrase: "We believe in God, all others must bring data." The message was that every decision had to be backed up with statistical proof.

Distribution was slow to adopt SPC and other tracking mechanisms since most distributors were smaller firms that could not afford the technology and did not have IT firms supplying appropriate systems for their business. In the 1990s distribution-focused ERP systems began springing up, and in 2000 and 2001, e-business tools directed at distribution functions were being developed either as bolt-ons to ERP or as part of the ERP offering. The potential for a fully connected distribution operation with all the data collection techniques and monitoring programs necessary to allow performance measurement seemed within reach. However, many distributors did not understand what the opportunity meant, and few had gone very far to implement these systems.[2]

The completely connected distribution firm would have to build an information flow that "mirrored" the forward flow of material, facilitated the existing flows of information, and integrated all sources to achieve the firm's performance goals. The average firm found itself in a race to create a network that was essentially a cyberspace mirror of its physical operations. As distribution firms came to understand the size and scope of the task, the race was on. Distributors like W. W. Grainger tried to seize the initiative, but the task grew as the firm got bigger, and it was unclear who would win the race.[3] As the savings described throughout this book demonstrate, however, the winner in building the network might be able to reinvent its distribution channel in its own image.

Real-Time Systems

A real-time supply chain network would connect every task and individual involved in the relationship between the customer, distributor, supplier, and logistics provider. This huge undertaking took in more than the internal connection within one firm. The enormity of the task led some to question its feasibility and others to seek industry alliances to pull it off. One thing was clear: no one was going to do it alone. Assuming a firm could break down its own internal barriers and then extend that openness to its supply chain, the key question became: "Where do we begin?"

It may seem odd to wait this long to discuss such a critical question, but the solution is so complex that the reader has to understand where the opportunities are before getting a feel for the answers. To understand where to begin, we should ask what the desired outcome should be. Answering that question gives us the metrics for measuring the e-channel and determining what the expected return will be for improved processes. Before embarking on an e-business initiative, we should have the end in sight. The end is given to us through performance metrics and system tracking.

Metrics must identify what the desired outcome of a process is and, to be really effective, attach a measurable value to differing levels of success. Most firms use revenue as a metric, but while increased sales are generally a good thing, this metric is too global. Most fashion clothing retailers experience their highest sales in December and January during their deepest discounting period. While high volume is critical for eliminating potential dead inventories before it is too late, if these firms continued their sales year round, they would not survive for long.

Real-time systems do offer savings. If measured correctly, they can be used to lead continuous improvement and maintain high standards once established. Previously we discussed the significance of cost justifying e-business investments; in this chapter we address the full continuum of metrics along the distribution channel and how e-business tools can be used to collect data, measure performance, and evaluate the distribution firm's contribution to the channel.

Customer Service Metrics

The supply chain begins with the customer. All metrics should be derived from the customer's needs. To be effective, therefore, customer service metrics should be comprehensive and quantifiable. To be comprehensive, metrics should include revenue, profitability, and efficiency metrics. Revenue metrics can be set up to track total sales volume, new product and market growth, and same-store sales. Profitability metrics focus on the income stream generated through serving certain market segments. Efficiency metrics determine how effective the firm has been at serving the customer's needs.

Total sales and sales increases over previous years divide into different areas that virtually all firms have tracked throughout their history. The total increase year over year is interpreted in terms of straight-line additional profits and economies of scale. To quantify the benefits, the firm has to establish a strategy for sales and then collect the proper data to measure the level of success in meeting the plan. Increased sales imply increased profits, simply because the firm will increase earned margins with each sale. The economies of scale theory discussed in Chapter 5 indicates not only that the firm should collect the standard margin on the increased sales, but that the margin percentage should also increase, since the increased sales will absorb additional variable costs (salesperson commissions, cost of goods sold, etc.) but may not generate additional fixed costs (managerial salaries, facilities, etc.).

Consider, for example, a firm currently generating a profit margin of $200,000 on $1 million in sales. This 20% margin includes fixed costs. If variable costs are 60% of the item price and the firm sold an additional $100,000 with no increase in fixed costs, the margin on the next $100,000 would be 40% (20% margin plus 20% in fixed costs not absorbed). Economies of scale are, therefore, counted on for a great deal of the benefit associated with increased revenue. As was demonstrated in Chapter 5, however, economies of scale are not guaranteed. The firm must measure how costs rise with respect to increases in sales to determine what benefit will be achieved. This information is critical if the firm is expected to invest additional resources for the sales increase. If economies of scale are not achieved, then the additional resources will cause an actual decrease in margins, possibly below the firm's expected return on investment or even to the point of losing money on the increase in sales.

The customer service representative (CSR) may be the final arbiter in this decision. Some customers will negotiate very hard when requesting bids for a large sale. The customer frequently has an inflated sense of the distribution firm's margin and knows the salesperson is anxious to make the sale. The CSR could become the customer's advocate in pushing for the sale. If the margin is given away on the expectation that economies of scale will make up for the lost profit and then the customer requests unusual delivery, does not pay on time, and, in general, increases the cost of the transaction, the large sale could turn into a large loser.

Same-store sales address part of the issue. Financial analysis places a great deal of emphasis on this, since an increase in same-store sales implies some economies of scale. The use of this metric implies there should be little to no increase in facility capacity for sales increase at a branch that is already in existence. A decrease in same-store sales in a firm whose total sales are increasing could be an indication that profitability is eroding, since new facilities generally take some time to become as profitable as the firm would like.

The Key Performance Indicators (KPIs) associated with increased sales should therefore capture both increased revenue and profitability at the same time. One such metric is same-store sales. Another metric is increased sales for certain product segments. Some products have a lower cost to serve or are favored by customer groups that are less costly to serve. Other metrics measure sales on new products that promise growth and prevent the firm's total product offering from becoming obsolete.

Efficiency metrics measure the firm's effectiveness in meeting customer expectations. Fill rates, discussed in Chapters 8 and 9, are efficiency measures. Fill rates can be measured at the item, customer, company, planner, and branch level. Fill rates at item level tell the firm how important products are performing. When matched up with an appropriate return on investment (ROI), the fill rate can be used to guarantee customer service on products that are significant to both the customer and the distribution firms.

Fill rates taken at the customer level can be used to measure the firm's success at serving large or otherwise important customers. One supplier was required to meet very stringent fill rates by home center retailers. Although the higher fill rate for this customer segment was more costly than the lower expectations of other customers, an Activity Based Management (ABM) study found that the customer's high-volume purchases and insistence on carrying only A items actually led to a lower cost of service. Even though the customer tended to be extremely aggressive on pricing, the ABM study seemed to prove that the customer was more profitable than other, lower volume customers. If the study was correct, the firm was justified in supporting the higher fill rate demanded by this customer.

The problem with customer service metrics lies in the last phrase "if the study was correct." Customer service metrics are a slippery slope that holds many uncertainties. Customers frequently do not know what they want or do not understand what they get. That makes the collection of metrics even more important. If a company collects metrics that support customer service from the customer's viewpoint, not only does the firm come to understand what kind of performance it has achieved— it also understands that information can, and should, be shared with the customer. Once customers understand what the supplier metrics are telling them, they look for the same answers from the supplier's competition. Less organized competitors with no proof of performance will not be able to hold customers if they cannot provide such metrics.

Planner and branch fill rates identify areas for improvement. If the company is not achieving its overall fill rate, an investigation into planner or branch fill rates may reveal that a planner is not following procedure or is unnecessarily altering forecasts, or that a branch is not informing the planners of upcoming events or is otherwise neglecting the flow of critical customer information. The problem with these types of metrics is that they frequently exist in isolation, without other global metrics, and are used to "assign blame" rather than to seek improved customer service.

The fill rate metrics should be set up in a hierarchy that starts with what the customer sees and drills down to operational levels such as planner and branch levels, to find opportunities rather than assigning blame.

Internal Operations Metrics

Once the customer metrics are established, the next set of metrics must be connected to these front-end metrics. Internal operational metrics must be driven by the customer service metrics. Internal operational metrics fall into three major categories: physical processes, financials, and purchasing/planning. We will address purchasing/planning later. Financial metrics like ROI, return on assets (ROA), days sales outstanding (DSO), and a myriad of others have long been available in most IT systems. The use of financial metrics goes beyond the scope of this book. It is critical to recognize, however, that along with inventory, accounts receivable is one of the largest assets distribution firms manage. Faster exchange of information, as in the e-channel, will make a critical difference in managing financial flows.

Some of the e-business tools for increased information velocity include electronic funds transfer (EFT) and automatic faxing. Many financial firms have already put Internet-based tools in place to collect funds in real time. The key to success, financial analysts say, is to keep your DSO below your payables so that you in net effect work off your supplier's money rather than having your customers working off your financing. For smaller companies, keeping accounts receivable and accounts payable in balance is simply a matter of survival.

An e-business example: One large distributor uses automated faxes to shorten cycle times (DSO) on its accounts receivable. The automated fax goes out to the customer immediately after the transaction takes place instead of a mailed invoice. The estimated time reduction in getting the invoice to the customer is two days. The due date has not changed, and many customers will still hold the invoice to manage their own funds, but many (especially successful small contractors) will pay as soon as they receive the bill. The reduction has resulted in a one-day decrease in DSO. The net savings from the decreased postage paid for the automated fax system and the one-day reduction in DSO has resulted in an average annual decrease in accounts receivables of nearly half a million dollars.

Operational metrics focus on cycle time. Long, variable lead times, as was discussed in earlier chapters, are very damaging to a firm's success. Longer lead times reduce forecast accuracy, and customer service suffers as a result. Lead times are a function of supplier performance and internal operations. Suppliers will be addressed later in this chapter; internal lead times can be greatly influenced by e-business.

Internal lead times in distribution include the time required for information signals from the sales function, quoting, design work, picking, shipping, receiving, scheduling, and invoicing. The first cycle time faced by the firm is the signal from the sales force. Forecast accuracy aside, the length of time that it takes to get a message from the sales force adds time to the customer fulfillment cycle. This additional time gets reflected in customer service (longer delivery lead times) or inventory (an additional day's availability).

Sales force automation software (SFA) focuses on getting information to and from the sales force in a minimal amount of time. One firm had a slow ERP connection that forced its sales force to take the customer's order, then get off the phone with the customer to check availability and pricing. The delay for the customer was one to three hours, depending on how many other calls came in while the CSR searched the system for the required information. The impact on the firm was an unmeasured loss in sales associated with the customer calling competitors while waiting for the quote and an increase in inventory necessary to meet customer demand in shorter time windows because the customer's delivery expectations began when the call was initiated. Sometimes the customer would call late in the day and would not get the callback before the next day; however, the customer still expected a two-day delivery starting from the initial call, so the distribution firm had to carry inventory for the shorter average time window created by the slowness of the IT system.

The solution was a faster system with a Graphical User Interface that made navigation easier for the CSR. The requirement was the new software and an increase in hardware capacity to handle the increased load on the system caused by the more demanding program. The result was increased sales due to a more immediate response and retention of the customer on the phone until the quote was complete. Another benefit was decreased inventory as customers' expected lead times were in effect increased by the amount of time that formerly went to the CSR's offline information search. Finally, CSRs were able to increase sales without an increase in personnel due to the more efficient process, which led to economies of scale.

Another firm had an extensive quoting system that required considerable engineering expertise to carry out. A customer would send a motor in for repair and ask for a quote to determine whether to approve the repair. The exercise was extremely information intense. First the product had to be checked in and photographed, and the problem diagnosed. Second, the engineers had to assess the solution (repair) and then draw up a list (by hand) of the parts necessary to repair the item. Third, existing inventory had to be pulled for the repairs and set aside to prevent its being pulled for another job (there was no way to reserve the inventory in the IT system). Fourth, nonstock product had to be determined for order after a manual check of what products would be needed for repair. The list of products used inside a motor was stored on microfiche that had to be periodically updated, since the manufacturer may have declared some parts obsolete and now had newer replacement parts. This step was particularly important because a change in one part could necessitate a change in others, thus changing the entire job. Finally, once all activities and parts had been identified, the quote would be drawn up by hand and faxed to the customer. The quoting process was part science and part art, and many projects required that previous repairs of this nature or on this motor be pulled and examined. Previous quotes gave an appreciation of repair time and so forth for pricing purposes. Previous work records on the motor ensured that previous changes or repairs were identified and that other work that had been performed by the repair shop did not get included in any warranty responsibility.

The process was enormously complex, which meant there were many hidden costs in this manual process. The costs included extra inventory to cover the parts set aside while new parts come in. The time-consuming and tedious job associated with paper handling was also expensive. The engineers had to fill out customer data that would have already been in an automated system. Common parts that were always used on a motor had to be filled in each time, costing time and risking errors. Mathematical calculations were done on a calculator and transferred to the paperwork, again taking time and risking error. Errors made in preparing the quotes could be repeated in future quotes. Microfiche was a very slow and error-prone way to gather specs. Previous history that had not been captured caused warranty problems.

The solution was a quoting system that maintained standard forms connected to a database system that linked customer information, former repairs, standard parts, and warranty information into the quoting process. Inventory was put on a real-time WMS that allowed for soft commitment of parts to jobs within time windows so that if a new part was coming in before the soft commitment became hard (needed for the repair to begin), the soft-committed part could be used to satisfy immediate requirements. The microfiche problem remained in the short term, but manufacturers were moving more and more information to the Internet, where the system would be able to immediately access it. The database program was able to access these Internet sites and link to product lists. Quotes became more accurate, inventory decreased, and errors were reduced without any reduction in customer service. The cost was the adoption and retooling of quoting software, new servers to handle the Internet connection and increased system needs, and redesigned processes within the firm for managing the quoting process. Quotes were then tracked for accuracy and sources of errors noted for continuous improvement efforts.

The foregoing demonstrates the effect e-business can have on sales and quotes. The warehouse is typically one of the major target areas for e-business, since many errors and lead-time problems start in the warehouse. Lead times in the warehouse include receiving, picking, and shipping. Receiving encompasses unloading, break-bulk, check-in, inspection, and put away. Lead times increase when product is ordered in difficult-to-unload quantities or forms, such as ordering a heavy, unwieldy product (pipe) and having it delivered in a van rather than a flatbed truck. The flatbed would allow for the use of a forklift to remove the product; a van would require a team to hand carry the item. Other lead-time drivers in receiving include poor or noncompatible labeling from suppliers, handwritten receiving rather than bar code scanning or automatic receiving, understaffed or poorly designed inspection procedures, and put away with poorly trained or overtaxed warehouse personnel with no IT support for product location.

One manufacturer had a problem with suppliers shipping goods in vans that could not be unloaded without considerable effort. A terminal was in place for receiving, but due to security concerns, only certain employees had clearance to use the system. The company was moving to 24/7 operations, and frequently security-cleared personnel were not working, so product would be unloaded and set aside until someone was available. The IT system also had to relabel product since suppliers did not use a compatible numbering system and many did not label at all. The warehouse had a high turnover, and experienced workers were placed in shipping (closer to the customer), leaving receiving to wait when experienced people were needed or forcing them to guess, which introduced error into the system from the start of the warehousing process. Finally, after product was checked in and cleared in a lengthy quality control process, the product was put away. However, the system did not provide a storage location for the product, which caused inventory to be stored in multiple locations. Often, when the same product was stored in multiple locations, some of these products would be lost for great lengths of time. The cost was increased human effort, lost merchandise, increased cycle time, increased inventory to cover missing or slow-processing merchandise, reduced responsiveness to customers, a decrease in data accuracy that increased forecast error, increased employee frustrations (turnover), and an increased need to expedite in order to meet regular customer orders. Expediting was more work intensive, since it typically involved single items and a more thorough search by the most experienced employees. Since the warehouse was already operating beyond capacity, the expediting process further slowed warehouse operations and increased the need to expedite. The result was a whirlpool that was swallowing the operation.

The solution was a real-time WMS that tracked merchandise, directed pickers to product, communicated with suppliers as to delivery requirements and problems, speeded receiving cycle time through simplified processes that could be entered into standard scanable forms, and reduced errors through connection to a Radio Frequency Identification bar coding system. Supplier deliveries were tracked and the variability of their deliveries calculated. The system maintained a control chart on deliveries to indicate if something was going wrong with a supplier. Too many deliveries occuring outside a tolerance range were flagged for investigation so that problems could be rooted out before too much damage occurred. Receiving time and errors were also tracked.

On another example, a large distribution firm faced problems with its picking and shipping interface. The pickers had to find product without direction as to location, which was doable for experienced workers but difficult for new hires. Even experienced workers had to deal with the fact that pick slips were not in order of best route through the warehouse and would require back tracking. A picking slip was printed with the order when the CSR entered the sale, but the picking slip had no relationship to the layout of the warehouse. If add-ons were added to the order during the picking process, they would have to be taken care of later. Multiple orders could not be picked together to shorten travel because the confusion in keeping orders straight would have resulted in a decreased customer service level. The picked orders had to be staged and rechecked, since the complexity of the pick led to many errors. To make matters worse, the warehouse was laid out according to where space had been available during the receiving of new products. Heavy product was frequently placed on high shelves, slowing the picking process and increasing risk of injury. Fast-moving products would be stored anywhere, including the most inaccessible locations of the warehouse.

The shipping process posed other challenges. Staging areas were not well defined. Product could be removed from the staging area with an improper pick slip. Proper product information was not always affixed to the product. An investigation would have determined how the product got where it was, and where it was going. If the received products were staged in an out-of-the-way area, they might get forgotten for great lengths of time, increasing cycle time. The labeling process was largely manual. Counts were manual, and a recheck of what was picked was required to ensure good customer service. Shipping was sent "best route," which was largely a guess since there was no software available to select carriers based on current trucking conditions. Freight rating errors were common when workers applied the higher rate used to ship premium products to other products that should have received a lower rate. Customers were not given advanced shipping notices (ASNs), which led to additional investigation work for the sales force when customers called to inquire about orders that had already been shipped. Invoicing was slowed on local deliveries since the process could not begin until a signed form came back from the customer. The slower invoicing process could add a day or two to the billing process (increased collection times).

The costs of the shipping problems included inventory to cover for lost products that had to be reshipped, additional financing for slow invoices, personnel costs to run down customer inquiries, and a variety of customer service losses from delivery quality problems. The firm determined that considerable savings could be achieved through more efficient information handling.

The solution was to institute a WMS and connect it to the sales process through the ERP system. The system would route pickers, send ASNs to the customer, lay out the warehouse (including staging areas), and control and track all movement of product in the warehouse. Bar coding was essential to enable the tracking of orders. Control charts were used to track picking time, errors, and fill rates after order initiation. The fill rate on orders that have already been promised is a measure of warehouse efficiency, since shortages after product has been promised are caused by picking, receiving, or shipping errors.

Process Control Charts

One of the best methods for controlling internal operations and the purchasing/planning function is the control chart alluded to earlier. A control chart can be established that outlines the point at which a process needs investigation. When the control limits are breached, the system issues a report that warns operators that something is wrong. The control chart has existed for a very long time.[4] Control charts are commonly used in manufacturing processes to determine when parts are not being made to specifications.

The "Six Sigma" movement championed by Motorola took control chart monitoring of processes to new heights when it mandated a quality target of less than 3.4 defects or mistakes per million operations.[5] The target is a measure of process capability. If we take a sample of performance on a regular basis and determine statistically how that performance represents the process in general, we can determine if the process is working as planned. "Six Sigma" set a high standard for the target by allowing very few defects. Such programs enjoyed enormous success in manufacturing. The "Six Sigma" process used statistics to establish the control lim-

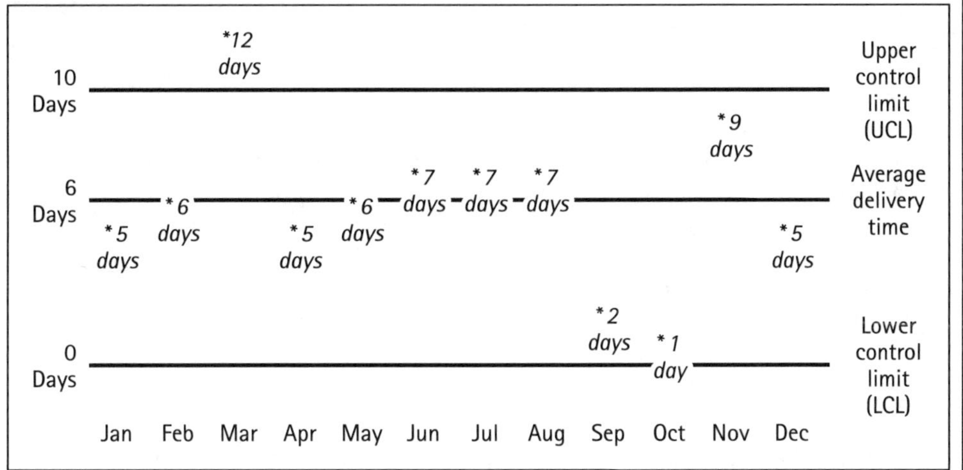

Note: Asterisks are observations of supplier lead times.

its in a dynamic chart. Control charts in distribution can also be established using statistics, or the limits can be determined based on managerial goals.

An example would be the common "a day's work in a day" that many firms seek. If one hundred orders arrive in a day, the firm wants to process them in one day. The goal prevents orders from running over to the next day and eventually causing bottlenecks or customer delays. A control chart that tracks how many orders get carried over from one day to the next could monitor progress in meeting such a goal. If more than a certain number get carried over, the process would be deemed out of control. Other examples would include monitoring errors per pick, time per pick, receiving errors, and supplier shipping problems. A sample control chart measuring supplier delivery times is presented in Figure 10.1.

The chart can be interpreted based on how many times the control limit is breached, which side is breached, and any consistent patterns the supplier shows on one side or the other of the requested delivery time. If, for instance, the supplier consistently ships on the high side below the control limit, the supplier may not be able to meet the requested delivery date. Purchasing/planning will need to investigate the cause and make a determination as to whether the supplier can improve or should be replaced, or whether inventory policy must be adjusted to the supplier's actual capability. The upper control limit (UCL) is considered to be the point beyond which the supplier is considered worth investigating. The lower control limit (LCL) is the point at which the supplier is exceeding the goal by such a large amount that the company should reevaluate the chart and adjust the expectation downward, perhaps.

The chart can be constructed based upon management-established goals or set up statistically. If management sets the goals, the center line might be the supplier's estimated lead time. The UCL might be the most time the company wants to allow before penalizing the supplier, and the LCL might be the earliest they will allow product to arrive. Under Just in Time (JIT), the customer might require the supplier to deliver in two days (center line) within a plus (UCL) or minus (LCL) limit of two hours. The UCL is designed to prevent stockouts and limit the amount of buffer inventory the customer has to carry to protect against supplier failure. The LCL is designed to prevent inventory buildup through unneeded inventory arriving too soon.

Statistical estimation of the limits is also possible. The customer can track supplier performance and determine what the average delivery time is and track the control limits based on the number of standard deviations from the mean that occur in the supplier's performance at any one time. Changes in average lead time or in the direction or magnitude of error can be cause for investigation. The strength of this approach is that it can be easily automated on many systems. Statistical Process Control goes beyond the scope of this book, and the reader is referred to the many excellent texts available.[6]

In each of the preceding cases, a study was conducted to determine the best solution and the cost of implementation. Many management teams balk at the cost of thoroughly investigating and preparing for implementation of e-business solutions. The costs usually include an initial study to choose a solution, the cost of hardware and software to implement the solution, implementation itself, and training after installation.

Skipping any of the steps, however, can be costly. The initial study should determine not only an appropriate solution but the operational requirements that the new system must meet and the processes that must be changed to make the new system a success (and how to make these changes). The initial study should also create a road map for implementation and develop a training plan for the firm. If a solution is implemented without a thorough understanding of the environment, the wrong solution may be selected, implementation may fail, the mission of the system may not be understood well enough to introduce appropriate training, or all of the above.

Although the hardware/software and implementation steps cannot be skipped, they can be poorly implemented. Hardware and software are often underpowered in the interest of saving money. These weak systems frequently are not able to meet the objectives as originally designed or get overwhelmed as soon as the firm grows. Upgrades are often nearly as expensive in equipment and time as the original installation, and much can be lost in the interim while the firm has to struggle with the existing system.

Implementation also gets shorted. The company frequently relies too heavily on the IT provider for implementation in order to avoid pulling critical people away from their other jobs. The damage, as we stated before, is a system that does not match your needs. This problem is very common and does more damage to distribution firms than virtually all the others combined.

Training is often shorted the most. Coming at the end of the project, when the budget has already been completely rewritten due to cost overruns, the training budget usually takes up the slack. The solution is usually an attempt to "train the trainer" and have inside people train the rest of the firm. This procedure usually fails because the trainers are not given sufficient training, have other responsibilities that prevent them from getting out in the field to train others, and lack adequate teaching skills.

Purchasing/Planning Metrics

Before internal operations has opportunity to meet or miss customer needs, planners have to anticipate the need for inventory and ensure it is available to promise. Available to Promise (ATP) refers to whether inventory is on the shelf or scheduled for receipt before the customer needs it. There is an old saying in sales: "Nothing happens until somebody sells something." Another goes: "You can't sell from an empty wagon." Sales and planning are tied together, and their metrics reflect both complementary and sometimes conflicting goals.

Forecasting involves anticipating needs as was discussed in detail in Chapter 8. The successful forecast is a combination of data collection speed and accuracy. The former is tailor made for e-business solutions; the latter requires a combination of human and machine processes. Data collection speed requires quick entry techniques that can be quickly transferred back to the system. If the firm maintains inventory for the customer (VMI), scanning at the customer's site by the salesperson or the customer increases not only information velocity but also accuracy. Customer Relationship Management (CRM) software can also be implemented to allow the salesperson to input expert opinion to make the forecast more accurate.

A large equipment distributor had problems forecasting. The customer base had varying needs, since products were purchased for original sale and for aftermarket supply. The large sales associated with original equipment were easier to forecast, since the customer ordered through the distributor to the manufacturer in a make-to-order system. Once a machine was sold, however, the aftermarket supplies were more problematic. In this as in many applications, the aftermarket was much more profitable, with margins running between 40% and 80% while the original equipment had margins between 10% and 20%. Each aftermarket sale was considerably smaller but had an ongoing profit stream.

The demand for parts to sell (aftermarket) and for repair seemed very difficult to predict since machines could go down at any time. When a machine was down, there was little time to react, and a stockout could do considerable harm to a valuable customer, since a construction crew and other major equipment might also be idled while waiting for the down machine. Forecasting, although difficult, was therefore critical to prevent stockouts without carrying an unprofitable amount of inventory. The company used more powerful forecasting techniques (regression, combination) and applied a control chart to the forecasts to warn planners when there might be a problem brewing with the forecast for any particular product. The control chart was based on the Mean Absolute Deviation (MAD), and control limits were set tight so as to guarantee quick reaction to forecast error problems.

Another major area to measure with purchasing/planning is obsolescence costs. There are two types of obsolescence: functional and physical. Physical means the product was damaged in the warehouse through an accident or as part of the production process. Physical, for the most part, is out of the planner's control.

Functional, however, is caused by product becoming obsolete because it has been surpassed by another model or because customers are no longer interested in the product. It is the planning department's responsibility to work with suppliers and anticipate upcoming model changes, and to avoid replenishing soon-to-be-discontinued products into inventory. Planners should also track the number of customers buying a product and watch for signs that a product may soon lose all its customers. Branch managers and marketing also bear some responsibility for informing planners of upcoming changes in a product's status. Branch managers and their sales force may have advance warning of a customer going bankrupt for instance. Marketing may develop a plan to push a new product line that will make another product obsolete. Notifying planners well in advance will allow for a phased drawdown on the endangered product's inventory. Ultimately, however, the obsolescence issue must be monitored and controlled by planners.

Other common planning metrics include inventory turns, ROI, ROA, number of days on backorder, number of backorders, and number of stockouts. Some of these metrics are redundant to some degree or outside of a planner's control. ROI or ROA on inventory, for instance, is under the planner's control (with cooperation from sales), but not ROI or ROA on total assets. The more metrics a firm collects, the clearer the picture the firm has on its operations. If the metrics are collected for assigning blame instead of seeking continuous improvement, however, the more metrics are collected, the more stressed planners and other personnel become.

How Visibility Improves Inventory Management

Throughout this text, we have stressed the importance of information management in controlling and reducing inventory. The control metrics discussed above focus attention on the accuracy of processes. As demonstrated in other chapters:

> More Accurate Processes = Less Need for Inventory to Meet
> a Customer Service Goal

Information that is inaccurate or incomplete translates directly into inventory that must cover up mistakes. Tracking systems with appropriate metrics provide visibility into the how the system works and empower the firm to operate with fewer assets (less inventory) and still achieve or exceed its customer service objectives. We have discussed a few metrics for measuring critical processes from the distribution operations perspective. Each of the same metrics applies equally to the customer and supplier, and to the operations of the supplier's supplier. The complete linkage of the supply chain through e-business tools such those pictured in Figure 10.2 will allow metrics to be compared and adjustments to be made to build the most efficient supply chain possible.

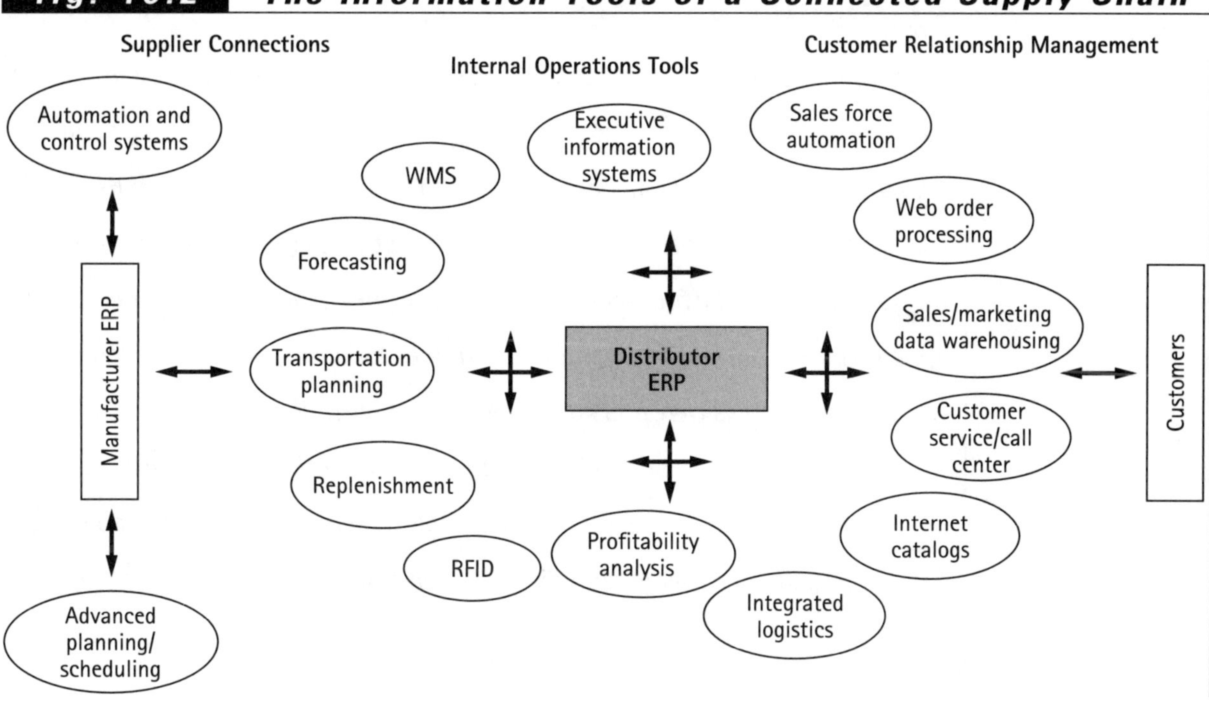

Source: F. Barry Lawrence and Ramesh Krishnamurthi, "Supply Chain Systems Laboratory: Simulation of Supply Chain Systems," Texas A&M University (2001).

The information tools should enable the collection and interpretation of metrics. These metrics should also be interpreted and connected with supplier and customer metric collection systems. Many ERP systems and their bolt-ons (bolt-ons surround the ERP systems in the diagram) do not yet have all the proper metrics presently available, but they will soon. In the meantime, the firm can write special programs for metric collection or conduct it offline through spreadsheets.

The popular buzzwords "system visibility" refer to the connection of measurement and tracking systems that provides the ability for the firm and its supply chain partners to "see in real time" how customer service processes are performing and how profitable those processes are. Customer expectations are increasing with no end in sight. Information-blind firms will struggle in the dark as higher demands destroy their ability to respond and make a profit. Those firms that create visibility will improve those things that need improvement, leave alone or eliminate ones that do not hold value, monitor and control the need for inventory, and outperform the competition at a lower cost. In the short term they will even see higher-than-expected margins as their competition holds down customer expectations with poor performance. In the long term, they will control their destiny while their competitors are consolidated or fail.

Distributor Retrospective

Rogers and the two manufacturing managers decided that moving all operations to real time would be the proper response. They soon discovered that getting there would expose all the rocks in their operation. They had to design a system that collected the right metrics and then used those metrics to drive performance. If they did not know what the firm should do to improve, they could not automate it on the system. First a team was brought together at the management level to determine what the firm's goals were and how to make them operational. Operational teams then had to interpret the strategic goals and work with other teams to integrate all actions to support the strategic goals. New tools were introduced (WMS and Radio Frequency) and processes were studied and then redesigned to support strategic goals.

Issues to Consider

1. Describe "real-time systems" and their importance to the supply chain.

2. What are the three major categories of internal operational metrics?

3. Discuss how the use of an integrated Warehouse Management System (WMS) could reduce cycle time, improve inventory accuracy, and reduce warehouse expenses.

4. Describe the recommended steps to follow in preparing for the implementation of an e-business solutions system.

5. What are the types of inventory obsolescence and what are their primary causes?

6. Discuss why a completely connected supply chain will result in a more efficient supply chain.

Notes

1.   W. E. Deming, "Out of the Crisis," MIT Center for Advanced Engineering, Cambridge, Mass., 1986.

   ———, "The New Economics: For Industry, Government, Education," MIT Center for Advanced Engineering, Cambridge, Mass., 1993.

2.   Robert Preston, "E-Biz Transforms Companies . . . But Not Fast Enough," *Internet Week* 9 (March 26, 2001).

3.   "Grainger Lightens Its Digital Load," *Industrial Distribution* 90 (3): 21–24.

4.   W. Shewhart, *Economic Control of Quality of Manufactured Product* (New York: D. Van Nostrand, 1931).

5.   P. S. Pande, R. P. Neuman, and R. R. Cabanagh, "How GE, Motorola, and Other Top Companies Are Honing Their Performance," *The Six Sigma Way* (New York: McGraw-Hill, 2000), 5.

6.   James A. Evans and William M. Lindsay, *The Management and Control of Quality,* 3rd ed. (St. Paul, Minn.: West Publishing, 1996).

Supply Chain Management and E-business

part

4

Standardization and Successful E-business Relationships

Distributor Perspective

Sam Abrams is the owner and chief executive officer of TenCo Electric Company. Headquartered in Jackson, Tennessee, TenCo is an electrical distributor with annual sales of $235 million. In the past, TenCo has used a legacy system to manage its inventory and to perform certain financial functions. Sam is interested in installing a state-of-the-art information system, but he has taken the position that the cost of such a system must be justified by increased profits. Sam has attended trade association meetings in which he has heard many "horror" stories regarding the implementation of information-processing systems. Sam wonders how TenCo can avoid repeating such mistakes. Also, in the back of his mind is the thought that TenCo may not really need a new information-processing system. How should Sam and TenCo go about developing a strategy to implement a state-of-the-art information-processing system?

Introduction

When the e-business movement first began, the first challenge it had to meet was the development of standards. The problem was neither new nor unexpected. The standards issue has bedeviled information technology throughout its existence. The Phoenicians developed the alphabet as a necessary requirement for carrying out business transactions in a format everyone understood and could agree upon. The Arabic numerical system was also adopted worldwide to make common calculation possible for business, science, and many other purposes. In recent years, the European Union has been working to develop a common currency. Each of the foregoing examples is a form of information exchange. The process is greatly hampered when we do not speak the same language, count the same way, or exchange the same document types in our transactions.

The movement toward standardizing business transactions has had a powerful impact on world commerce. Each standardizing effort from ISO 9000 to using the dollar as a base currency for valuing other currencies has led to powerful and usually beneficial change. However, before we conclude that standards are a necessary condition that will always win out, we must consider situations in which standards have failed. Standards tend to fail when cherished cultural beliefs clash with the need for a single way of doing things. Language is perhaps the most prominent example. Business transactions are more hampered by language barriers than by any other force, but rather than agreeing to use a single language, we have forced our business mechanisms to bend to cultural norms. Customs and currency are other examples. Even the euro has had to struggle against antistandardization forces. Conformity is considered a way to lose our national individuality. Those things we cherish the most tend to force our other systems to bend to their will.

The history of standards is very instructive as we look toward our future relationships and how e-business tools will be used. Logic dictates that we should standardize all communication: forms, data, formatting, and so on. Major industry groups such as Rosetta.net were developed to facilitate the standards movement. Where these consortiums have run aground, however, is over the issue of how far standards should go. Many manufacturers have resisted standardization, since they believe a standardized product is a commodity. This position is analogous to the early resistance in Europe to a single currency (the euro) on the basis of losing national identity. Brand equity is the key differentiator for manufacturers, especially in the Internet world.

Some distributors have also resisted the standards movement on the basis of competitive advantage. If a distributor controls a channel, it wants its suppliers to do business its way so that the supplier will have difficulty working with others that do not use the same processes. This is analogous to countries that refuse to allow education or other promotion of multiple languages so that the only way for suppliers to participate in your market is to use your local businesses. Many countries encourage their children to learn English as a second language to penetrate the huge U.S. market. When you are big enough, you can force the world to do things your way. Long term, however, this can be a difficult strategy to maintain.

The real issue going forward is to differentiate between things that are important to intercompany cultures that cannot be changed for competitive or other reasons, as opposed to those things that can be standardized without risk of damaging relationships. When relationships between supply chain partners are put at risk by standardization, relationships are going to win. In the near term, however, many things that are not important to relationships will be declared significant reasons not to standardize. Firms that have not prepared themselves for e-business will resist standardization because they are too far behind in the development of consistent systems and fear that the freedom standards will provide to the e-business movement will cause them to lose competitive advantage to better-prepared competition.

All firms need to understand the difference between data and processes that will ultimately be standardized and those that will not, so that they can begin to move toward the standards that make sense and are likely to be implemented first. Failure to act will force a firm to go through its own standardization at the same time competitors have started moving at Internet speed. Information technology firms and industry consortiums are coming to understand the difference between what should be standardized and what cannot be. It serves the interest of many IT firms to support standards so they can start developing and selling their products.

Industry consortiums are interested in a healthy economy for the firms that support them and therefore, will also adopt, standards that will support a strong competitive position for the majority of their members. The recent failed attempt to eliminate distribution from the supply chain hammered the point home to distribution associations that their members could not afford to lag behind the e-business movement. Some members will continue to resist, but the majority will support their efforts. In other words, the standardization movement will go forward.

Those relationship-based activities that cannot be standardized will not be standardized. IT providers will be forced to customize for each application. This may seem impossible with so much to be done in e-business, but eventually someone will get around to those things that give small subsets of firms a critical edge. These "boutique"-type solutions will make the most interesting applications, creating an explosion of creativity that will offer services not even imagined today. Such customized relationship-based solutions come from the tacit knowledge discussed in Chapter 7 and are the source of true competitive advantage. Explicit knowledge can, and to a great extent will, be standardized. Any company that intends to derive its competitive position from explicit knowledge that is rapidly being converted into standard offerings must be prepared to fight for low-cost leadership, which is a viable strategy but one that only a few firms can win, and which most would rather avoid.

Back-Office Integration

The standardization arena is currently focused on back-office integration. In the e-channel, this occurs wherever two firms meet to carry out a transaction. The back-office integration function has long been the responsibility of salespeople, but the automation opportunities associated with these activities have raised awareness of the redundancies and costs that these human-based processes carry. In the e-business world, this interface is critical to a fully connected supply chain.

fig. 11.1 *Shifting Knowledge Types*

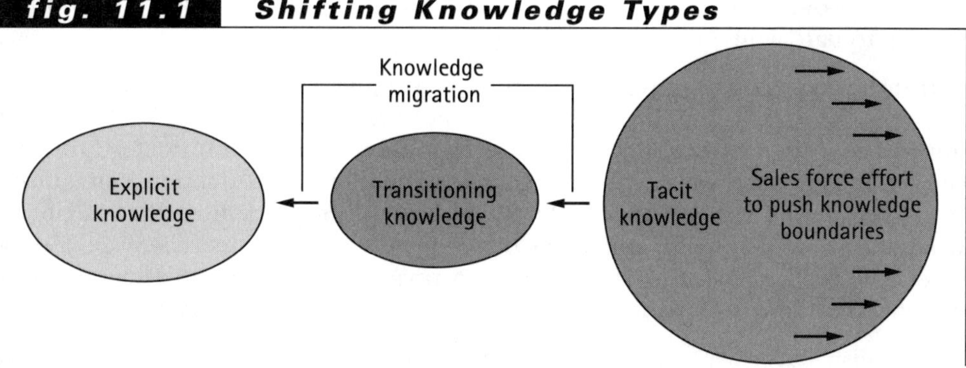

Source: F. Barry Lawrence and William Christensen, "The Boundaries of Knowledge," adapted from course lectures at Texas A&M University, 2001.

As explained in Chapter 7, these junctures between e-business tools like ERP and CRM, are the major communication ports handled by salespeople at most firms today. Salespeople are important keepers of tacit knowledge, the knowledge that provides competitive advantage. Customer Relationship Management (CRM) software seeks to turn tacit sales force knowledge into explicit knowledge. The shift will cause the sales force to further extend the boundaries of tacit knowledge. The extension of tacit knowledge will give the firm competitive advantage, as what was formerly tacit becomes explicit and a commodity. Commodities, as defined earlier, will not hold a competitive advantage in e-business (see Figure 11.1).

One large distributor assumed that basic operational knowledge was a given among salespeople and, therefore, a commodity that would not continue to provide competitive advantage. If the sales force was to continue to create unique value for customers, it had to start offering a higher level of information. In addition, the rote task of commodity information delivery had to be made explicit and offered through the Internet. Simple information like inventory availability, pricing, and product specifications was put on the company's website for the customer to access. The reduced need for salespeople to provide this information allowed time for them to develop more extensive tacit knowledge about the customer's operations, such as required fill rates from their own customers and product information too complex to go on the Net.

The two challenges the distributor faced were placing the simple information on its website (transitioning tacit knowledge into explicit knowledge) and increasing tacit knowledge. Inventory availability created problems with hardware and software that could operate in real time. If information on the Web was not up to the minute, the customer might buy material thinking it was available when in fact it had been sold minutes before the order was placed.

Pricing was complicated as well. The firm had a complex series of discounts for different customer types. The program would have to match each customer to the appropriate discount. All the different configurations of customers, products, and discounts would require computer space and speed to access. Keeping the information up to date would also be a challenge.

Transferring technical information from the supplier to customer through a website was also challenging. Since every supplier had a different way of formatting information, the firm had to reformat all supplier technical information to get a consistent look to its website. Formatting determines how information is organized. If a door were displayed as part of a building materials catalog, the distributor would not want the dimensions of the door presented at the top of the page in some cases and at the bottom in others. Other formatting issues included the length of data fields and their placement for reading by the information system.

If the distributor's system is going to read in the information from the supplier and each supplier uses a different format, the distributor's system has to adapt for each possible configuration. Consider electronic invoicing, for example. If one supplier wishes to invoice electronically and puts the date at the top of the page in abbreviated numerical format (02/02/01) and another puts the date at the bottom of the page in complete verbal form (February 2, 2001), the distributor's system has to be able to look in both places and for both formats. Consider how many places on a page a date could be placed (dozens or more) and how many forms the date can take (three or more). The date alone could require formatting for thirty or more different searches. Multiply this by all possible combinations of dates, pricing, product descriptions, types of artwork, and volume of information, and the programming problem explodes.

The system-to-system connection is greatly facilitated by standards. To date, many applications are still unresolved due to the lack of standards. Where standards do not exist, people have to take on the task of developing them. Think for a minute how many people in a typical firm spend their time on rote tasks like invoicing, inventory status reporting, filling out sales orders, and updating accounting records. The e-business movement promises to eliminate these massive transactions costs but cannot do so without some agreement on standards for information exchange.

Standard setting is both a global issue (solvable by IT providers and professional associations) and an individual one. If the standard is one that affects a great many, industry associations can solve it. As an example, electrical distributors and manufacturers formed the Industry Data Warehouse (IDW) to address the length of data fields. If the standard is individual, however, the solution becomes the responsibility of the channel's members. Quotes, for example, present many problems for distributors and manufacturers alike.

One small distributor that does a great deal of repair work found job quoting to be very challenging. The customer would send in the item for repair, and the distributor would put together a quote. Since the repair item was typically associated with one manufacturer and carried a warranty, all parts needed to come from that supplier. The problem was that the distributor had to use a certain form to place orders with the manufacturer. These forms, which differed tremendously from manufacturer to manufacturer, played a major role in the pricing portion of the quote. Product identification numbers, customer information, warranty details, product specifications and descriptions, and many other types of information were placed in different places and configurations on the various forms. Not only was it impossible for the distributor to come up with a common form for its information system, but invoicing was forced to be manual since pricing could not be automatically pulled from the disparate forms. Customer invoices had to be compiled by manual inspection of the different forms and rekeying into the system. Supplier invoices were paid in the same fashion. The keying and rekeying was very expensive in terms of man hours and keying errors.

The high cost of nonstandardized systems will continue to be one of the most troubling issues for industry associations, IT providers, and supply chain partners. The number of problems that can be solved by IT providers and industry associations is limited to a small subset of the total. The remainder will be solved through standardizing of business processes that must be driven by the supply chain members themselves.

XML and the Search for Standards

This text is not so much a technical manual as an operational analysis of what IT systems in general, and e-business in particular, will do to redefine distribution. XML, however, has been discussed a great deal as a panacea for the standards problem, so we will briefly address its true value for standards setting.

XML (eXtensible Markup Language) is the child of SGML (Standard Generalized Markup Language), a computer language designed to transport massive amounts of data through information systems developed by the military.[1] Its sibling, HTML (Hypertext Markup Language), also derived from SGML, enabled the Internet.

XML was developed under the auspices of the World Wide Web Consortium (W3C) in 1996 to address the above need for standardized communication in a business-to-business environment. It was designed to overcome the limitations inherent in traditional data exchanges, such as flat files delimited by commas. These "record by record" exchanges lead to fields that have no universally apparent meaning and therefore need extremely complex mapping in order for another application to understand the data. The end result is a point-to-point solution (different for each relationship) for each company's exchange of data with another company. Considering how many customers a typical distributor handles (thousands), and how many suppliers (hundreds), one can quickly see that point-to-point solutions would increase exponentially with the number of customers/suppliers. Eventually, the relationship map would overwhelm efforts at information automation (see Figure 11.2).

XML overcomes the limitations of traditional data exchange mechanisms by providing a standard way of describing, processing, and presenting data. The markup tags are semantic in nature and reflect the data they encapsulate. This makes XML both human- and machine-readable. XML emphasizes what the data really is, thereby providing avenues for automating B2B communication, using a set of tags that identify data types for easier reading.[2] XML goes a long way toward solving some of the problems associated with EDI and its predecessors but is only part of the solution. XML does not address several key areas of information exchange.

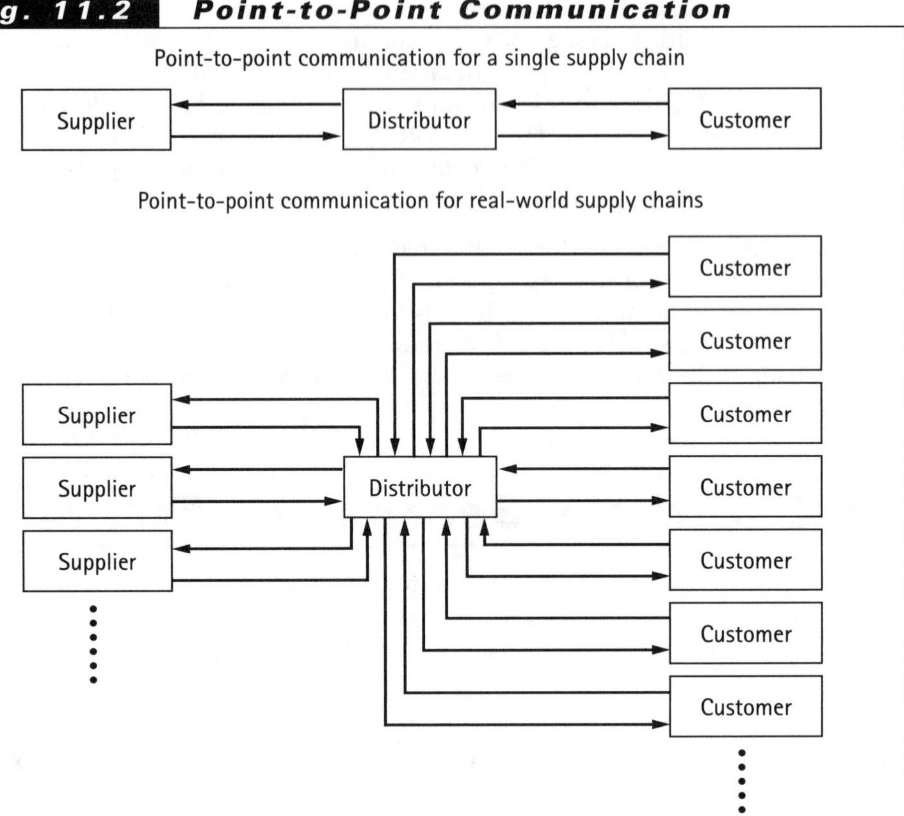

In traditional EDI, the medium for information exchange was typically a VAN (Valued Added Network), and the alphabet and words were required to conform with standards like ANSI X12 and UN/EDIFACT. Transaction sets defined using these standards took care of the grammar, dialog, and business processes. The ANSI X12 and UN/EDIFACT embody a business dictionary of transaction sets in the context of business processes. Traditional EDI embodied more than just data definition, as it also included the implementation guidelines in the transaction sets.

The role played by XML when compared with traditional EDI is small. XML is just a standard that governs how data is to be represented. It only provides the alphabets to define a vocabulary of business processes. It does not impose or attempt to specify the standardized use of the vocabulary. In other words XML is not a dictionary, only a means of formulating one. There are several pieces missing from the solution. The missing links include the words, grammar, dialog, and business process representation.

The dictionary is the representation of product or other information that can be used as a common language for exchange of data. The rules for dialog and business processes have to be agreed upon by the supply chain partners. This can be done on a global level, such as an industry rule on how documents are to be formatted, or it must be agreed upon individually by the two transacting parties. Those rules that can be set up globally can be programmed by IT providers for multiple users, thereby making the setup less expensive. In situations in which the information exchange can create a competitive (strategic) advantage, the partners may decide on a customized solution.

EDI Past, Present, and Future

The missing parts of the XML/e-business solution are going to take time to develop and many major players might not participate. Those with EDI solutions already in place might not be interested in supporting change that does not improve their current situation. Many large firms pushed through EDI implementation by forcing smaller ones to comply. How the smaller firms implemented EDI did not really matter to the large firms. EDI remained expensive (the cost of VANs) but was viewed by some as less expensive than investing in new technology.

The EDI standards groups spent years agreeing on and formulating transaction sets. At the end of the 1990s, XML was not in a position to replace traditional EDI. The corresponding tag sets did not exist in a common standardized dictionary yet. Organizations like Rosetta.net, CommerceNet, and O.A.S.I.S were trying to leverage the extensible nature of XML to fill in the missing links. The basis for organizations such as Rosetta.net was, in fact, the development of a master dictionary to define properties for products, partners, and business transactions, coupled with common business specifications. As organizations rushed to solve the problem, each in its own way, the problem quickly became less about the lack of standards to fill in the missing links and more about a slew of competing standards.

Conclusion

In the midst of all this XML-driven change, many thought EDI would be taken to the Internet. The Internet was viewed as less expensive than VANs, and many believed EDI would be absorbed as part of the XML/e-business movement. The final solution was still unclear at the end of the 1990s. One thing was clear, however: the solutions offered through standardization groups, EDI, and XML would only partially solve the problem. Each business would have to look to its own internal operations and make them as standard as possible. This meant that continuing to do business with your partners as it was done in the past would now have to be reevaluated from both a strategic and tactical (process-by-process) angle.

Distributor Retrospective

After many internal battles revolving around what would have to be given up and what could be taken advantage of under e-business, Sam Abrams had a better understanding of the issues involved in developing and implementing a strategy for a state-of-the-art information-processing system. Sam saw the need for back-office integration and began to see that until his company understood itself, it could not understand what technology should be adopted or how. He felt overwhelmed by acronyms like XML and HTML but also felt that before he launched initiatives to alter his core processes, he had better learn the lingo! He started teams on process-mapping the business while he read a primer on XML and searched the Net for information on Rosetta.net and similar groups.

Issues to Consider

1. Discuss why the issue of channel control has delayed the development of standards.

2. Which of the two types of knowledge do salespeople typically possess, and why is this knowledge important to their company?

3. Discuss the challenges faced by distributors in placing information on the Web.

4. Why is the development and adoption of standards important to e-business?

5. Discuss the advantages and limitations of the current generation of XML.

Notes

1. Powell E. Robinson, F. Barry Lawrence, R. Narayan, and S. Jayavelu, "Measuring the Value of Standardization," Information Systems Consortium for Supply Chain Integration, Texas A&M University, vol. 1 (September 2000): 100–189.

2. Ibid.

12

Performance Metrics in the Connected World

Distributor Perspective

Horace Burke is vice president of sales at Cameron Supply, a $75 million general line distributor. In a recent meeting with a major customer, American Manufacturing (AM), the customer asked for a price reduction on one of Cameron Supply's major product lines. AM also indicated dissatisfaction with certain aspects of Cameron's customer service. After the meeting, Burke was concerned. He strongly believed that Cameron Supply provided considerable value to both its customers and suppliers. Yet, Cameron Supply had little "formal" documentation of its customer service activities. Burke suddenly realized that Cameron Supply could not translate its present customer service metrics into financial measures. How could he convince AM as well as other customers that Cameron Supply adds value to its supply chain partners by factually demonstrating this value?

Introduction

The customer (especially the end user) is now in control of the supply chain. Supply Chain Management (SCM) and Just in Time (JIT) have redefined all distribution channels to emphasize the final customer's needs. When it comes to consumer channels, this means that the supply chain with the greatest product/service value will win. For the Maintenance, Repair, and Operations (MRO) channels, it means that relationships that maximize channel efficiency will be the most successful.

As companies strive to add value and prove that value to other supply chain partners, it becomes necessary to address what customer service metrics a company should collect and how it should use them. Several functional areas of a company need to collect and evaluate metrics.

Purchasing makes many of the key decisions that drive inventory levels and responsiveness. Salespeople have long been evaluated on productivity, originally through revenues and more recently through margins. While the switch to margin and Return on Investment (ROI) metrics is good, the sales force must be engaged in and held responsible for accurate forecasting. Operations contributes to the supply chain through process cycle time reduction and increased inventory accuracy. Transportation faces many of the same challenges operations does and contributes to the efficiency of the supply chain in much the same way. Each function must view its predecessor as an information customer and seek to make that customer more successful through the collection and proper dissemination of information that makes the entire supply chain more successful.

Finally, the company needs a translation of efficiency measures into financial terms so it can evaluate the costs and benefits of improving processes. Early TQM efforts often failed because the financial evaluation of quality improvement frequently killed important initiatives. This may have led to the mistaken belief that financial metrics should not be applied to information technology since that same technology is often part of a continuous improvement program. The financial evaluation of service metrics is important, however, when prioritizing the next initiative to undertake or deciding whether to implement a simple inexpensive solution or go on an expensive full-scale assault. Financial measures must use the holding costs of inventory, stockout costs, additional human effort, and as many other parameters as are deemed meaningful in evaluating how and when to change a process. Looking at the cost of current operations can generate these financial measures. The firm should then be continually asking how new technology or improved processes would change those costs.

Chapter 10 addressed the connectivity of measures and introduced the concepts surrounding metrics collection. This chapter examines some of the most common measures for process efficiency as they apply to various functional departments in an SCM initiative. We examine each functional area in turn and describe important measures that were introduced elsewhere in this text and how they can be used in a connected supply chain. To manage the process, metrics must be generated by the company information system and updated in real time.

Control and Measurement

A scorecard, or set of measurements, should be comprehensive. *Comprehensive* means that no critical process goes unmeasured and all measured processes are interconnected by those measures to achieve a universal end goal. The problem at many firms is that goals are often based on mistaken assumptions or on a set of conditions that no longer exist.

Mistaken assumptions are often built into measures when managers do not understand their own processes or the logic behind how they interconnect. Many large manufacturers have had trouble connecting manufacturing and distribution processes because each uses its own information system. Manufacturing may be operating on a legacy MRP system that has been in use for many years, while distribution may be struggling with a new ERP system. Manufacturing divisions are often unwilling to part with their existing system, since the new ERP system is unproven and such systems have often suffered from high-profile failures at other firms.[1] Many manufacturing divisions have experienced supplier shutdowns due to new ERP introductions by the supplier and are unwilling to risk the same problem in their operations.

The lack of connectivity requires certain assumptions be made in manufacturing metrics. One assumption often introduced is that the cost of manufacturing product should be based strictly on raw material cost and man/machine hours. As discussed earlier, this type of logic will cause manufacturing to buy raw materials in larger amounts and produce in larger production runs. The larger raw material purchases will get quantity discounts from suppliers and spread freight over more products, thereby reducing product cost. The longer production runs will spread the cost of the setup (changeover of machines for a new product) over more pieces and so further reduce product cost (on paper). The problem with this methodology is that it ignores the holding cost of the inventory bought and produced in large amounts. This leads to an average inventory that is considerably higher than would be maintained under a smaller order size. Figure 12.1 demonstrates this relationship.

The larger average inventory exists in both raw materials that are purchased in large amounts and in distribution inventories that are received after large production runs. The figure demonstrates that average inventory sits on top of safety stock, since safety stock on average never leaves inventory. Regular inventory does leave, however, and, if we assume the inventory is depleted at a somewhat steady rate, the average inventory is half the production or order amount. The large average inventory is only part of the problem, however. The large production runs also increase the amount of time between orders, which, in turn, increases forecast error (longer-term forecasts are less accurate than shorter-term ones) and lead-time variability (the longer the production run, the more opportunity for problems to occur). Increased forecast error and lead-time variability will cause stockouts, which will lead to increases in safety stock (see Figure 12.2).

The cost decrease brought about by larger orders is, therefore, often an illusion, but manufacturing has no way to determine this without a signal from distribution of what its true needs are and a thorough understanding of the firm's actual cost

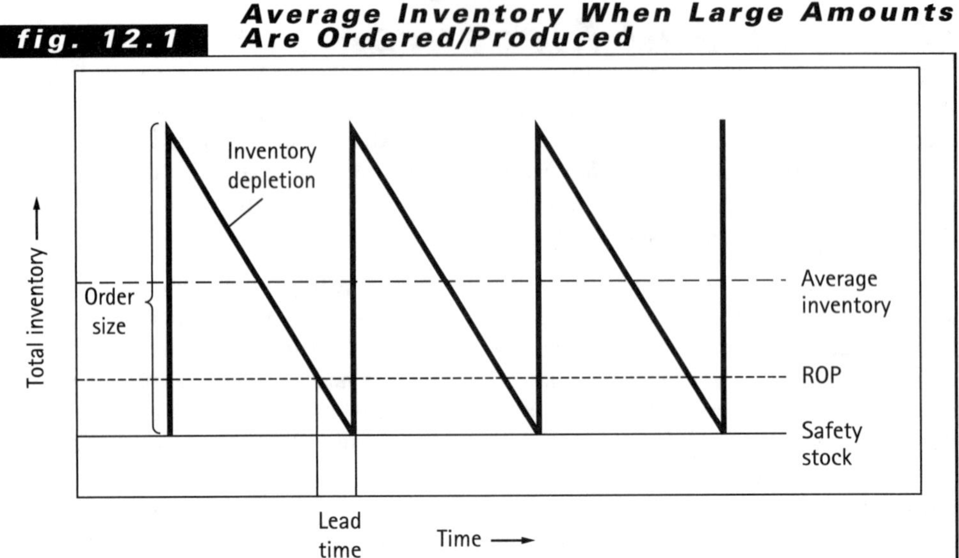

fig. 12.1 *Average Inventory When Large Amounts Are Ordered/Produced*

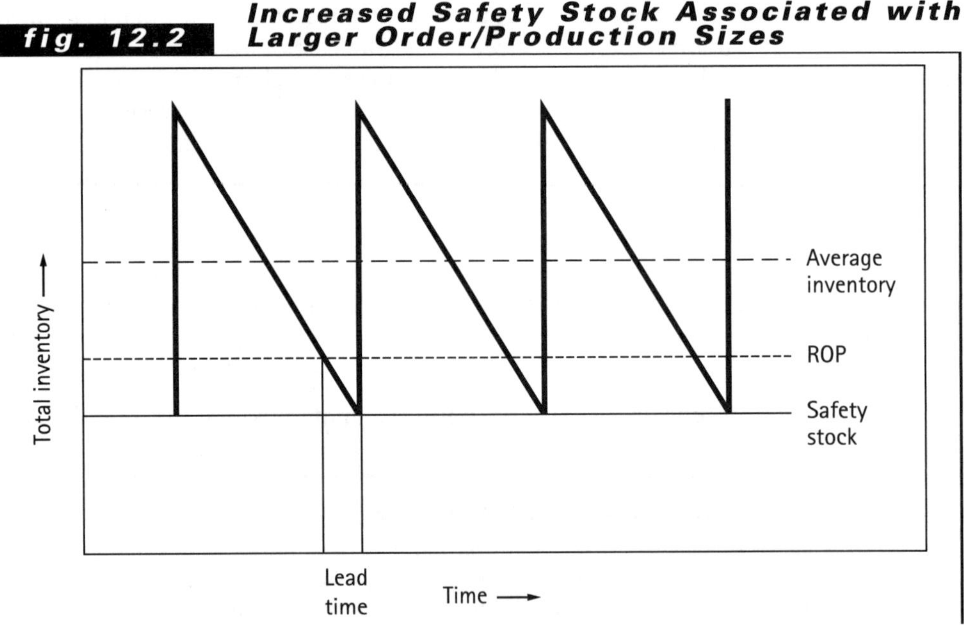

fig. 12.2 *Increased Safety Stock Associated with Larger Order/Production Sizes*

structure. In the absence of such metrics, false assumptions will drive production planning. The ideal pattern would be to drive better production planning with more accurate information exchange and measurement of the success of such processes. If we can achieve a smaller production run, the manufacturing savings associated with large production runs and raw material buys might be more than outweighed by inventory reduction and customer service improvement (see Figure 12.3).

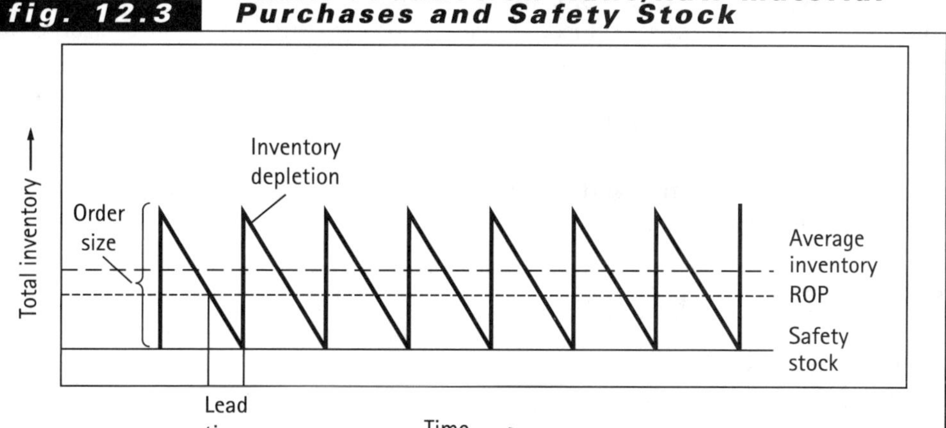

fig. 12.3   ***Small Production Runs/Raw Material Purchases and Safety Stock***

The drive to push average inventory down by reducing purchasing/production amounts is the essence of Just in Time. The reader will note not only that there is a large decrease in average inventory, but also that this only includes processes directly under control of a single firm. The demand during lead-time inventory (the difference between the ROP and safety stock) is based on the amount of time a supplier takes to deliver material. If distribution ordered in a more regular pattern and exchanged better information with the manufacturer, the manufacturer, through its own continuous improvement process, could reduce lead time (further decreasing demand during lead-time inventory) and, in so doing, the variability of lead time (further decreasing the need for safety stock). Managing and controlling processes in one firm is beneficial, but managing it across the supply chain is even more so. This information management across the supply chain is the definition of SCM. When we set inaccurate measurement systems based on false assumptions, we guarantee failure of SCM and JIT, not only in our firm but also across the entire supply chain.

Another problem is setting expectations based on one environment and then applying those same goals and associated metrics to future scenarios. Often a firm that is in a strong marketing mode, attempting to grab market share, will measure its sales force and branches based strictly on revenue. This "increase sales at any cost" methodology is commonly employed when reaching a certain critical mass is essential to achieving profitability or even survival in the market. The nature of the dot-com marketplace was such that Amazon.com had to achieve critical mass before it could reach profitability.[2]

If a firm cannot reach a sufficient number of customers, it may be unable to attract critical suppliers. In other cases, a firm may have built in new manufacturing capacity that cannot be justified without increased sales. Some firms are in a high-growth mode because their parent firm is preparing to sell them and interested buyers care more about market reach than profitability. The list of reasons goes on and on. The problem is that no firm can continue to be unprofitable indefinitely, and eventually the sales force must be expected to meet profitability as well as revenue goals.

Deriving the right set of goals or Key Performance Indicators (KPIs) is therefore a complex science that must connect all aspects of the firm and yet at the same time be understandable to all. Each function must see its role in terms of how it fits the overall plan and how it supports those functions that depend on its performance. Supply Chain Management theory simplifies this process by making the customer's needs the focus. All KPIs must be driven by the customer's requirements, and those requirements must control and "drill down" to all the distributor operations and through to the manufacturer.

Marketing and Sales

At many firms, sales metrics are being redefined to move away from a revenue-driven environment to one that emphasizes profit, cash flow, and customer service. The classic revenue methods focused on cash flow to some extent but principally on increasing profits through increasing sales (and hopefully economies of scale). A new paradigm that first defines customer service and then seeks to meet requirements while reducing operational costs is replacing the classic approach.

As has been discussed extensively in this text, one of the largest contributors to operations cost is forecast error. Cycle times (lead times), forecast error, and freight are the only reasons inventory is necessary at any firm.

Forecast error metrics should capture the total error (Mean Absolute Deviation, or MAD), identify any bias in the forecast (Mean Forecast Error, or MFE), produce a system for flagging a poorly performing forecast (tracking signal), and produce reports that allow experts to evaluate the weaknesses of the forecast. For each of the measures there are alternative methods of calculating error, and the system should capture as many as possible to offer the user the greatest flexibility.

Forecasting can be affected by goal setting. Motivational goals for the sales force should be handled separately from the forecasting system, with an override capability if necessary. An example would be for management to increase sales faster than forecasted by introducing a customer promotion or special compensation for the sales force. The forecast should continue to operate normally and be adjusted based on expert modification. The modified forecast would then be evaluated by the forecast error measures. A useful report would evaluate the modified and nonmodified forecasts to determine which was more accurate. Management could then use this report to evaluate the accuracy of its expert forecast.

The sales force makes a considerable contribution to profitability through its efforts to sell specific products. Revenue enhancement should be measured for cash flow purposes, but the sales force should also be measured on lead times to the customer and sales profitability. *Lead times* refers to the efforts the sales force puts into reporting timely information to purchasing, and to their negotiation of realistic customer expectations from the firm's operations divisions. Timely information is critical to effective forecasting. The sales force should be as automated as possible, and reporting lead times should be recorded by the system.

Customer expectations are increasing with the advent of Just in Time (JIT). JIT has led to a continual narrowing of time windows for delivery. When combined with wide supplier windows, the results can lead to decreased profitability for a particular customer due to the increased service expectation. Customers frequently use JIT in conjunction with a sole sourcing promise to hold down prices and avoid paying any service premium. The information system should allow for estimation of profitability for the customer under different service and volume levels.

The salesperson should be able to enter the delivery expectations (order size and frequency) and receive a profitability report. If the system captures supplier lead times and freight rates, the calculation is straightforward. The system could then evaluate the salesperson on contribution to profitability, and reward structures could be built around the measures. Salespeople tend to be very effective at maximizing performance measures if they are directed at the right target.

Purchasing

Purchasing has one of the most profound effects on the supply chain and yet is one of the most poorly understood functions. One frustrated executive, upon hearing his purchasing division was being hamstrung by a sales force that was more powerful than the buyers, asked: "How am I supposed to measure purchasing effectiveness?" The answer is that you cannot, unless proper tools are in place and the system can drive metrics that encompass each division's responsibilities and any influence they exert on other divisions. This implies that stand-alone metrics on one division will not give a true picture of that division's performance. Purchasing cannot be effective at buying if the sales force does not provide timely information, if customers change orders unexpectedly and management always gives in, if management is not willing to invest in the proper technology, or if any of a variety of other issues exsist.

While the significance of the purchasing function has continually increased (especially since the advent of JIT), the buyers still find themselves at a disadvantage when dealing with the sales force. Sales groups tend to wield great power due to their direct relationship with the customer. The sales force frequently uses this power to influence purchasing. Unless external influences are measured, purchasing metrics will not give a true picture of how this critical function is being performed. The good news is that in a connected supply chain change orders can be tracked, poor sales force forecasting can be measured, external parties changing purchasing decisions (safety stock levels, forecasts, etc.) can be recorded, and so forth. This will require a great deal of work, but to achieve the benefits of a connected supply chain and to be able to measure the effectiveness of different potential decision processes it must be done.

Purchasing's principal concern is inventory status as it relates to overstock and obsolescence or to customer service failures like stockouts. Common metrics for customer service include timeliness of delivery, the number of stockouts, expedites, back orders, and fill rates. For inventory planning, the most common metrics include ROI, Return on Assets (ROA), obsolescence, yearly holding costs (by item, vendor, customer, and product classification), forecast error, and product quality.

Stockouts are the most difficult and important customer service metric to measure. The fill rate can be assessed a number of different ways. The most common one is the absolute percentage of parts shipped on time. This item fill rate is not a good measure of supply chain efficiency. For most customers, the order fill rate is more significant, since a process usually needs multiple items to function. Order fill rates are usually much lower than item fill rates, since each item added to the order lowers the order fill rate by a multiple of the item fill rate. This is a particularly devastating measure in a distribution environment.

Take, for example, three products that are always shipped together. If the item fill rate per SKU on the order is 90%, then the order fill rate will be 72.9% (90% times 90% times 90%). Since many distribution orders may contain anywhere from ten to thirty SKUs, the order fill rate at distribution firms could easily be below 50%. A few firms track (but do not publish) order fill rates. These firms report order fill rates in the low seventies. Since those who collect this data are likely top performers, the outlook for order fill rates in distribution leaves much room for improvement. As SCM progresses, companies will come to be measured by their order fill rates, and the competition to improve inventory management will intensify.

An even more difficult goal to meet is the 0–1 fill rate. With a 0–1 fill rate, the order was either filled completely or is listed as a complete failure. For item fill rates, this means that if you shipped ninety parts out of one hundred, your fill rate for that shipment was zero. From a customer standpoint, this type of measure can make a great deal of sense. Manufacturers may not be willing to start a production run if all raw materials are not present, since they will be forced to set up again later when the additional parts come in. A contractor may not be willing to put a roofing crew to work on a project that will have to be halted midway due to missing materials. This 0–1 methodology considerably reduces fill rates. If it were used on an order fill rate policy where any item shipped incomplete on an order would cause the entire order to be listed as a failure, the effect would be to reduce distribution order fill rates even further.

Many customers are already demanding items be filled complete (0–1 methodology, becoming common in manufacturing raw materials), and others are demanding fill rates be order based (becoming more common in retail). It is only a matter of time before the two are combined. A proactive firm will measure all levels and report the best (item fill rate) for as long as possible while working behind the scenes to improve the others before they are demanded. If a stronger measure can be made respectable before the customer demands it, the distribution firm could report it and gain competitive advantage. One distributor started reporting order fill rates before the competition even started measuring them. The distributor then suggested to customers that they demand the same from the competition. While competitors scrambled to produce the numbers they lost credibility.

A third possible way to measure fill rate is at the line item level, but each line is evaluated separately. If an order contains five line items with a required quantity of ten each, the total order quantity will be fifty items. If three of the line items shipped are in quantities of five per line item and the remaining two line items are filled with ten as required, the total items shipped will be thirty-five. If the fill rate is measured this way, it will be 70%. While this calculation is mathematically correct, it does not meet the customer's requirements.

A more appropriate way to measure this example would be to measure each line item as either being filled 100% or not. If the line item is filled with any quantity less than what the customer ordered, it should be measured as a complete miss, or a zero fill rate. Each line item in the order would be measured using this more critical method. For the three incomplete lines, divided by the total number of lines on the order (five), the result is a 40% fill rate. While it could be argued that the customer probably didn't need all of the items at one time anyway, the fact remains that the order was incomplete. To argue otherwise is an exercise in rationalization, which will not produce real customer satisfaction.

On-time delivery (not back ordered) has to be tracked based on the customer's needs, and not on what is eventually agreed to between the customer's purchasing group and the supplier's sales department. A more effective way to measure on-time delivery is for the distributor's information system to capture two dates, the date required and the date promised. The date required is the date by which the customer has said he needs the product, and the date promised is the date negotiated between the customer and the inside salesperson, or customer service rep. The distributor's ability to meet the customer's required date is the harshest measure of the two, but it is useful in determining the distributor's ability to meet customer requirements. Measuring the distributor's ability to meet the promised delivery date is the more relevant in evaluating the distributor's processes. If the customer calls on an item with a stated three-day lead time and agrees to wait four days, a stockout has occurred and must be captured for continuous improvement purposes. This leads to some problems, however: some items have a standard lead time of a few days and if necessary can be ordered from suppliers for same day delivery. To carry an inventory in this case would be wasteful. One approach to the problem is to measure the fill rate at different points in the process and watch the effect on sales and customer satisfaction to determine what the proper mix of fill rate measures should be.

For most products, if an item fill rate is collected at order initiation (when the customer calls in), the items should be available. This makes the order initiation fill rate most important. On the other hand, if the item can usually be easily accessed from the supplier or another location, then the most important fill rate may be the fill rate at the time the pick slip is delivered to the warehouse. Each item has to be evaluated separately. Some items should have a 98% order initiation fill rate and a 100% rate at picking since the customer expects the firm to stock the item and does not expect a stockout once promised delivery. Other items should have an 85% fill rate at order initiation and 100% at picking since they can be sourced easily in the time window and the customer expects the item to be in stock. Still other hard-to-procure items should have a 70% fill rate at order initiation and 90% at picking since both the distributor and the customer understand the difficulty of getting these items and the high probability of supply chain failures.

These relationships are very complex, and the only way to mathematically derive the fill rates would be to manipulate them and measure customer reaction and profitability. This process is called simulation and can be done through a computer replication of the business environment or through actual changes made to the business process. The latter is very expensive since the only way to find out how positively or negatively the customer will react to different fill rates at different points in the process is to actually change those fill rates and suffer the consequences.

The computer simulation technique requires incorporating the firm's fill rate process and potential customer reactions into a computer program and then running it on the current fill rate policies, and then on any others of interest. Customer reactions would also be changed for each scenario to represent the best- and worst-case scenarios as well as many in between. The simulation, in order to be effective, must consider as many "real world" variables as possible. These can become quite numerous; they will increase the amount of time it takes to set up the simulation and make operating it more difficult (requiring greater expert assistance). Many software packages are now available to assist in simulation development, but the drawback will always be whether they accurately represent the firm's environment. Most offer the ability to add specific variables and change others, but the process is still complex and requires the efforts of good simulation programmers and internal company specialists from the affected functions (sales, purchasing, etc.). Spreadsheets can also be used but are often more cumbersome. They do have the advantage, however, of being easily understood by the firm's operational specialists.

Many times what appears to be a stockout may not, in fact, be one. Some customers are merely shopping, and even if the item had been in stock, a sale may not have occurred. For effective purchasing decision-making, the firm must track stockouts (separating the real from the perceived) and then determine their cost.

The information system should also track the number of expedites, back orders, and lost sales. Lost sales will require a delineation between lost opportunities on a "buy" where the customer would definitely buy the item if in stock and situations where the customer would only have bought if the price was the best they could find. This type of tracking requires a sophisticated setup of screens that easily allows the salesperson to record whether a call was a lost sale or a simple inquiry. Some distributor ERP systems provide the ability to enter a customer inquiry as a quote that can be converted to an order with minimal keystrokes. If a quote is entered into the system and the customer then decides to place the order, the inside salesperson can quickly convert the quote into a sales order. If the quote is entered into the system and several days pass, the inside salesperson could then follow up with customers on his outstanding quotes to find out the status of the inquiry. This may be an effective way to determine if the order was lost, for what reason, and maybe where the order was placed. This information would be very useful in identifying how and why an order was lost.

Back orders should be counted in terms of number of customer orders in back order and the length of time (days) orders are spending on back order. The days on back order should be traced back through the supply chain directly to originating suppliers. All suppliers should be tracked, and the variability associated with their ability to fill back orders should be assessed. Expedites should be measured as to how many expediting situations occur, cost of expediting, and as to whether expediting was successful in averting back ordering.

Finally, the system should apply the cost structure to each set of metrics to determine the cost to the firm of that level of back orders, expedites, or lost sales. The resulting information will enable sophisticated planning for investment in inventory or new technology such as e-commerce or RF tracking to reduce cost.

Inventory metrics must measure the status of inventory across the aggregate, vendors, product classifications, and customer groups. For purchasing, inventory management focuses on ROI, which applies to each of the above areas. The aggregate investment in inventory and its turn ratio affect the company's ability to serve the market and invest in new opportunities. The firm would like to minimize inventory investment so funds could be used to maximize other opportunities. On the other hand, the firm wants to maintain its current customer base and, therefore, may need a significant inventory investment to do so.

Aggregate methods rarely provide sufficient detail for purchasing to determine how they should go about minimizing their inventory investment. One more detailed measure would be to consider the amount of inventory invested with a vendor and compare that with the margin contribution the vendor has made to the firm. Dating, where the vendor postpones payment or interest charges for a specified period of time, should also be considered so that the amount actually invested in inventory is considered along with the total amount of inventory carried from the vendor. Vendors with dating programs should not be penalized for advance purchases made to take advantage of the dating period. Vendor metrics allow purchasing to assess vendor performance and share that information with suppliers. Suppliers can then respond with programs that facilitate the relationship and enhance the supply chain.

Product classification measurements allow purchasing to determine the investment in a product class as compared to its margin return. This measure becomes increasingly important as more firms (particularly distributors) divide their purchasing and marketing groups along product lines. One of the most difficult decisions purchasing faces is what new products should be added to inventory and when. Vendor and product class metrics are useful for determining where to add new offerings.

Customers are also being divided up based on margin return and service requirements. Dedicated inventory for JIT programs, or matrix pricing, where different prices are offered to different customers or for different volumes, has become common in distribution and other related fields. Since margins and service levels (cost) differ greatly between these environments, purchasing needs to be able to examine the inventory used to support different customer groups with metrics that allow an assessment of the ROI on those groups.

For each group or class being measured, the metrics captured should be inventory turns, ROI, ROA, and obsolescence. Inventory turns are an overall measure of inventory health. Turn gives a sense of but not the direct relationship between items, product classes, customers, and vendors and their impact on ROI, ROA, and cash flow. The measure actually is a combination of cash flow and ROI. A fast-turning item, for instance, may generate a strong cash flow but not be profitable. While ROI and ROA make good intuitive sense, cash flow must be considered directly. Cash flow is the lifeblood of a firm and should not be taken lightly.

A final consideration is the ABC classification of inventory. The operations group uses inventory classification for controlling the physical flow of goods and is most interested in classification schemes that capture movement, size/weight, or similarity between products. Purchasing, on the other hand, needs classification schemes that capture ROI. As was demonstrated elsewhere in this text, there should be a direct relationship between the metrics mentioned above and the calculation of ABC classification.

Operations

The operations (warehouse management) team is principally concerned with lead times and accuracy. If purchasing has correctly identified supplier capabilities and the sales force has correctly forecasted customer needs, the operations division is only concerned with efficiency in picking, receiving, and shipping goods.

The picking process is driven by layout and information systems issues. The layout of the warehouse should follow the popularity, similarity, and size philosophies. Pickers spend 60% of their time in transit between items. To increase picking accuracy and minimize human effort, the information system must maintain the layout of the warehouse and provide for directed pick activity.

Popularity puts items with a high pick frequency at the end of rows and in the "golden zone" for picking. The golden zone is the area between the shoulders and the knees where picking can be done with a minimum of bending and stretching (reduced chance of injury). Similarity places items that are commonly picked together near one another. The size philosophy refers to the need to store large, bulky items in places where they can be picked with minimal risk. The layout has to be planned in advance, then mapped onto the information system for maintenance.

Technology plays a major role in picking procedures. RF technology, carousels, and conveyers will continue to bring decreased cycle times and increased data integrity to the picking process. As the technology continues to advance, the focus will be on metrics that measure cycle times (picker routing) and picking accuracy (data integrity).

The same metrics will be applied to receiving and shipping processes. Data integrity will focus on checking in merchandise as accurately as possible (bar coding will play a major role) and efficient put away so the product is available for use as fast as possible. Any delay will add to lead-time variability, one of the major safety stock drivers. The shipping process seeks to guarantee on time delivery and order accuracy. Measurements will be customer exceptions for inaccurate or late shipments that can be traced to shipping activity (late delivery, inaccurate shipments).

After measuring the shipping accuracy of their suppliers, some distribution firms have found it to be so high that the time and cost of physically counting all incoming shipments far exceeds the value of any shipping errors discovered. If the supplier's shipment history, based on measuring shipping accuracy over time, is so good, the distributor can then consider making that supplier a "dock-to-stock" supplier. Dock-to-stock means that the incoming shipments from these suppliers bypass the normal receiving process and are instead taken and put on the shelf immediately upon arriving at the distributor's dock. This process can dramatically reduce the time that product sits in receiving, which should also quickly make the product available for sale. Another benefit is that speeding up the physical movement of the product should also increase inventory turns.

Obsolescence applies to operations as well as purchasing. In operations, however, the focus is on physical as opposed to functional obsolescence (purchasing's concern). Physical obsolescence refers to theft or damage caused by the operations division. This type of obsolescence should be separated from the functional kind, which is caused by poor forecasting leading to overbuys that cannot be disposed of before new product introductions.

Where product is modified as part of the value add process (common in distribution as well as manufacturing environments), metrics must focus on the conversion process. Cycle times for value add focus on machine and staging setup times and processing run times. The length of the cycle for a manufacturing process or the setup time for machines can be tracked so that continuous improvement programs can be applied.

Other metrics include quality measured through statistical process control (as in the now famous Six Sigma programs pioneered by Motorola and others), accuracy of the order (another quality issue), scrap generated by the process, and equipment failures.

Transportation

Transportation metrics focus on asset control and delivery expectations. On the asset control side, fleet utilization measures the percentage of time a fleet is in use. The first measure is idle time for vehicles. The second is back hauls, where a truck goes out fully loaded but returns empty or at least not full. For most firms back hauls represent a considerable loss in fleet productivity. While idle time can be used to determine whether the fleet can be downsized, back hauls are a scheduling issue.

If vehicle routing is optimized, and the best possible routes and loads are planned, back hauls will be minimized as far as internal firm operations go, but there will still be times when the load is not full. Some companies resort to other measures for fleet optimization such as contracting out their back hauls or using back hauls for "reverse logistics" by bringing in returns, repairs, or shipping materials on the back haul. While these measures can increase utilization, they rarely completely eliminate the back haul problem. This is a complex asset management problem, and the information system should track utilization so that creative thinking can be applied.

The fleet can run full but still be used in an inefficient fashion. Poor maintenance can lead to equipment downtime, poor scheduling or picking procedures can cause an increased number of "hot shots" (emergency runs) to customers, and inefficient scheduling or loading can increase the number of runs or the cost per run. The information system must track on-time delivery (after leaving the warehouse), the number of expedites or "hot shots," total fleet run cost, and cost per run so that comparisons can be made for improvement processes.

Executive (Financial)

Executive reports need to give a "view from 10,000 feet" with drill-down capability. Purchasing aggregate measures should include performance measures for inventory (turns, ROA, ROI) with drill-down capability for more detailed information (functional obsolescence, category ROI) and customer service (fill rates, etc.). For sales and marketing, aggregate measures should include forecast accuracy and contribution to profitability through success on targeted sales programs.

Operations and manufacturing measures should include overall cycle time to deliver an order, quality of shipment or product, and physical obsolescence. Transportation reports would give an aggregate assessment of fleet efficiency. Each of the functional areas should have drill-down capability for executives to further explore the underlying causes of performance failures.

Executive measures should include the cost of process failure or sub-optimal performance. Holding costs should be assessed and reported on inventory, stockout costs on customer service failures, employee time on changeovers, number of errors caught by customers and their nature, and so forth.

Connecting the Supply Chain through Metrics

The metrics collected at each firm must be extended back to its suppliers and customers. Customers need to see true performance on agreed-upon metrics from distributors so that they understand where problems lie and can act proactively to improve their operations and possibly those of the distributor. One example is forecasting: If the customer sees problems in the accuracy of distributor forecasts versus what the customer actually bought, the customer can then work with the distributor to provide better information in those scenarios where bad forecasts are causing excessive inventory for the distributor (and thus higher costs for the customer) or stockouts.

This sort of exchange is SCM at work as originally envisioned. As has been repeatedly stated before in this text, this sort of relationship does not exist between most distributors and their customers (unless Vendor Managed Inventory is present). The problem is twofold: trust and technology.

In the 1990s, the technological problems related to sharing information looked insurmountable. By the next decade, however, these problems were being solved on a daily basis. The technological capability of sharing metrics and other important supply chain issues with customers would lead to the ability to outperform competitors. With the technology just around the corner, the key issue becomes trust. Trust, as we discussed in Chapters 4 and 5, and elsewhere, will be the most difficult issue for firms to wrestle with in the e-business rollouts.

In many channels, the trust issue is not as severe between supplier and distributor. Principally through franchise agreements (electronics and electrical channels are good examples), many distributors and suppliers are ready to connect and share metrics. An example here is the supplier report card where the distributor gives the supplier performance metrics on lead times, fill rates, etc. that when improved will make the distributor more successful. Many distributors rank suppliers based on their performance on various metrics, but this methodology has to be handled carefully since it can easily become an adversarial tool. One distributor surveyed its branch managers on supplier performance and then used the data to elicit discounts in future negotiations. The data was opinion-based, and its use was adversarial. The result was an air of distrust that did not encourage SCM initiatives.

Ultimately the supply chain will be "transparent," with end-user customers demanding visibility for all relevant progress and metrics measuring that progress on their orders, made available in real time. This environment was still mostly a dream at the turn of the twenty-first century, but the technology was becoming available and once something becomes possible, someone generally does it. The dot-coms set out to make this happen before the technology or channels were ready and failed as a result. Their failure should not be taken to mean that real-time visibility will never happen, but that it will happen, when the technology and aggressive channel members make it happen.

Conclusion

Today's information systems are moving from the role of "historian," where they tell us what happened, to the role of planner, where they suggest what should happen. Eventually we will complete the process, and the information system will decide what will happen. The line will be crossed when information systems are reliable enough (i.e. capable of gathering the right information and using statistical and algorithmic estimation) to handle the vast majority of operations decision-making. Rather than replacing people, the system will take over the mundane tasks (scheduling, forecasting, assessment) and free people up for more creative tasks (customer relationships, process improvement, or process redefinition) that offer competitive advantage.

Deciding on data to collect and reports to generate is an important step. Data collection techniques keep improving, and most systems capture the right data. It just is not always stored for a sufficient amount of time, does not come in quickly enough, or is not accessed for the proper analysis. Analysis planning has to take place first to determine what we want to know and what we need (in terms of data and report generation) to get that knowledge. Then data collection, storage, and access are more easily understood.

To decide what data to collect and how to interpret it, we must first determine how it is to be used. Collecting data and running reports that are not used is a waste of resources. Collecting data and running reports that are based on incorrect assumptions and therefore lead the firm in the wrong direction are a threat to survival. Setting KPIs requires an understanding of the firm's objectives, available data, processes, customer and supplier relationships, and role in the supply chain. Once understood in the broader context, KPIs can and must be connected to give the firm and its customers and suppliers an understanding of how to improve service and minimize cost.

Distributor Retrospective

As indicated in this chapter, the success of an MRO supply chain depends on the extent to which supply chain partners can add value to other supply chain members and can prove that such value is being added. Thus, it is important that Cameron Supply develop an understanding of how performance metrics should be collected and how these metrics should be utilized. It will also be important to translate these performance metrics into financial measures so the managers of the firm have a basis to determine the costs and benefits that are generated by their performance activities. Metrics that give an understanding of the true competitive position of Cameron will enable the firm's managers to better determine the extent to which their firm adds value to its supply chain partners.

Issues to Consider

1. Discuss the four principal functional areas of a distribution firm and why it is important to have effective customer service metrics for each.

2. Discuss the effect on holding costs when large amounts of product are ordered/produced.

3. Describe how forecast error and lead-time variability can cause stockouts, and the effect stockouts can have on safety stock levels.

4. How is information linked to the effectiveness of the supply chain?

5. Discuss how and why the sales force can exercise influence over the purchasing function. What are the possible results of this influence?

6. Discuss the various ways that fill rate can be measured. Describe which of these you think is the most appropriate.

Notes

1. Andrew Osterland, "Blaming ERP," *CFO Magazine* (January 2000):1–4. http://www.cfo.com/article/ 1,4616,0l1lADl1684,00.html (accessed October 1, 2001).

2. Saul Hansell, "Listen Up! It's Time for a Profit: A Front-Row Seat as Amazon Gets Serious," *The New York Times,* May 20, 2001 (Late edition, Sec. 3):1.

E-distribution Strategy

Distributor Perspective

Ivan Rogers is the CEO of an electrical distributor with annual sales of $40 million. Recently Rogers was interviewed by the editor of a trade publication and asked to describe the core competencies of his firm. After some thought, Rogers described the core competencies of his business as follows: providing credit to his customers, having the ability to buy in bulk and sell in smaller quantities, maintaining inventory, having technically trained salespeople who can sell technical products, and offering competitive prices to his customers. Later Rogers attended a trade association meeting sponsored by the National Association of Electrical Distributors and participated in a seminar on core competencies. The seminar leader stated that core competencies have the potential to create above-average profits. Rogers became perplexed. How can a core competency create above-average profits? The margins of his firm have declined! Do the activities that Rogers described earlier to the trade publication editor as being the core competencies of his firm have the potential to create above-average profits?

Introduction

E-distribution has been described as being similar to Oklahoma after the 1889 land rush. While some lots had been fenced to keep trespassers out, most of the Oklahoma territory was unmapped. Enormous opportunities were seemingly available for those individuals willing to take risks and to make the gamble. Similarly, the e-distribution environment is one that requires considerable risk and involves a gamble on the part of the participants.[1] How firms successfully compete in an environment that involves a considerable degree of uncertainty is an important question. Can a plan of action be developed that will minimize the risks and uncertainties? Andrew Grove, former CEO of Intel, argues that e-commerce has created a new challenge for CEOs in many industries, involving the need for continual change and quick strategic decisions that are essential if the firm is to survive. According to Grove, these challenges create paranoia for CEOs because they must continually articulate a clear vision of their firms during times of change.[2] In addition, these CEOs must also spend a significant portion of their time positioning the company in the minds of customers, employees, industry partners, and the popular press, remaining on constant alert to survive the substantial competition and uncertainty of electronic commerce. For example, PointCast was a purveyor of "push technology" that continually updated information on a computer screen throughout the day. A few years ago, PointCast and its technology were very "hot." At one time, the PointCast network had 1.5 million users, $5 million in annual revenues, and a list of significant advertisers. Also, PointCast had raised $48 million in funding from venture capitalists and had a market valuation of $240 million. However, many of PointCast's customers subsequently realized that push technology clogged up their corporate networks and ordered their employees to discard PointCast from their personal computers. Eventually, PointCast was unable to obtain additional capital despite several attempts to do so and was reorganized as another firm, InfoCast.[3]

In this chapter we present a number of important and useful strategies that industrial distribution firms involved in e-distribution can use to manage change. These concepts are developed through a strategic management process that allows managers to understand the competitive forces present in a dynamic environment and the ways to develop a competitive advantage in such an environment. In fact, the challenge of developing a competitive advantage is greater today than it has been historically. For example, a new competitive landscape is developing in the twenty-first century as a result of the technological revolution in e-commerce and the increasing globalization of firms. This technological revolution has placed an increased importance on product innovation and the ability of firms to rapidly introduce and distribute new goods and services to the marketplace.[4] By offering *valued* goods or services to customers, firms can increase the probability of earning above-average profits. Thus, the strategic management process assists organizations in identifying *what* they intend to achieve and *how* they will do it. A senior electronics distribution executive has stated that, unfortunately, most senior managers in industrial distribution firms spend their time "doing" rather than "thinking." They are involved with short-run situations and tend to neglect the long-run issues facing their firms.This executive has emphasized the importance of the "thinking"

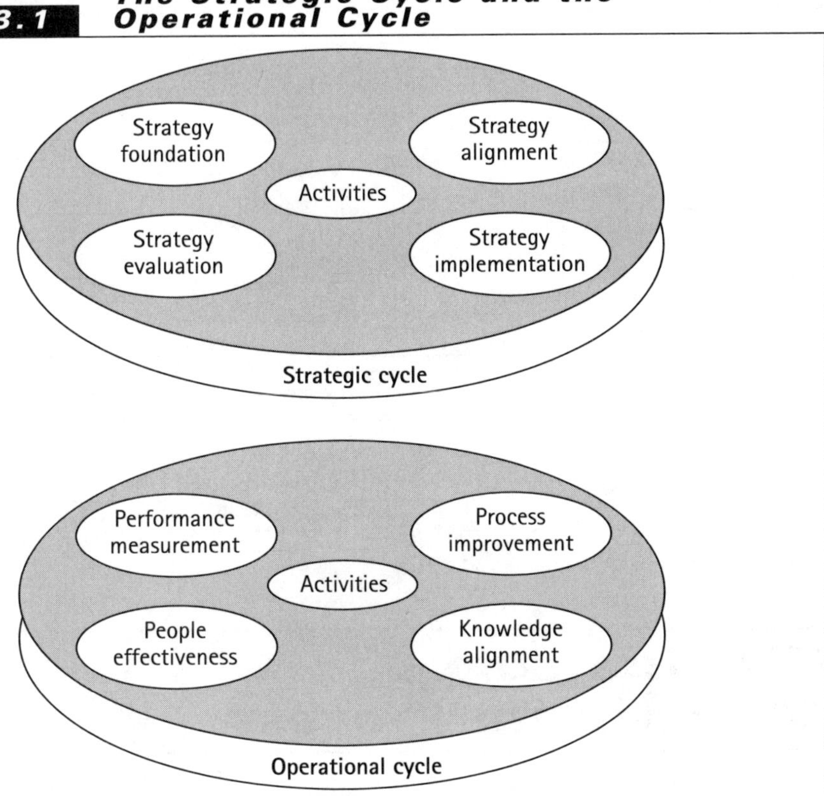

component when it comes to how a particular firm can utilize a strategic management process. Figure 13.1 describes two cycles that occur in organizations, an operational cycle and a strategic cycle.

The operational cycle focuses on tactical or short-run activities and involves people effectiveness, process improvement, the alignment of knowledge within the organization, and performance measurements. The strategic cycle involves strategic or long-run activities and includes strategy formulation and implementation, the alignment of strategies, and strategic evaluation. The focus of this chapter is both traditional and contemporary. In keeping with tradition we discuss the elements that comprise the strategic management process. These elements are depicted in Figure 13.2. We develop a contemporary treatment by discussing how business practitioners, especially those in industrial distribution, can understand and utilize the strategic management process.

Our focus is on how top managers can determine the value-creating potential of their firm's resources and capabilities in order to develop core competencies that will help them gain a competitive advantage through a strategy–structure match, and earn above-average profits.

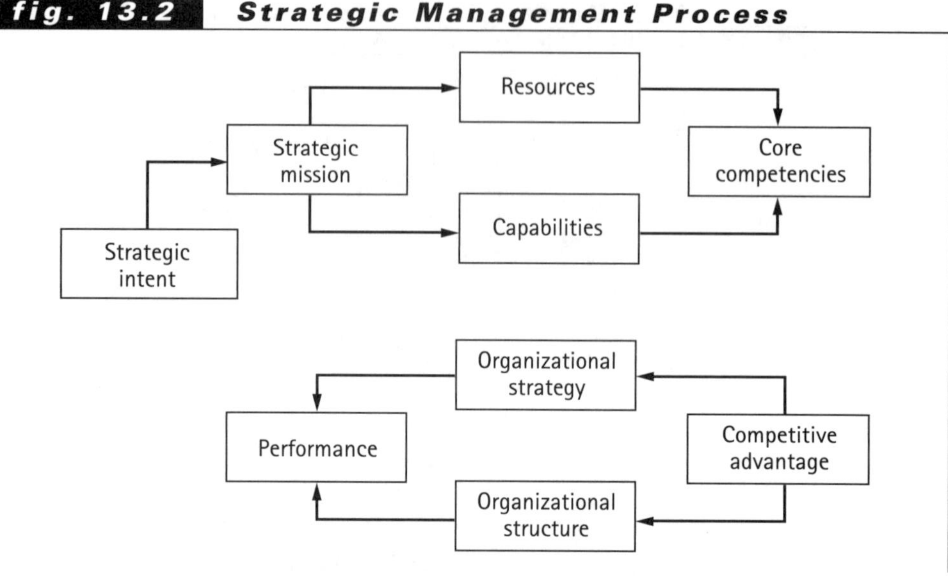

The Strategic Management Process

A review of the strategic management literature indicates that ten distinct schools or models of strategic management have been developed.[5] From the 1960s through the 1980s the external environment of a particular firm was believed to be the primary determinant of strategies that firms should select to be successful. During this time frame, two competing strategic models gained prominence.[6] One model, the strategic choice approach, argued that the effectiveness of a firm's strategies resided in the choices made by managers as they selected certain strategies and structures to implement a particular plan of action.[7] The other model, the industrial organization (I/O) approach developed by disciples of Joe Bain, argued that the industry in which a firm competes has a stronger influence on the firm's performance than do the choices made by managers inside the organization. Grounded in economics, the I/O model argues that the firm's performance is determined by economies of scale, barriers to market entry, diversification, product differentiation, and the degree of concentration of firms in the industry.[8] The I/O model also argues that firms should locate in the most attractive industry because it is presumed that firms tend to have similar strategic resources that are mobile across companies. Thus, competitiveness can be increased only when firms find the industry with the highest profit potential and learn how to use their resources to implement the type of strategy required by the structural characteristics of the industry.[9]

Recent studies indicate that the actions and characteristics of a firm determine 36% of its profitability while approximately 20% is determined by the industry in which the firm chooses to operate.[10] Today, the most widely held model of strategy management is the resource-based model, which presumes that each organization is a collection of unique characteristics and capabilities that provide the basis for its strategies and that these resources and capabilities can be dynamically managed to attain above-average profits. Thus, the resource-based model argues that a firm's performance is determined by its unique resources and capabilities rather than by the structural characteristics of a particular industry.[11]

We have included the characteristics of the resource-based model in the strategic management process model presented in Figure 13.2. In the following sections, we discuss the elements of the strategic management process, beginning with the concept of strategic intent.

Strategic Intent

The concept of strategic intent was developed by Gary Hamel and C. K. Prahalad in 1989 to define the framework for a firm's strategic mission. Strategic intent is the leveraging of a firm's internal resources, capabilities, and core competencies to accomplish the goals of the firm; it exists when all employees of the firm are committed to the pursuit of a specific and significant performance criterion.[12] For example, the strategic intent of Coca-Cola is to have a "Coke within arm's reach of everyone on the planet."[13] Strategic intent occurs when employees of a particular firm fervently believe in their products and are totally focused on their firm's ability to outperform its competitors.[14]

Strategic Mission

A firm's strategic mission flows from its strategic intent and is externally focused. An effective mission is formed when the firm has a very strong sense of what it wants to do and what ethical standards will guide behaviors of the firm's employees in achieving its objectives. The strategic mission is a statement of the firm's unique purpose and the scope of its operations. Together, strategic intent and strategic mission yield the insights required for a firm to identify its resources and capabilities and to formulate and implement its strategies as well. The mission of a particular industrial distributor is "to deliver the right product, at the right price, to the right customer, at the right time."

Resources

The resources of a firm involve tangible, intangible, and human resources, as depicted in Table 13.1.

table 13.1	The Resources of a Firm	
Tangible	**Intangible**	**Human**
*Financial	*Technology	*Specialized skills and knowledge
*Physical	*Reputation	*Communication
	*Culture	*Interactive abilities
		*Motivation

Tangible resources are the easiest to identify and evaluate because financial and physical resources can be identified in the firm's financial statements. However, historic cost valuations provide little indication of an asset's market value. For example, the critical issue in the 1994 battle between Viacom and QVC to acquire Paramount Communications was the value of Paramount's movie library. The library was valued on Paramount's balance sheet as a capitalized film production cost less accumulated depreciation, while the market value of the movie library was considerably higher in value.[15]

Although the balance sheet provides a starting point for an analysis of the tangible resources involved in creating a core competency, it is important to go beyond the accounting numbers and examine the basic facts needed to evaluate the potential of their resources for creating a competitive advantage. For example, to state that the fixed assets of an industrial distributor are $250 million is of little use in determining their strategic value. Where are the assets located? What are their capabilities? Their age and type? How flexible are they in terms of product/service variations? In essence, the value of any durable resource is the net present value of the cash flows that the resource can generate. Such an analysis determines how the greatest value may be gained from the resource—by using it within the firm or by selling it to another company. A strategic assessment of tangible resources can be accomplished by answering two important questions: 1) What opportunities lie in using fewer resources? (Can certain assets be pruned?) and 2) What are the possibilities for employing existing assets more profitably? For example, Federal Express increased the productivity of its huge distribution network by taking over the management of distribution activities of other firms.

Over time, most tangible resources become less important to the firm in terms of their contribution to value added and as a basis for achieving a competitive advantage.

Intangible resources are the invisible assets of a company with respect to financial statements. General accounting principles do not require U.S. companies to include intangible resources on their balance sheets. Yet in 2001 the brand valuation of Coca-Cola was $69 billion and that for Microsoft was $65 billion.[16] Brand names and other trademarks are a form of reputational assets in that their value is in the confidence they instill in customers. This value is reflected in the price premium that customers are willing to pay for the branded product over that for an unknown or unbranded product. Reputation may be attached to a company as well as to its brands. As an example, an industrial distributor may have an excellent reputation for on-time delivery and customer service. Technology is another category of intangible resource. The central issue in valuing technological resources is ownership—does the company own the technology or is it employee owned?

In the environment of today, the value of companies has been shifting from tangible resources—the bricks and mortar—to intangible resources, such as patents, customer lists, and brands. These are the keys to shareholder value in a knowledge economy, but our accounting system does little to acknowledge the shift. Ignoring these intangible resources may have been fine thirty years ago, but not anymore. Investors need a sense of the value of these resources and whether expenses to support them, such as advertising, are really productive. If financial statements do not take stock of a firm's intangible resources, then top management cannot allocate capital intelligently, analysts cannot properly evaluate the companies they cover, and investors cannot get a fix on the market. As stated by Jonathan Low, senior vice president of Cap Gemini Ernst & Young, "You end up with the blind leading the blind."[17]

Human resources are the productive services that human beings offer a firm in terms of their skills, knowledge, reasoning, and decision-making abilities. In essence, human resources are the *human capital* that is employed within a firm. Research has indicated that human capital in an organization is durable and can be created through investments in training and education. Research has also indicated that the ability of employees to harmonize their efforts and to integrate their skills is influenced by the culture of the organization. While an expanded discussion of organizational culture is beyond the scope of this chapter, it may be defined as the values, traditions, and social norms of an organization. Organizational culture has been identified as a strong intangible resource that tends to define human resources in an organization.[18]

Capabilities

Generally, resources are not productive on their own. For example, a brain surgeon is almost useless without a radiologist, anesthetist, nurses, surgical instruments, imaging equipment, a surgical team of other physicians, and a host of other resources.[19] Just as individuals have the capability to ice skate or speak a foreign language, organizational capability refers to a firm's capacity for undertaking a particular productive activity. Thus a capability is the capacity to integrate sets of resources to perform a task or activity. Examples of capabilities for an industrial distributor are the quality and effectiveness of customer service; expertise in purchasing raw materials, inventory management, sales, and motivating employees; effective use of logistics management techniques; the ability to motivate, empower, and retain employees; and responsiveness to market trends.[20] Through continued use, capabilities become stronger and more difficult for competitors to understand and imitate.[21] Some of the more socially complex capabilities include the interpersonal relationships, trust, and friendships among managers, and between managers and employees of the firm's suppliers and customers.

Generally, the value of capabilities in forming a competitive advantage increases as the task for which the capability is substituted becomes more complex. Also, the more invisible capabilities are, the more difficult it is for firms to locate substitutes, and it is even more difficult to imitate another firm's value-added strategy.[22] Next we discuss how core competencies are developed from resources and capabilities.

Core Competencies

Once the managers of a firm understand the resources and capabilities of their firm, they can identify their core competencies. However, not all of a firm's resources and capabilities have the potential to be the basis for a competitive advantage: to have this potential, they need to be valuable, rare, costly to imitate, and nonsubstitutable.[23] Resources and capabilities are *valuable* when they allow a firm to take advantage of opportunities or neutralize threats in the firm's external environment; they are *rare* when only a few firms possess them; they are *costly to imitate* when other firms either cannot obtain them or are at a cost disadvantage in obtaining them compared with the firm that already possesses them; they are *nonsubstitutable* when they have no equivalents. When the preceding four criteria are met, resources and capabilities become core competencies that serve as a source of competitive advantage for a firm over its rivals. As such a source, core competencies can create above-average profits, create barriers to entry, utilize the strengths and resources of suppliers and increase customer responsiveness.

An interesting question regarding core competencies is: "How many core competencies are required for a firm to have a competitive advantage?" The management consulting firm McKinsey suggests that its clients utilize three or four competencies in which to frame their action plans to achieve a competitive advantage. Trying to nurture and support more than four competencies may prevent the firm from developing the focus that is required to fully exploit its competencies.[24] A review of the research literature on core competencies and competitive advantage tends to support the McKinsey's recommendation of three or four competencies.[25]

Core Competencies of Electrical Distributors

It is often difficult for managers to determine the core competencies of their firms. Some managers just do not understand the definition of a core competency and will describe the firm's mission statement or identify a function of the firm, such as sales or operations management, without determining if the competency is valuable, rare, costly to imitate, and nonsubstitutable. Recently, the Thomas and Joan Read Center for Distribution Research and Education at Texas A&M University conducted a research study to determine the core competencies of electrical distributors. The study began with the selection of ten electrical distributors with sales for the year 2001 ranging from $10 million to $50 million. Next, a senior top manager from each firm was interviewed and asked to identify the distributorship's core competencies, and then to provide the names of one supplier and one customer with the understanding that these firms would be contacted to participate in identifying the core competencies of an electrical distributor. Next, top managers from each supplier and each customer whose name had been provided were contacted and asked to identify the core competencies of an electrical distributor. The specific name of the electrical distributor was not provided to either, the supplier or to the customer. In essence, managers of the suppliers' and customers' firms were contacted and asked the following: "You have been identified as a supplier (customer) of an electrical distributor. We cannot give you the name of the particular electrical distributor that provided your name. Would you provide us with what you believe to be the core competencies of an electrical distributor."

Thus, the study involved thirty firms—ten electrical distributors, ten suppliers, and ten customers. A definition or explanation of the term *core competency* was not provided to the participants unless they specifically requested one. Interestingly, none of the electrical distributors, none of the suppliers, and only two of the customers requested such a definition. After the thirty firms had been surveyed, their responses were aggregated and tabulated. The following tables list the core competencies of electrical distributors as reported by the distributors themselves, their suppliers, and their customers. Table 13.2 describes the responses of the suppliers:

table 13.2	*Core Competencies Reported by Suppliers*
O	Carrying inventory
O	Working with suppliers to manage customer relationships
O	Having technically trained sales personnel to sell technical products
O	Providing customer service

Table 13.3 describes the responses of the distributors themselves:

table 13.3	*Core Competencies Reported by Distributors Themselves*
O	Providing customer service
O	Carrying inventory
O	Having product specialists to assist in selling
O	Having technically trained sales personnel to sell technical products
O	Offering competitive prices

Table 13.4 describes responses of the the customers:

table 13.4	*Core Competencies Reported by Customers*
O	Providing customer service
O	Offering emergency deliveries
O	Offering low prices
O	Having knowledgeable inside salespeople
O	Having outside salespeople with product knowledge
O	Carrying inventory

The study participants who stated that customer service is a core competency for electrical distributors were asked to expand their definition of customer service. Table 13.5 provides these specific responses.

table 13.5	*Definitions of Customer Sevice as a Core Competency*
O	Providing one-stop shopping
O	Providing credit
O	Offering the ability to buy in bulk and to sell in smaller quantities
O	Providing technical support
O	Meeting customer's delivery requirements
O	Maintaining inventory
O	Retaining salespeople with product knowledge
O	Providing customer service at the lowest cost

An analysis of the preceding responses indicates that they describe or identify a function of the firm, such as sales or operations management, without determining if the response is truly a core competency. Is the competency valuable, rare, costly to imitate, and nonsubstitutable? Later, members of the Texas A&M Industrial Distribution program faculty who were familiar with electrical distribution and with the process of identifying core competencies developed their own list. Table 13.6 lists these core competencies.

table 13.6	Core Competencies Listed by Texas A&M University Industrial Distribution Faculty
○	Superior technical know-how
○	Reliable processes
○	Close external relationships

Superior Technical Know-how. A technical competency involves a deep understanding of a subject area. Such an understanding arises from an early, substantial, and continuous involvement in that area. This knowledge is valuable if competitors do not have a similar knowledge base and if the knowledge can be converted into a value-add for customers. The personnel of an electrical distributor have technical and product knowledge regarding electrical products and components that has the potential to be a significant core competency.

Reliable Processes. A reliable process delivers an expected result quickly, consistently, and efficiently with the least possible inconvenience or disruption to customers. It involves the ability to combine various inputs to customers in order to customize a product that will meet a customer's particular need. Electrical distributors have the potential to develop reliable processes in order entry, order processing, inventory management, logistics, and the ability to "break-bulk."

Close External Relationships. Close relationships among suppliers, distributors, customers, and professional organizations such as banks yield several benefits. Suppliers can suggest ideas for new product developments or execute rapid design changes. Distributors can provide market access and customer information. Customers can suggest new competencies that can be developed. Siemens, a German manufacturer of electrical and other capital goods, markets its products to over 120 countries. Siemens's close relationship with Deutsche Bank, a major German bank, provides the firm with ample low-cost financing for its customers, enabling Siemens to make many international sales.[26] Tristate Electrical & Electronics Supply advertises on its Web page that it can "assist customers in arranging financing."[27] These types of close external relationships can be a significant core competency for electrical distributors.

Competitive Advantage

The premise of the resource-based strategic management process model is that a competitive advantage allows a firm to generate above-average profits by offering value-added products and services for which customers are willing to pay. Firms achieve a competitive advantage by combining their resources and capabilities into core competencies, which provides the means for creating these value-added products and services. Competitive advantages emerge when profitability differences occur between firms. The source of changes in profitability may be external or internal to a firm. Sources of internal change include changes in customer demand, prices, and technology. Also, some firms have the ability to respond to external change more quickly and effectively by exploiting that change. Sources of internal change are the creative and innovative elements that occur within firms.

A Sustainable Competitive Advantage

A competitive advantage becomes sustainable when the firm's competitors cannot imitate it or do not understand how it is developed. Once established, a firm's competitive advantage is subject to erosion by competition. The speed with which competitive advantage is undermined depends upon the ability of the competitor to challenge by either innovation or imitation.[28]

Organizational Strategy

A strategy is a plan for interacting with the competitive environment to achieve organizational goals. Generally, organizational science researchers do not consider goals and strategies to be interchangeable. Instead, a goal defines where the organization wants to go, and strategy defines how it will get there.[29] Researchers have developed classifications, which are called typologies, to provide operational definitions of strategy. Two widely used typologies are Porter's Generic Strategies[30] and the Miles and Snow Typology.[31]

Porter's Generic Strategies. Porter conceptualized that organizations cope with competitive forces by using three generic strategic approaches to outperform other firms: (1) overall cost leadership, (2) differentiation, and (3) focus. According to Porter, no organization can successfully perform at an above-average level by trying to be all things to all people. Porter proposes that management must select a strategy that will allow an organization to attain a competitive advantage. Which strategy management chooses depends on the organization's strengths and its competitor's weaknesses. When an organization sets out to be the low-cost producer in its industry, it is following a cost-leadership strategy. Success with this strategy requires that the organization be the cost leader and not merely one of the contenders for that position. Organizations can achieve a cost advantage by efficiency in operations, economies of scale, technological innovation, low-cost labor, or preferential access to raw materials. Examples of firms that have utilized a low-cost strategy include Wal-Mart and E. J. Gallo Winery.

An organization that seeks to be unique in its industry in ways that are widely valued by buyers is following a differentiation strategy. It might emphasize high quality, extraordinary service, innovative design, technological capability, or an unusually positive brand image. The key is that the attribute chosen must be different from those offered by rivals and significant enough to justify a price premium that exceeds the cost of differentiating. Organizations that have differentiated themselves include the supercomputer manufacturer Cray (technology), the cosmetics firm Mary Kay (distribution), and L. L. Bean (service).

The first two generic strategies seek to achieve a competitive advantage in a broad range of industry segments. The focus strategy aims at either a cost advantage (cost focus) or differentiation advantage (differentiation focus) in a narrow segment. Thus, management will select a segment or group of segments in an industry (such as product variety, type of end buyer, distribution channel, or geographical location of buyers) and tailor a strategy to serve them at the exclusion of others. The goal is to exploit a narrow segment of a market. An example of a cost-focus strategy is Stouffer's Lean Cuisine line, while focuses on calorie-conscious consumers seeking high-quality products and convenience. A university that appeals to working students by offering night classes is an example of a differentiation-focus strategy. Research suggests that a focus strategy may be the most potent for a small business firm. This is because a small business does not have the economies of scale or internal resources to successfully pursue one of the other two strategies. Also, a focus strategy may be the best strategy for most industrial distributors because of the niche nature of the particular channel in which they operate.

Miles and Snow's Typology. The Miles and Snow Typology is based on three premises. The first is that over a period of time successful organizations develop a systematic, identifiable approach to environmental adaptation as they focus on three types of problems: (1) an entrepreneurial problem, which deals with the definition of market-product domain, (2) an engineering problem, which involves the organization's technical services and/or products, and (3) an administrative problem, which arises from structure and process issues. The second premise is that four identifiable strategic orientations exist within an industry: Defenders, Prospectors, Analyzers, and Reactors. According to Miles and Snow, Defenders emphasize a narrow domain by controlling secure niches in their industries. They engage in little or no product/market development and stress efficiency of operations. Prospectors constitute the other end of the continuum; they constantly seek new opportunities and stress product development. Analyzers exhibit characteristics of both Defenders and Prospectors. Finally, Reactors do not follow a conscious strategy and are viewed as a dysfunctional organizational type. The third premise of the Miles and Snow Typology is that the Defender, Analyzer, and Prospector strategies, if properly implemented, can lead to effective performance. Much depends on the internal consistency among the three elements of the adaptive cycle. Each type emphasizes different functions to produce a set of sustainable, distinctive competencies. The Reactors lack a coherent strategy. Therefore, the Miles and Snow Typology proposes that Defenders, Analyzers, and Prospectors will outperform the nonadaptive Reactors.

An important question is whether one strategy is better than another. Or in other words, does one particular strategy yield a higher performance than another strategy? For example in Porter's Generic Strategy are there performance differences between the cost leadership, differentiation, and focus strategies? Similarly, in the Miles and Snow Typology are there performance differences between a Defender, Prospector, and Analyzer?

Is One Strategy Better Than Another?

About seventy-five years ago, the biologist Ludwig von Bertalanfy began a study to investigate the movement of organisms within a biological system. Von Bertalanfy formulated certain concepts concerning the organism as an open system. These included the principle of equifinality, expressed in the statement "the same final state can be reached from different initial conditions and in different ways."[32] Bertalanfy's work has spawned two opposing theoretical arguments in the strategic management and strategic marketing literature. One such perspective is that an organization can achieve an outcome by a variety of strategic actions or strategies.[33] The other perspective is that there is one best strategy.[34] Three recent empirical studies, however, have argued that there is no best strategy.[35] In other words, the principle of equifinality applies to strategic management, in that no one strategy is inherently better than another. What is important is the manner in which the strategy is implemented. A number of studies indicate that in 95% of all cases, failed strategies result from an inadequate implementation.

Organizational Structure

Organizational structure refers to how the various parts of an organization are arranged to achieve consistency and coherence. The seminal work on structure is Weber's description of the ideal organizational structure, which he calls *bureaucracy*.[36] The proper use of an organizational structure can contribute to a firm's strategic competitiveness.[37]

Mechanistic and Organic Structure

Burns and Stalker discovered a relationship between the external environment and an organization's internal management structure. They found that, when the environment is stable, rules, procedures, and a clear hierarchy of authority characterize the internal structure. Organizations, under these stable environments, are formalized in their structures and decision-making is centralized. Burns and Stalker called this a *mechanistic* structure.[38]

In rapidly changing environments, the internal organization is much looser, free-flowing, and adaptive. Rules and regulations often are not written down, or if written down, are ignored. The hierarchy of authority is not clear. Decision-making authority is decentralized. Burns and Stalker used the term *organic* to characterize this type of management structure. [39]

Burns and Stalker also learned that as environmental uncertainty increases, organizations tend to become more organic, which means decentralizing authority and responsibility to lower levels, encouraging employees to take care of problems by working directly with one another, encouraging teamwork, and taking an informal approach to assigning tasks and responsibility. Thus the organization becomes more fluid and is able to adapt continually to changes in the external environment.

Effect of Context and Design on Organizational Structure

Researchers have discovered that two other major factors affect structure: context and design. Context is the situation in which an organization is operating. Contextual factors include organizational size, technology, internal culture, the environment, and national cultural factors. An organization's context is simultaneously within and beyond its control. For example, an organization may decide to increase its size and then do so. However, once size is expanded, it influences the structure of the organization. Thus, a firm's choices can influence its context, but the context in turn can influence the firm. Design is the choice an organization makes about how it is to be structured, and it is a political issue. An organization's design does not form automatically but develops out of managerial decisions. Structural dimensions include such factors as formalization, specialization, standardization, hierarchy of authority, complexity, centralization, integration, coordination, control, and professionalism.[40]

Organization Structure and Competitive Advantage

The organizational structure of a firm influences how the tasks of an organization will be accomplished. However, organizational structure alone does not create a competitive advantage. Research indicates that a competitive advantage occurs when there is a proper match between the strategy of an organization and its structure. This research indicates that a firm's structure should be designed to support its strategy. Figure 13.3 depicts the findings of a significant study conducted by Alfred Chandler. In his study of seventy large corporations, Chandler found that changes in an organization's strategy create new organizational problems, which in turn require either a new or redesigned structure that matches the new strategy.

fig. 13.3   **Chandler's Strategy–Structure Relationship**

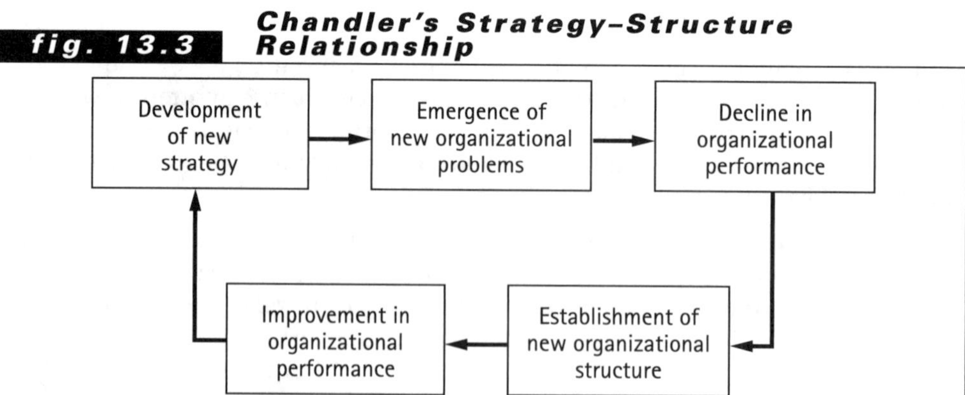

The Structure–Internal Processes Match for Industrial

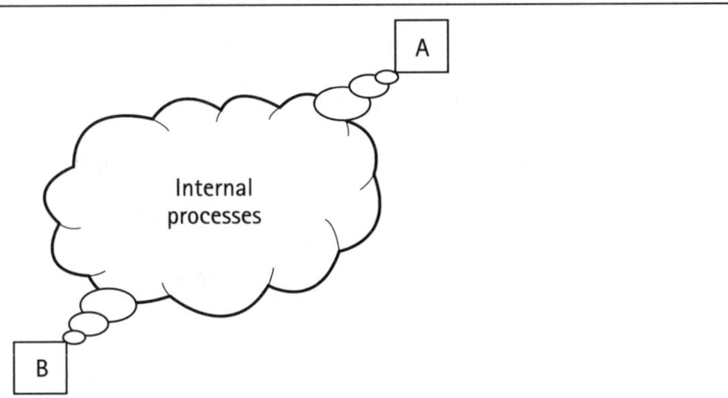

Chandler's study indicated that the firms in his study followed a consistent sequential pattern: the development of a new strategy, the emergence of new organizational problems, a decline in profitability and performance, the development of a more appropriate organizational structure, and a recovery to more profitable levels.[41]

Industrial distributors may be able to relate to the strategy–structure match by considering Figure 13.4.

In the preceding figure, an industrial distribution firm is at Point A and wishes to move to Point B. In doing so, it will develop a new strategy that will entail new or different skills and activities. If these go unrecognized, then there will be a mismatch between the industrial distributor's new strategy and the processes within the firm. Such a mismatch can create implementation and performance problems.

Conclusion

The e-business movement has given distribution its new organizational problem: how to connect the supply chain and offer information management leadership. The cloud of internal processes will have to be mapped and upgraded or eliminated. The customer and supplier must be connected and the technology understood to move toward improvement in our processes.

The firm must face its new strategic plan in this new connected world. In fact, we must skip a few steps and determine where we want to be in the future before making the investments associated with e-business. Strategy development is the starting place for the e-distributor and will need updating as the shifting sands of technology and new supply chain expectations change the distributor's world.

Distributor Retrospective

It is often difficult for managers to determine the core competencies of their firms and how to utilize these competencies to earn above-average profits. By pursuing the steps for strategic planning, Ivan Rogers will gain a better understanding of what is involved in developing core competencies for his electrical distributorship. That understanding will have to grow and develop as the market continues to change.

Issues to Consider

1. Why is the challenge of developing a competitive advantage more difficult today than it has been historically?

2. Discuss the operational and strategic cycles that occur in organizations.

3. Discuss how firms can use the two elements of the strategic management process: strategic intent and strategic mission.

4. Compare and contrast tangible, intangible, and human resources, and explain why they are important to a distributor's ability to develop and sustain competitive advantage.

5. Describe what core competencies are and what criteria must be met in order for them to create competitive advantage.

6. In reviewing the core competencies of an electrical distributor as identified by their suppliers, their customers, and by the distributors themselves, where are they similar, where do they differ, and why?

Notes

1.   Amir Hartman, John Sifonis, and John Kador, *Net Ready* (New York: McGraw Hill Publishing, 2000).

2.   Andrew Grove, *Only the Paranoid Survive: How to Exploit the Crisis Points that Challenge Every Company* (New York: Bantam Books,1999).

3.   L. Himelstein and R. Siklos, "The Rise and Fall of an Internet Star," *Business Week,* April 26, 1999, 88–94.

4.   For an expanded discussion of management challenges in the twenty-first century see Peter Drucker, *Management Challenges for the 21st Century* (New York: HarperCollins, 1999) and David Sull, "Why Good Companies Go Bad" *Harvard Business Review* 77 (4): 42–52 (1999).

5.   Henry Mintzberg, Barry Ahlstrand and John Lambel, *Strategy Safari: A Guided Tour through the Wilds of Strategic Management* (New York: Free Press, 1998).

6.   Robert Hoskisson, Michael Hitt, W. P. Wan, and D. Yiu. "Swings of a Pendulum: Theory and Research in Strategic Management," *Journal of Management* 25: 417–456 (1999).

7.   John Child, "Organizational Structure, Environment, and Performance," *Sociology* 6:1–22 (1972).

8.   Joe Bain, *Industrial Organizations* (New York: Wiley, 1959).

9. Michael Porter, *Competitive Advantage* (New York: Free Press,1985).

10. J. L. Stimpert and I. M. Duhaime, "Seeing the Big Picture: The Influence of Industry, Diversification, and Business Strategy on Performance," *Academy of Management Journal* 40: 560–583 (1997).

11. A. Seth and H. Thomas, "Theories of the Firm: Implications for Strategy Research," *Journal of Management Studies* 31: 165–191 (1994).

12. G. Hamel and G. K. Prahalad, "Strategic Intent," *Harvard Business Review* 67 (3): 63–76 (1989).

13. "The Merlin Factor and Strategic Intent," *Fast Company,* January/February 2000: 86.

14. S. Sherman, "Stretch Goals: Asking for Miracles," *Fortune,* November 13, 1995, 231–232.

15. "The Value of a Movie Library," *Financial Times,* October 5, 1994, 8.

16. "The 100 Top Brands," *Business Week,* August 6, 2001, 60.

17. Neil Gross, "Valuing Intangibles: A Tough Job, But It Has To Be Done," *Business Week,* August 6, 2001, 54–55.

18. Jay Barney, "Organizational Culture: Can It be a Source of Sustained Competitive Advantage?" *Academy of Management Review* 11: 656–665 (1986).

19. This example was adapted from Robert M. Grant, "Toward a Knowledge-Based Theory of the Firm," *Strategic Management Journal* 17 (Winter Special Issue 1996): 109–122.

20. Most certainly, this is not an exhaustive listing.

21. Jay Barney, "Looking Inside for Competitive Advantage," *Academy of Management Executive* 9: 52–66 (1995).

22. Jay Barney, "Firm Resources and Competitive Advantage," *Journal of Management* 17: 99–123 (1991).

23. Jay Barney, "How Firm's Capabilities Affect Boundary Decisions," *Sloan Management Review* 40, issue 3: 137–145 (1999).

24. Thomas Stewart, "Core Competencies, Competitive Advantage, and Success," *Fortune,* February 15, 1999, 65.

25 Thomas Brush and Kendall Artz, "Toward a Contingent Resource Based Theory: The Impact of Information Asymmetry on the Value of Capabilities in Veterinary Medicine," *Strategic Management Journal* 20: 223–250 (1999).

26. Mark Goldstein, "Dynamics of Core Competencies in Multinational Companies," *Industry Week,* September 21,1998, 75–80.

27. www. tristate-electric.com/about/corecompanies.htm (accessed 4/11/02).

28. Jay Barney, "Firm Resources and Sustained Competitive Advantage," *Journal of Management* 17: 99–120 (1991).

29. Ellen Chaffee, "Three Models of Strategy," *Academy of Management Review* 10: 89–98 (1985). Henry Mintzberg, "Patterns in Strategy Formulation," *Management Science* 24: 934–948 (1978).

30. Michael Porter, *Competitive Strategy* (New York: Free Press, 1980).

31. Ray Miles and Charles Snow, *Organizational Strategy, Structure and Process* (New York: McGraw-Hill, 1978).

32. Ludwig von Bertalanfy, *Kritische Theorie der Formbildung* (Berlin, Germany: Schaltz Publishing, 1925). Later translated into English as *Modern Theories of Development* (New York: Macmillan, 1930).

33. Ray Miles, Charles Snow, Andrew Meyer, and H. J. Coleman, Jr., "Organizational Strategy, Structure, and Process," *Academy of Management Review* 12: 607–621 (1978).

34. Andrew Van de Ven and Robert Drazin, "The Concept of Fit in Contingency Theory," in Barry Staw and Larry Cummings (eds.), *Research in Organizational Behavior,* vol.7 (Greenwich, Conn. JAI Press, 1985).

35. Daniel Jennings, Daniel Rajaratnam, and F. Barry Lawrence, "Strategy-Performance Relationships in Service Firms: A Test for Equifinality," working paper, Texas A&M University 2001, Daniel Jennings and Samuel Seaman, "High and Low Levels of Strategic Adaptation: An Empirical Analysis of Strategy, Structure, and Performance," *Strategic Management Journal,* 15: 459–475 (1994), David Doty, William Glick, and George Huber, "Fit, Equifinality, and Organizational Effectiveness: A Test of Two Configurational Theories," *Academy of Management Journal* 36: 1196–1250 (1993).

36. Max Weber, *The Theory of Social and Economic Organizations,* trans Talcott Parsons (New York: Free Press, 1947).

37. Danny Miller and Jay Whitney, "Beyond Strategy: Configuration as a Pillar of Competitive Advantage," *Business Horizons* 42: 5–17 (1999).

38. Tom Burns and G. M. Stalker, *The Management of Innovation* (London: Tavistock Publications, 1961).

39. Ibid.

40. Richard Daft, *Organization Theory and Design,* 6th ed. (St. Paul, Minn,: West Publishing, 1996). Richard Hall, *Organizations: Structures, Processes and Outcomes* (Englewood Cliffs, N.J.: Prentice-Hall, 1996).

41. Alfred Chandler, *Strategy and Structure* (Cambridge, Mass: MIT Press, 1962).

Case Studies in E-business

ERP/E-business and the Small Distributor

Case Study: Ray Distributing

Keith Rainwater was tired. He had been trying to work out his information needs for a long time and he was still confused. He had purchased Ray Distributing, a small fishing distribution company, in the mid-1990s and discovered the company's information-handling capability to be woefully inadequate. As an industrial engineer, Keith knew something about state-of-the-art distribution management but was frustrated that his information system did not have the capabilities needed to support his ambition to build a world-class distribution operation.

Keith decided to approach the problem by putting the customer first and building a system that supported customer service while maintaining profitability. He wanted the company to grow and thought that the Internet offered opportunities but was concerned about integrating the Internet into his ERP system. Keith wanted information to flow smoothly from his customers all the way back to his suppliers, especially Ray Manufacturing. Ray Manufacturing was an internal production system that produced new products for Ray Distributing to sell. Ray Manufacturing was Keith's most profitable operation, and connecting it to the customer was one of his highest priorities.

"Well," Keith said to himself, "I've done my research. I guess I'm going to have to make a choice and live with it."

Background

After a successful career at Dow Chemical, Keith Rainwater had decided that he wanted to do something on his own. He looked around for a small business to buy, and Ray Distributing came to his attention through a real estate agent. Not only was the company a good buy—Keith was an avid fisherman and Ray Distributing was located in his hometown of Victoria, Texas, which made it all look like fate.

The previous owner was ready to retire after many successful years. Business had been flat for the past few years, and Keith was unsure whether the problem was that the business had reached its peak or merely needed a new infusion of energy. Keith knew he had that energy and had faith he could get things moving again.

It took a little while to understand how to manage a small business, in contrast to his work at Dow Chemical. Customers had more personal relationships with the sales force, employees were motivated differently, training fell entirely on Keith's shoulders, and virtually everything from keeping the books to putting away inventory as it came in needed his attention. Keith soon found himself working long hours and worrying about things that would never have occurred to him when he was at Dow.

The hard work started paying off, however, and the business began to grow again. Keith wanted faster growth at first, but then he experienced an explosion of nearly 50% in sales, taking the company from $3 million to $4.5 million in a year. Some of the growth could be attributed to Keith's improvement efforts and some to a strong economy, but the effect was a tremendous strain on his operations. Keith decided that after his experience with such growth, he wanted to maintain steady manageable growth in the 10–20% range.

An interesting opportunity presented itself in 1997. An Internet start-up had approached Keith about providing fulfillment for its website. E-business made sense in fishing distribution. Fishermen were very particular about their gear, would do research to determine what new offerings were available, and were very loyal once something worked. This combination of research and loyalty was tailor-made for e-business. Keith made an agreement to work with the dot-com and at the same time began work on his own website. The dot-com would sell directly to the final consumer while Keith's site was designed to sell only to retailers.

Customer Relationships

Ray Distributing's customer base consisted of two major types. One was the large to midsized sporting goods retailers that maintained a fishing goods department. The second group was more diverse and consisted of bait shops and small grocery stores in coastal towns that sell fishing equipment. The sporting good retailers tended to be larger on a per capita basis and were more sophisticated in terms of inventory management and business-to-business communication. As a rule, the bait shops were less sophisticated but tended to trust Ray to control a great deal of their fishing supply business.

Ray maintained an outside sales force of two to three salespeople, with Keith also making calls on important customers. Keith himself targeted the large retailers and was constantly on the lookout for opportunities to bring in new business. The sales force traveled by car and, in addition to taking orders, frequently made deliveries. A sales call might consist of dropping off an order, unpacking and putting it on the shelf, taking an inventory of products in the customer's location, and preparing a reorder. The Ray Distributing salesperson would help maintain the appearance of the display, which was frequently provided by Ray Distributing.

Vendor Managed Inventory

A major portion of Ray Distributing's business fell under the heading of Vendor Managed Inventory (VMI). Although the larger retailers frequently maintained their own inventories, many of the bait shops allowed Ray Distributing's outside sales force to take counts and reorder as they saw fit. This inventory maintenance activity was a classic example of VMI. The advantages to VMI from the distributor's point of view are closer control of customer inventory and better information for planning.

Closer control meant that Ray Distributing knew about a shortage as early as possible and could make sure the inventory was there before a stockout occured. The process was good for both the bait shop and Ray Distributing, since it prevented lost sales for both. The faster and more consistent reporting of demand patterns back to operations also allowed for better planning and inventory management at Ray.

Integrated Supply

Ray Distributing also acted as a fulfillment house for a large distributor that managed inventory for very large retailers. The larger distributor contracted to handle all replenishment for a broad category such as sporting goods, agreeing to manage the entire department but then setting up agreements with specialized distributors to handle areas outside of its expertise. Ray Distributing would handle fishing supply, another might handle weights, and so on. The contracting distributor might handle none of the categories, or only a few, outsourcing the rest. For the customer, the entire department was now managed externally with only one purchasing point of contact.

The arrangement was similar to Integrated Supply in Maintenance Repair and Operations (MRO), in which a distributor would set up an agreement to serve all MRO needs for a customer. Commonly referred to as the integrator, the lead distributor will put together a second-tier set of suppliers, including distributors and manufacturers, to handle areas outside the distributor's area of specialization. Integrated Supply had enjoyed great success in MRO and was spreading into other distribution fields.

The Internet

Keith had plans for the Internet as well. The dot-com business was steady but not overwhelming. Meanwhile, dot-coms in other channels were falling apart as they proved unable to develop critical mass before their funding ran out. Keith was convinced that his market would be influenced by the Internet, but was still confused as to how much and when. He decided to use the Internet with his traditional market by offering his catalog over his own website. Since the catalog was paper-based, Keith was able to set up a Web presence at a minimal cost (no need to put the entire catalog on the Web).

Offering the catalog over the Internet was a very conservative move designed to prevent any channel conflicts with his retail customers. The catalog was only offered to retailers; the site essentially registered these retailers and then the catalog was sent to the retailers. The Internet was essentially acting as an outside salesperson in territories that the Ray Distributing sales force could not reach. Keith's business outside southeast Texas started to grow. International business (formerly well outside Ray Distributing's reach) also started coming in.

Eventually, Keith decided that the Internet business he generated through his own activity was better than that generated through the dot-com. He began to question the value that the dot-com added to his business and eventually decided to go it alone. The dot-com had difficulty meeting its obligations to Ray Distributing and was more concerned about putting together an IPO (initial public offering) for the stock market. The dot-com formed an alliance with another fishing distributor, and Ray Distributing and the dot-com parted company.

Enterprise Resource Planning

Ray Distributing's Enterprise Resource Planning (ERP) system was a Microsoft Windows–based package that was very capable of handling financials and human resources but had considerable shortcomings when it came to operations management. The system did not have an effective forecasting methodology, no warehouse management capability, and no ability to assist in purchase order size or reorder point logic.

Forecasting

Forecasting at Ray Distributing was principally based on moving averages. The length of the forecasted period was based on payment terms offered by the supplier. Suppliers frequently offered better terms for 120 days' notice on orders. The forecast, therefore, had to look forward far enough in the future to plan beyond the payment terms.

The Ray Distributing forecasting procedure, using their ERP system, was as follows:

1. Print out stock status report. Check for "low numbers" (need recognition) and compare with month to date figures to get a "feel" for potential trends (trend and seasonality analysis).

2. Calculate the percentage of the year to be forecasted (time bucket) and multiply it by the previous year's usage. Adjust for trend, based on expert opinion.

3. Factor in on-hand quantity. Delete marginal products.

Forecasting was time intensive so in the interest of assuring maximum attention to top-selling products, Keith proceeded down the product list with some prioritizing of fast movers. The procedure made little use of more advanced forecasting tools. The "feel" for potential trends in step one and expert opinion in step two, along with the prioritizing of fast movers, created a system that was largely opinion based. Keith knew that the lack of tools to assist him in these decisions was leading to suboptimal decisions and was consuming a great deal of time. Keith wanted a more scientific approach. He developed a best-case scenario that would act as the model for whatever information system upgrade he decided to pursue.

Keith's proposed procedure was as follows:

1. The information system would maintain the forecasting procedure in real time, automatically providing predicted quantities for any requested number of periods into the future.

2. The preferred forecasting method would be exponential smoothing.

3. The forecast would be continuously monitored by error measures. These measures would raise a flag if the forecasting technique were underperforming.

The existing ERP system was not going to be able to support this effort. The system was not capable of capturing data far enough back and manipulating it for better forecasting techniques. The system also did not contain forecasting methods such as exponential smoothing. Finally, it did not capture measures of forecast error, so there was no way to track forecast accuracy.

Keith decided to set up the system using spreadsheets. The ERP system did allow for downloading of information to spreadsheets, but the process was slow and somewhat cumbersome. Keith was forced to download the data, allow the spreadsheets to do the analysis, and then upload the results to be used for purchasing decisions.

Reorder Point Calculations

The Reorder Point (ROP) contained within the ERP system was called the "safety level" and was set based on managerial opinion. To make such a call the manager would need an accurate forecast in order to determine what demand would be during the supplier's lead time, obtain a measure of how accurate the forecast was (to know how much additional inventory was needed for forecast error), and gain some idea of supplier performance (to determine how much inventory would be necessary to prepare for suppliers missing delivery dates). The ERP system was not capable of performing any of these calculations, so expert opinion was once again necessary to set the ROP or "safety level."

Keith decided to build his spreadsheet models to create a more accurate ROP. When he downloaded data for forecasting, he also had the spreadsheets keep a running measure of forecast accuracy: the Mean Absolute Deviation (MAD). MAD could be used as a surrogate for the standard deviation of the forecast, and Keith would use it in his ROP calculation. He also kept track of supplier delivery performance and used it to develop a performance metric for suppliers.

The spreadsheets then combined the forecast error, supplier performance metrics, and demand during lead time to develop a new safety level. Since the forecast would increase in the summer and decrease in the winter (by the same token supplier performance and forecast error would decrease in the winter), Keith had created a dynamic safety level that moved with his business and prevented him from carrying excessive inventory in the winter and not enough in the summer.

The additional downloading was minimal, since he only had to collect supplier performance data and had far fewer suppliers than products. However, uploading information back to the system became more intense now because he had to develop the new safety level as well as the new forecast information. The whole process was too work-intensive. In addition, Keith realized that although the new system would help him make better inventory decisions going forward, he also needed something that would deal with current inventory problems.

ABC Analysis

The new system would be work-intensive at least until a new ERP system was developed that could automatically handle all the tasks under the new procedure. Keith was not sure such a system would be easy to locate. In the meantime, he designed an interim purchasing and classification system as follows.

1. All products would be categorized by Return on Investment (ROI), with ROI defined by yearly total margin earned divided by the amount of inventory that had been paid for by Ray Distributing. Many products sold before the company had paid for them, resulting in a favorable cash flow position for the company. For inventory control purposes, the amount of money currently invested in inventory was regarded by Keith as more important than the actual total inventory in stock on any individual item. ABC classification was, therefore, established as:

A—Those items whose total margin/committed inventory investment ratio was greater than 200% (roughly the top 40% of all products).

B—Those items whose total margin/committed inventory investment ratio was less than 200% but whose sales were greater than $400 per year (emphasizing cash flow, next 20% of all products).

C—Those items whose total margin/committed inventory investment ratio was less than 200% and which had total sales of less than $400 per year.

"A" items accounted for approximately 70% of sales, B for 20%, and C for 10%. Committed inventory investment (inventory that is already paid for) was 70% of the total inventory investment at this time, and inventory (both total and committed) was considered to be too high. Although C items only accounted for 10% of sales, they constituted 80% of the committed inventory. As a result, the new classification scheme targeted C items for elimination.

2. For reordering purposes, the inventory classes would be treated in the following manner:

A—Reorder whenever inventory falls below the amount needed to cover safety stock and demand during lead time (safety level = demand during lead time plus safety stock).

B—Reorder whenever inventory falls below the amount needed to cover demand during lead time only. Safety stock, by definition, never leaves inventory and can, as a result, cost up to twice as much as regular inventory. B items did not have sufficient margins to justify safety stock (safety stock = 0).

C—Do not reorder (safety level does not exist).

3. New products were assigned to their own class (R class). The class was subdivided between A, B, and C items for reorder until six months' performance could be tracked on them. A items constituted the top 10% in terms of sales, B the next 40%, and C the bottom 50%. A items could be reordered as needed, B would be treated on a case-by-case basis, and C items would not be reordered during the first six months. After the six-month introductory period, the items reverted to standard ABC status. The R classification was kept extremely flexible, however, since a group of new products might outperform the norm.

4. Every few months, Keith would look at exceptions to ABC classification. Exceptions might include items that ran counter to the season (waders in summer, beach toys in the winter) or, items that were critical to important customers.

5. Minimum order quantities for supplier and freight discounts would be met for A items but not for B items.

Since A and B items constituted only 60% of products, the new ABC classification scheme would reduce the total workload. The C items did not need to be downloaded and uploaded to the ERP system. In addition, the bottom 40% of the inventory was slated for elimination. The plan reduced both the levels of inventory and certain inventory maintenance costs. In addition, the new scheme made elimination of slow-moving inventory feasible before these items became obsolete.

Order Quantity

Once he knew what to order and when, the only remaining question for Keith was how much to reorder. Keith decided to use a combination of the popular Economic

Order Quantity (EOQ) and minimum order quantities mandated by suppliers and transportation providers. If the EOQ was greater than a key minimum, he would reorder to the EOQ. If it was less than the minimum, he made a judgment call about which was best. The EOQ and the minimum quantities were put into the spreadsheets to be driven by the forecast. Keith knew there were more scientific ways to match up the order amount with minimum quantities (he had heard of the EOQ with quantity discounts model) but decided they were too complex without better support from the ERP system.

Before using the EOQ, however, Keith still needed to know what his holding costs were, since they were a key component in determining the order size. Keith calculated it as shown below in Table 14.1.

table 14.1   *Ray Distributing Holding Costs*

Cost of Capital (Opportunity Costs)	20%
Obsolescence	5%
Storage	15%
Insurance and taxes	2%
Total	**42%**

Keith wanted a minimum Return on Investment of 20%, which became his cost of capital. The remaining costs were developed from his financial records and divided by the total investment in inventory. He decided on a purchase order cost of $75, which was on the low side of most industry estimates, but he believed that his system would be more efficient than others.

Other ERP Obstacles

The ERP system, given the recommended order quantity and safety level, could generate Purchase Orders (POs) automatically. Keith now had a viable system, but the uploading and downloading of order quantities, ABC status, lead times, etc., was time-consuming. Keith felt the system was necessary, but he wanted an ERP system that could carry out his program internally. In addition to the purchase planning problems, the system had some other issues:

1. His purchasing clerk had her progress slowed by incorrect SKUs on the sales order (one order may have multiple errors). They had to be handwritten since there was no way to direct load sales data from the field into the system. Keith was interested in an automated system that would allow scanning at the customer's site with a download to the ERP system.

2. Multiple price levels had to be handled through several screens (special pricing might not be up to date as well), and sometimes the purchasing clerk had to resolve these issues manually.

3. The salesperson might request an item that was no longer in the system.

4. Other problems:

    a. Screens would not scroll.

    b. Commission screen had to be passed through even when it was not needed.

    c. Ray's numbering system was easier to use than the manufacturers'. The system was not able to translate (match) Ray's numbers with those of suppliers.

    d. The system was case sensitive, and any products with lowercase letters would be out of alphabetical order, thus increasing the clerk's search time.

Keith knew he would need a new system, so he began his search. The new system would need to interact with Ray Manufacturing, however. Ray Manufacturing was very profitable and growing faster than the standard distribution operations. He therefore placed a great deal of emphasis on a system that could integrate manufacturing planning into the complete process. Smaller ERP systems were not noted for their manufacturing planning capabilities, so the search might be difficult.

Ray Manufacturing

Ray Manufacturing (RM) was responsible for making products that would be sold through Ray Distributing. Rather than competing with larger manufacturers, however, RM focused on offering unusual products that could be easily built and distributed by Ray Distributing. The most popular items were fishing lures constructed from plastic worms and hooks, and fishing leaders made from basic materials such as steel line and floats. The workforce was composed of retired individuals who worked on a contract basis and would pick up the materials each week and assemble the products at home. RM also kept a few employees at the warehouse to package the finished products and maintain a raw materials inventory.

The workforce was extremely flexible because they worked when needed and did not work when demand was off. The problem was, therefore, predicting demand so that these high margin products would not stockout. RM also gave Ray Distributing a branded product that tied customers to the firm.

Keith had developed a Bill of Materials (BOM) on each product. A BOM is a tree that describes what goes into a product (see Figure 14.1). If the product is planned for manufacture, the BOM notifies the scheduler what raw materials will be needed at what point in the manufacturing process. Keith did not want to miss sales on key RM products because of raw material shortages. Keith wanted Ray Manufacturing to be notified of the forecasting and purchasing decisions made at Ray Distributing in time to obtain the necessary raw materials and to manufacture the products. He wanted the system to work through the BOM and check raw materials to make sure that nothing was overlooked.

Keith was not sure whether to keep his BOMs off the system and respond through human evaluation of orders coming from Ray Distributing or to integrate the systems and have RM's inventory managed by Ray Distributing's ERP system. Managing RM's scheduling would require the ERP system to have an MRP (Materials Requirement Planning) system embedded in its programs. MRP systems were the original

fig. 14.1   *A Sample Ray Manufacturing BOM*

Item: K-3   Description: Ray's 3-Hook Kingfish Leader

Item Component List

	Component	Description	Unit Measure	Quantity
1	FS08T	AFW .02″ DIAM SS WIRE	FT	5.170
2	85M-5/0	BULK HOOKS FOR PKG	EA	3.000
3	802-1/0	ROSCO BLK SWIVEL,F/K	EA	1.000
4	KING LDR BAG	$4\frac{1}{2}$ × 8″ BAG, for R	EA	1.000
5	OATP 1511	$1\frac{1}{2}$ × 1.1 LABELS UPC	EA	1.000
6	STAPLES	STAPLES, 5000/box	EA	0.083

systems that ERP was derived from and were, therefore, better tested and developed over the years. The issue was finding a system that could manage MRP and distribution at the same time. Many larger systems could do so, but locating a capable smaller system would be difficult.

Other Suppliers

The ABC system was going to create certain channel issues as well. For example, some manufacturers with long-term relationships had multiple products that were not doing well in the inventory classification. In one case, virtually all products from a manufacturer were C items. Keith saw this as both a risk and an opportunity. Less powerful manufacturers could be manipulated into helping to reduce Ray Distributing's inventory in order to maintain a presence. Since the ABC was based on ROI, anything that would raise the ROI would improve the product's stature. Inventory reduction through the return of slow movers, price reductions, improved payment terms, or shared promotions could all improve margins on a product and were controllable by the supplier. Now that Keith had concrete information, he could use it to make his suppliers partners in the effort.

On the other hand, some manufacturers might not pay attention to the ABC rules. If Keith dropped their slow movers, they might threaten to pull critical products from Ray Distributing. The information offered opportunities, but he would have to manage relationships carefully. Today's weak supplier might have a big winner tomorrow.

Connecting the Ray Distributing Supply Chain

Keith saw many opportunities to connect his supply chain. He marveled at the commonly held belief that small distributors were at a disadvantage under e-business because of system costs. Even with his underpowered system, he had been able to do things he knew larger distributors could not. If he could find a system with more functionality than his current one, he would be able to move at a much faster pace. Keith was already more agile than his large competitors. Things could only get better.

The areas that needed improvement were as follows:

1. Customer data collection and transferal: Keith wanted to see customer information deposited directly into his information system as quickly as possible. At that point, the information had to come back in written form from his sales force causing at least a day or two of delay to get it from salespeople who were visiting customers regularly. Those customers who were visited less often might not register demand patterns for weeks or more. When the salesperson did return the information to Ray Distributing, it was in written form, further slowing the process and leading to opportunities for keying and rekeying errors.

2. Purchasing automation: The purchasing function was being exchanged between the ERP system and the spreadsheets. Keith wanted the entire process to be run on his ERP system.

3. MRP scheduling: Ray Manufacturing needed a system that could pull real-time information from Ray Distributing and expand end products through a Bill of Material into raw materials that would ensure uninterrupted supply.

Opportunities to integrate Warehouse Management Systems (WMS) and other bolt-ons would be considered in the process as well.

Conclusion

Keith smiled as he thought about the possibilities. New ERP providers were popping up regularly, and he had already contacted some that claimed they could meet many of his needs. The trick was to put the pieces together correctly. The ERP system was the heart of the Ray Distributing information network, but by no means was it the only issue. Keith might decide to buy bolt-ons for some other functions such as MRP or WMS. The key was compatibility, and not leaving any holes that would prevent the complete connection of the supply chain.

Money was an issue, but the cost of the systems was dropping fast and he believed a complete system would be affordable for even the small distributor very soon. Keith's work in inventory management had already made clear what his needs were. Now he only had to find the systems.

"Still, how I design this thing will determine my competitive position for a very long time, since changing will be difficult and expensive," Keith stated. "I want to get it right the first time." The search began.

Issues to Consider

1. What methods could Keith use to connect the customer more closely to his system?

2. What benefits should Keith achieve by connecting the customer with his internal operations?

3. What contributions could Keith's suppliers make that he may not be considering?

4. Discuss the implications of Keith's decision to avoid working with the dot-com companies.

5. What connection and benefits might be realized by automating Ray Distributing's VMI relationships? How could VMI be automated?

6. What challenges will Keith face in integrating his e-business presence into his ERP system?

7. Is Ray Distributing making a mistake by not offering its catalog over the Web to all possible customers and not just retailers? Why or why not?

8. Evaluate Ray Distributing's current forecast methodology and discuss its strengths and weaknesses. Next, evaluate the proposed methodology. Suggest any potential improvements and the cost differentials between the existing method, Keith's, and your own.

9. Evaluate the ABC methodology both in terms of cost effectiveness and relationships. Suggest potential improvements and their impact on costs and on relationships with suppliers and customers.

Connecting the Supply Chain

Case Study: My Plumbing Supply

Note to the reader: The material in this case is based on a real company from a channel other than plumbing supply. Other than the name and product line, all other elements are accurate. This case does not represent the state of the plumbing supply market.

The project manager surveyed the landscape. He could not imagine how this would ever come together. After a myriad of consultants and implementation of a new information system, the company seemed no closer to achieving the logistics objectives they had laid out ten years before. The information system had in fact set them back quite a few years and cost a fortune to boot. Now even bigger things were afoot, and a plan called Demand Management was finally crystallizing for managing customer needs. He would be responsible for making that plan a success—no easy feat given the complexity of the firm and the pressure everyone was under to bring so many initiatives together at once. He would have to be part politician and part magician to get everyone behind this enormous undertaking.

No one could say that My Plumbing Supply (MPS) was a sleepy little firm. From ten sales branches in the 1980s it had grown to over fifty separate operations by 1999, spanning sales branches, distribution centers, and manufacturing plants in both the U.S. and Canada. This phenomenal growth had brought with it phenomenal growing pains as well. The company now dominated the market with somewhere between 30% and 40% market share, but the company's operations were far flung and procedures differed from one location to another.

In the fall of 1999, MPS faced many challenges. The company had introduced new products to broaden its scope, another acquisition was on the horizon, and an ERP (Enterprise Resource Planning) implementation started in 1994 was still under way. The company felt that with or without the new acquisition, it was time for a new business model. The model to date had been to grow into market leadership through acquiring competitors, opening new branches, and increasing same store sales. The strategy had worked beyond expectations, and MPS now found itself the market leader in plumbing supply. Now the management wanted to focus on profitability and customer service. The MPS network now spanned the nation, with the only remaining potential growth area now being the Northwest. The new acquisition, if successful, would fill that gap. The task of linking together this huge facility and process network while maximizing customer service and profitability would be as challenging as building it had been in the first place. The ERP system had been an important first step in that direction, but much remained to be done both on and off the information system.

Background

The company had been purchased from two brothers in the 1980s by a large international holding company. The holding company wanted growth, and MPS management set out to achieve just that with a series of acquisitions that rocketed the firm to industry leadership in the space of just ten years. In the late 1990s, a huge opportunity presented itself. The owners of the third-largest plumbing supply company, Northwest Plumbing (NWP), put it up for sale. Although MPS had reached critical mass, the acquisition had some very attractive elements to it.

First, NWP held a dominant position in the only part of the country where MPS lacked a strong presence: the Northwest. Second, NWP had a manufacturing facility in Seattle, Washington, which provided added incentives: additional manufacturing capacity, which was needed by MPS, savings on shipping plumbing products, and the assurance that NWP would not be acquired by a competitor, which might pose a competitive threat.

In 2000, MPS acquired NWP and in the process expanded from fifty to eighty different operations. The IT system at NWP was different from the ERP system at MPS, so the two systems had to be consolidated. This meant turning off the NWP system and turning all operations over to the MPS system.

It was in this environment that MPS decided that all of its distribution/logistics demand management processes needed to be redesigned. Demand management means controlling the material movement process from beginning to end as it serves the end user. The goal of the process was to minimize system costs while maximizing customer service. Customer service had great importance for MPS and would not be compromised. In fact, the company wanted to improve it further. Cost minimization was not necessarily at odds with customer service, however, and management believed there were many opportunities in its network to decrease costs with little to no effect on customer service. With these two goals in mind, MPS set out to increase customer service and profitability simultaneously.

Connecting the Customer

Connecting the customer means first understanding the customer. In the plumbing industry, the customers fell into two distinct groups: home center stores and contractors. Home center stores had high expectations for customer service but only tended to order "A" items and typically provided more lead time than contractors. They also ordered in larger amounts and set very strict fill rates and delivery time windows. Some fined their suppliers for failure to meet fill rates or on-time delivery requirements. If the company did not correctly identify home center store demand before it hit as an order, the order size could easily wipe out branch and Regional Distribution Center (RDC) inventory. Cleaning out the RDC would lead to stockouts at many branches when the RDC could not refill its inventories on a regular basis. It was also not wise to carry "Just in Case" inventory at the branches, since safety stocks could easily explode from unpredicted demand. The company knew that in spite of the cost, safety stock was being used to buffer home center demand. The home center store business was, therefore, targeted as an area for cost savings.

Contractors were an altogether different type of customer. Contractors came in different sizes and predicting their demand patterns was complicated. Large contractors were sometimes better organized and could give some advance notice of their orders; at least they did a sufficient volume of business with the company to allow for better forecasting. Small contractors were more variable, since they often did not plan well for upcoming projects, might experience credit problems, frequently asked for orders to be changed, and often placed orders the day before they needed the materials. Large contractors and even home centers might do the same (with even more damaging results due to their order sizes), but this was nearly a standard practice for the small contractors. The large numbers of small contractors had some smoothing effect, in the aggregate, on their demand patterns, but their erratic orders led to an opinion among the MPS inventory planners that forecasting was impossible.

Meeting the twin goals of increasing customer service and decreasing costs hinged primarily on better inventory availability. In a customer survey regularly carried out by the company, all customer groups listed availability as the top priority. This expectation drove large inventories (a cost issue) at MPS. Even with the high inventory levels, meeting fill rates was still challenging since the difficulties with forecasting often put inventory in the wrong products or locations. The company had two objectives when it came to managing demand from the customer interface. The first was to properly predict demand from existing data and even enhance the data the system already had. The second was to provide a forward view of customer demand from both the customer and the sale force.

The first objective came down to using better data collection routines, more robust mathematical forecasting models, error metrics, and an inventory planning methodology for these forecast results. Data collection breaks down into two areas: that which is tracked and that which is not but could be. The data that was tracked included last year's sales in units by SKU (stock-keeping unit) and location (branch, RDC, or manufacturing plant). This tracked data could be upgraded, thus ensuring that the system had correct information for forecasting purposes.

Back orders led to incorrect forecasting because the customer may have desired a product in a certain period but negotiated for delivery at a later date due to inventory availability at MPS. The ERP system tracked sales both by when a product was sold and when it was first requested. The system did not keep track of back orders per se. Customers who ordered an item for next-day delivery and were told that it could not be delivered for two weeks might allow delivery in two weeks or might take their business elsewhere. This created two problems in data collection: back orders and lost sales. Capturing back orders was pretty easy even though the system did not track them. Most customers wanted next-day or two-day delivery. If customer demand was recorded on the date the order was placed rather than when it shipped, the back order problem was solved.

Lost sales were different. If a customer placed an order and a lost sale occurred, the system did not capture that information. This could lead to a repeat episode the following year. The demand, if real, needed to be captured for next year's forecast. The problem was the difficulty in telling the difference between a lost sale and a customer that was just "shopping." If a customer called and asked for price and availability, the customer might have bought but only if the price were right. The customer might call several suppliers and pick the one with the best price and availability. Even if the company had the best price, it might not get the sale anyway if that price was too high.

The information system needed a method for collecting lost sales. The method would have to be easy to maintain and not be a burden to the salesperson in the process of conducting customer service. The company had made one failed attempt to collect lost sales data by offering the salesperson "reason codes" for missed sales.

The salesperson would enter the reason code, which could be inventory availability, price, or a host of other problems. The reason codes were so complicated and time-consuming that the sales force tended to pick availability almost every time in the interest of saving time and getting on with the next sale. The reason codes also had no relationship with the forecasting data but were used primarily for management review.

The company felt that if the correct data were collected it could be stored in the file that the forecasting model used to make its mathematical predictions. The mathematical model the company used was based on the previous year's sales and an estimated percentage increase. One strength of the model was that since last year's sales were seasonal, the forecast would be seasonal. Another strength was that it did take trend into account through the estimated percentage increase. Its weaknesses centered on the fact that it assumed what happened last year (plus the increase) would happen this year. Forecast literature refers to this model as the "Naive Model," since it makes simplistic assumptions about changes. The model breaks down if the assumed increase is not correct or last year's demand for any period was an anomaly.

Both of these circumstances applied to MPS. Most products had growth rates different from the global number estimated for the model. Anomalies were commonplace: Home centers might open a new store. Returns might come in a month other than the one they were purchased in. A major customer might be lost or gained. Many such opportunities for improved information gathering existed. Other models would also be "fooled" by these events, but since they smoothed demand over multiple periods and years, they would tend to "smooth out" problems, reducing overreactions to anomalies. An example might be the opening of a new home center store sending demand on a product to 200% of the norm in July of the previous year. The naive model would predict sales at last year's 200% plus the trend multiplier (if the multiplier was 5%, this year's forecast would be 210% of normal).

A more scientific smoothing model would adjust based on previous years and the months immediately preceding the month in question. Depending on its smoothing parameter's setting, the forecast would still be higher than it should be, but only marginally rather than to the degree of the naive model. These sorts of anomalies were common at MPS, and the current forecasting model was struggling.

The firm had investigated the use of other models in the ERP system but had had disappointing results. The underlying data was problematic, and it was difficult to tell whether the problems stemmed from the data rather than the model and, if so, what could be done about the data. On further investigation, there were two culprits. The first was the data. The data in the system had integrity problems stemming from back orders and what seemed to be unpredictable demand. With the naive model, these anomalies caused problems in one period, but with more advanced smoothing models the problem was spread out farther. If a data problem came up, the naive model had one huge error in one period. The smoothing models, however, had less severe errors spread over several periods. If the data problem could be minimized, the smoothing model would hardly be affected, whereas the naive model would still get a good hit in the period where the anomaly occurred.

If the data collection problem were solved, the smoothing models would work better, and they were available in the ERP system. This meant no "surprises" for the system. In other words, the sales force had to be providing buyers with information that the system did not have in time for appropriate reaction. To be effective at providing such information, the sales force needed a methodology to respond to buyers in a consistent pattern that the buyers could understand and interpret consistently in forecasting.

This need was fraught with problems as well. In the past the buyers had made numerous attempts to get information like the planned opening of home center stores or the landing of large jobs like public projects to no avail. The sales force received such requests in the heat of a busy season and did not have time to respond. The problem was twofold: First, the request was difficult to meet since there was no standardized and well-understood company procedure to deliver the information. Forms could be made up but would take a great deal of time to fill out, and interpreting every possible sales scenario with such a form was problematic. The system also did not store the types of unusual events discussed here, so improved forecasting would be thwarted next year when the anomaly came around anyway. The second problem stemmed from the company mission. The sales force still believed the mission was to increase sales at all costs. Customer service was king, and filling out forms did not seem to meet the company mission.

To be effective, the request for better information had to be consistent, the sales force had to see it put to good use, it had to be easy to prepare and deliver to the planning group, the system needed a notation system that tracked and, if possible, reacted to unusual events in the coming year, and the cost reduction mission had to be understood by all. Some of these requirements could be met easily; others were more difficult, and some were going to be very complex to implement. The information system did not automatically collect or offer much of the needed data.

One critical tool consisted of forecast error metrics that could be used to drive safety stock decisions and determine whether the forecasts derived from the new mathematical model were indeed better than the current system. In the long run, the forecast error metrics would be used to determine whether the additional information gathered was leading to improved forecasts or whether the historical data and the mathematical model were sufficient. If the historical forecast were sufficient, it would mean a dramatic reduction in workload for the buyers. The system did not collect forecast error metrics, but it did provide the ability to code in mathematical equations so a formula could be put in for just that purpose.

A debate had been going on for some time in the company as to whether a forecasting bolt-on could solve these problems. The IT group was opposed to the plan, since the company was still struggling with the implementation of the ERP system, and the introduction of a bolt-on would consume resources and not guarantee results. Many bolt-ons had some of the functionality needed, but integrating that functionality into a system that produced results would require process redesign at MPS. IT felt this planning should take place first. They also felt that adopting the latest upgrade to the ERP system would be more effective, since they had been led to believe that the upgrade already provided the sought-after functionality.

The planning group was concerned that the ERP upgrade would not perform as promised, especially given the the current system's lack of performance capability. Consultants from the ERP provider had admitted that forecasting was not a strength of their software and had also recommended a bolt-on. The planning group was also concerned that the upgrade would require eliminating many of the modifications they had already made to the system. They felt this would send inventory planning backwards rather than bring about improvement.

Connecting Distribution and Planning

A better forecasting methodology would only solve some of the inventory planning process problems. Once a good forecast was generated and error metrics collected, the company then needed to determine how much inventory to carry, where, and in what form (safety stock versus regular inventory), how much to buy, and what service level to maintain. The information system ran off DRP (Distribution Requirements Planning) logic. DRP was derived from MRP (Materials Requirements Planning) in manufacturing and was originally intended to match distribution information flows with manufacturing scheduling needs. The DRP system ran off a "safety stock," which was in fact its reorder point (ROP). The ROP was determined by the buyers and inputted into the system.

Setting ROP manually presented some problems. The buyers found maintenance of the "safety stocks" in the ERP system to be extremely onerous. With so many products, the buyers were forced to input a safety stock and would most likely not revisit it until something went wrong. Problems were detected when a branch manager or buyer became concerned about the number or magnitude of stockouts that a product was generating. The safety stock would then be adjusted upwards based on the branch manager or buyer's best estimate of what it would take to fix the problem. This meant safety stocks only got adjusted upwards and revisiting them would be extremely time-consuming.

Since all products were seasonal, the safety stocks tended to get set at a level that would meet the risk associated with the highest demand periods. This meant that the safety stocks were at their highest point year round. The company's order pattern followed the classic set ordering pattern depicted in the famous "sawtooth" diagram, where a static reorder point was set based on assumed static supplier delivery times and demand variability (see Figure 15.1). The technique assumes suppliers' lead times do not vary over the year and that safety stock needs remain the same all year long. Order sizes are based on minimums for freight or supplier savings. The maximum inventory occurs when an order comes in and is depleted at a fairly steady rate until it hits the reorder point (safety stock plus estimated customer demand during supplier lead time). Average inventory is equal to safety stock (which on average never leaves) plus half of the order size. Safety stock is estimated based on how often and to what degree suppliers miss delivery requirements and on the amount of forecast error associated with the product.

fig. 15.1 *A Typical Inventory Reordering Pattern*

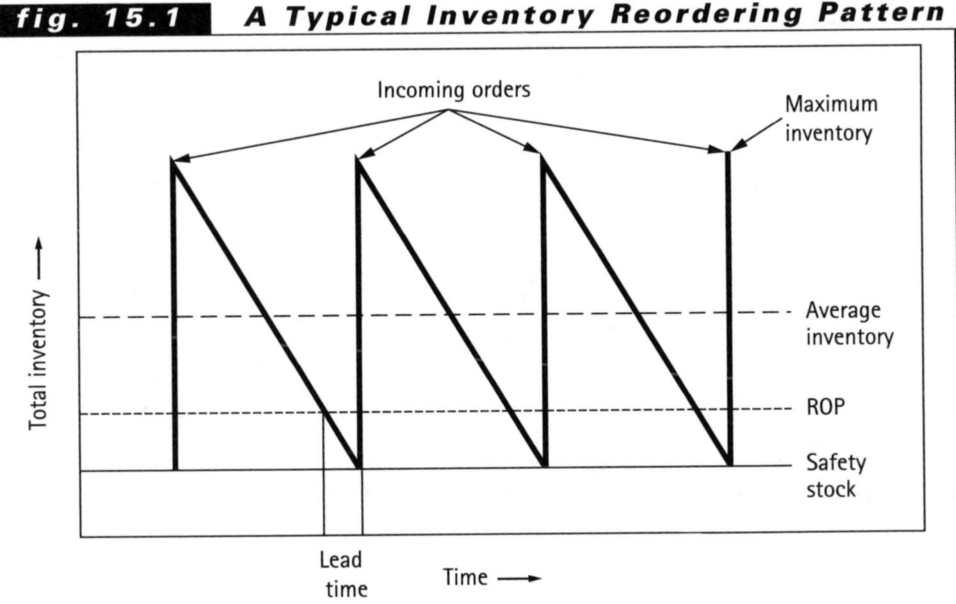

For MPS, the assumptions depicted in this graph were not valid. First, the supplier's lead time varied with the season and other factors. The length of supplier lead times increased in the summer (busy season), as did the variability of those lead times (due to strains on capacity). Forecast error also increased during the summer, since increases in demand usually led to bigger surprises when something unusual happened. The magnitude of demand and its variability (forecast error) were direct contributors to safety stock levels. The magnitude of lead-time variability was also a contributor, since the company needed safety stock for times when suppliers ran late. The remaining inventory, meant to cover expected lead time, would also be affected by the season since lead times got longer in the summer. The net effect was that instead of the static safety stock and lead-time inventory depicted in the figure above, MPS needed a variable safety stock and lead-time inventory like that depicted in Figure 15.2. The static nature of the DRP reorder point in the ERP system would not match real needs without continuous updating on the part of the buyers.

The company referred to this new ROP and safety stock as "dynamic," since it moved with business conditions. The safety stock and inventory for lead time during the busy season is higher. The static model created excess inventory during the slow season as depicted in Figure 15.3.

The problems associated with creating a dynamic ROP and safety stock were significant. The system could be taught to collect information on supplier deliveries and forecast error, but many feared the data collection process would fail. If the collected data did not accurately represent the environment, the safety stocks might not be sufficient to prevent stockouts or be higher than necessary. Some products were purchased from multiple suppliers where more expensive sources were more reliable

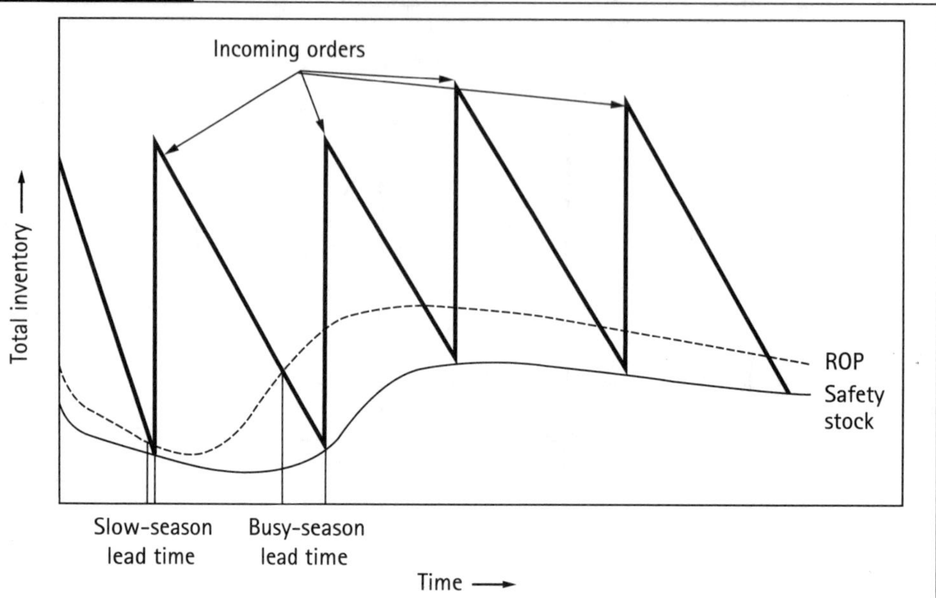

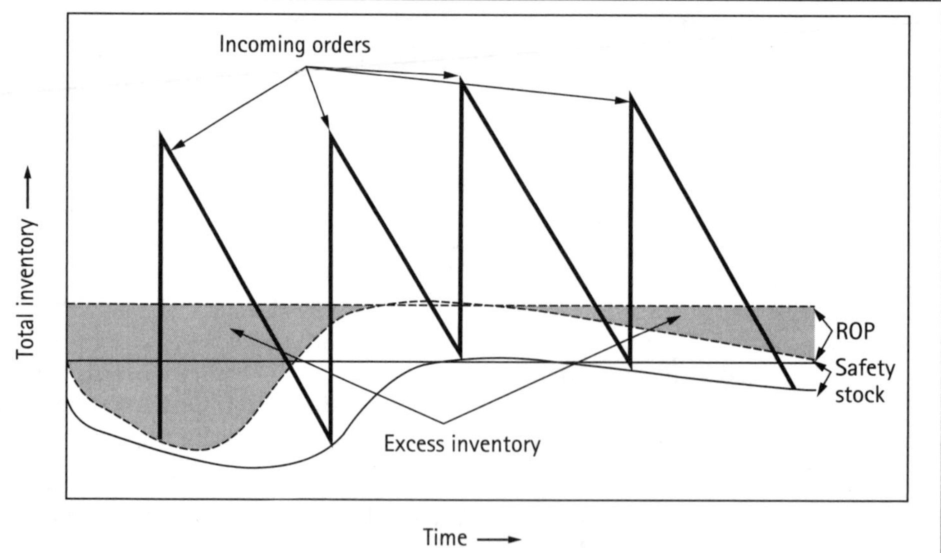

in delivery but could run from 40% to 100% higher on prices. The company used these suppliers as a backup to their regular suppliers. The buyers would go to these suppliers when their regular supplier could not meet the need. If the system were set up, which supplier should it rely on? If it relied on the regular supplier, it would generate larger inventories due to that supplier's limitations. If it relied on the alternative higher-priced supplier, it would generate inventories that would not meet customer service objectives, since the majority of orders did not go to that supplier. If it combined the two, the results would be unpredictable.

Assuming the ROP could be accurately set, the buyers then needed to decide how much to buy. The Economic Order Quantity (EOQ) assumes that demand is continuous (in other words, not seasonal and without trend). This was certainly not the case. In addition, the company had a firm belief in truckload shipping for two reasons. One was the perceived economic benefit (which was deemed considerable but not measured). The second was a competitive issue. The company liked to order in truckload amounts because their competition typically did not wish to (they lacked the volume to buy in truckloads). The perception was that truckload buys put the suppliers into a mode that would cause them to penalize those receiving less than truckload shipments. However, there was some uncertainty as to whether this was true.

The EOQ by itself would not provide sufficient insight to make the buying decision. In addition, the EOQ was not even present in the ERP system. The question was whether to code it in (a simple process) or to go to a bolt-on. Whichever solution was selected, the process would have to be supported by human expertise. As yet, decision-making programs that could capture the complexity of order size constraints like those present at MPS either did not exist or required an internal expertise the company simply did not have. Somehow, the decision process currently used by the firm—buyer judgment that differed from buyer to buyer—would have to be melded with mathematical models that the system or a bolt-on could provide and a consistent process developed.

Connecting Internal Suppliers

In addition to the problems with external suppliers, there were some rather specific problems with internal suppliers. Manufacturing was getting inconsistent messages from distribution due to the forecasting problems and the number of special orders put through by the sales force. Special orders were not evaluated for profitability and frequently required a complete line changeover to be carried out. Since the company did not have limitless manufacturing capacity, the specials could be very expensive. The erratic messages from distribution caused manufacturing to take defensive measures to survive.

Manufacturing had grown through acquisition as well. Each plant, as a result, had its own system for scheduling, loosely based on MRP logic. The DRP messages sent from distribution would be evaluated and based upon maintaining a somewhat level production plan. The manufacturing master scheduler would then determine what could be produced. This often led distribution to refer orders typically filled by manufacturing to vendors outside the firm. Frequently the special orders could only be sourced through manufacturing, which would cause considerable confusion for a time and ultimately tie up manufacturing resources for shutdown and changeover of lines. If the demands on manufacturing became too extreme, their lead times could stretch out further than those of external suppliers.

The disconnect principally came from the "hand-off" when distribution data was examined manually and then put into a schedule by the different manufacturing master schedulers. The planning group understood the process poorly, and sales force expectations of what manufacturing could do were often too high. The combination led to manufacturing having to do all their own planning, with no direct connection between the ERP system and manufacturing scheduling. Aggregate planning of resources for the following year's manufacturing needs came not from distribution forecasts but from manufacturing's own historical forecasts.

The Demand Management Solution

The demand management program set out to connect all information sources in the inventory replenishment cycle. This meant changes to the ERP system and to other company processes.

Centralized Purchasing

First and foremost, the company needed one group that was responsible for all purchasing activities. When the project began, branch managers and buyers had purchasing authority, and a great deal of "maverick buying" took place. Branch managers who feared stockouts would frequently buy truckload shipments from unauthorized suppliers without informing buyers. The practice was stopped and buyers were brought under one umbrella with a unified set of goals. Those goals were to consolidate slow-moving inventory at the Regional Distribution Centers (RDCs) and eliminate dead inventory from the company. The buyers were also charged with improving service levels on A and B items to elevate the entire firm's performance. A set of tools was developed to assist them in their efforts.

Combination Forecasting

The ERP system had all of its forecasting models tested, and the most powerful one turned out to be exponential smoothing for trend and seasonality. The system was switched over to this model, and Mean Absolute Deviation (MAD) was coded in for evaluation of the forecast. If an item forecast was performing well, the system would accept it without modification. If it was not, the system would notify buyers, who would investigate the cause and adjust the forecast based on their judgment.

The data collection process was improved as well. For use in the forecasting model, back orders were set into their actual demand periods. Plans for capturing lost sales were set in motion by a new interface that allowed the salesperson to interface with the ERP system in real time. At the end of an unsuccessful search the salesperson would receive a simple set of prompts that would determine whether the sale was lost due to availability or some other cause. The system did not try to enumerate the entire "other" category in the interest of saving the salesperson's time. Lost sales were also added to the forecast data file.

The planning group was also charged with maintaining a notation file that would flag unusual events from the previous year and notify the buyer that upcoming forecasts might be affected by the unusual event the year before. As part of combination forecasting, branch managers were charged with surveying their sales force on a weekly basis to determine if any large sales were expected, if the opening of new home center stores was planned, or if some other unusual event was forthcoming. The branch manager would then communicate with the buyer to prepare for any identified events. This communication was set to occur at the same time each week. Failure to inform buyers of events that could have been foreseen was directly tied to the branch in question.

Finally, the success of the forecast model both before and after expert modification would be measured by the error metrics. If combination forecasting was less successful than the pure mathematical model, it was suspended until performance deteriorated or a major event was reported from the field.

Reorder Point Logic and ABC Analysis

Before setting a reorder point and putting all these mechanisms to work, the company wanted to eliminate those items that did not require buyer attention. An ABC analysis of the inventory was coded into the ERP system. Based on sales and return on investment (ROI), it would determine what products should stay and which should be eliminated. A items would be carried at RDCs and branches with safety stock. B items would be carried at RDCs and branches, but safety stock would be limited at the branches. The assumption was that the RDC would react if a risk of stockout occurred. C items were consolidated at the RDCs, and D items were eliminated from inventory.

The resulting reduction in SKUs at many locations considerably reduced the buyer's workload. Since fast movers were easier to forecast, the items remaining after ABC consolidation and reduction frequently did not require expert forecasting. Since virtually all decision-making before the new system was expert based, the buyers were freed up to focus on better purchasing decisions and tracking of difficult products. The process also eliminated problem merchandise while it was still at C status and moving, before it hit D (dead). The combination of these benefits kept the buyers better informed and reduced the need to follow up on trivial matters. The result was an increased ability to focus effort on more complex problems.

Further reductions in inventory were achieved by coding a dynamic safety stock and reorder point for the A and B items. The ERP system's existing safety stock calculator did not work, so the company merely replaced the existing formulas with ones that did work. The process of collecting data from suppliers and performing subsequent calculations remained a problem, however, and buyers had to review safety stocks of products that might be at risk. Primary suppliers were set up for each product, and data collection and analysis were based on their performance.

Aggregate Planning

As a result of the new distribution planning system, a more reliable message was sent to manufacturing. Aggregate planning was driven by distribution forecasts rather than historical estimates from manufacturing that might not represent the end user's real demand. All manufacturing operations were also loaded on the ERP system, and a mandate went out that DRP and MRP would be used in the ERP system throughout the company.

Conclusion

The transition was difficult especially during the acquisition. Bringing multiple distribution and manufacturing systems onto one system, retraining many people, and redesigning processes in ways that others in the industry had never attempted would have been an incredibly difficult feat to pull off even under normal circumstances. Add in the acquisition, the inability of the ERP provider to provide much help, and the complexity of the market, and the challenge was nothing short of phenomenal.

At many times during the undertaking, the project manager wondered why he ever got into this mess and if it would ever be over. The new processes were in place or nearly so, but there was still so much to do. As he considered the new system, he knew the project had been worthwhile, but that due to its nature it would really never be over.

Issues to Consider

1. How will the new acquisition affect MPS's attempt to upgrade to Demand Management? Be specific: Consider the impact on IT resources, cultural issues, planning group responsibilities, customer reactions, and any other challenges the firm might face.

2. Discuss the tracking of back orders. Is the company's solution—recording sales in the forecast file at order date rather than ship date—appropriate? Can you think of any other means that could be employed to ensure proper tracking of back orders? How would you implement it?

3. Design a human/ERP solution for capturing lost sales. Consider the different customer types (large and small contractors and home center stores), use of salespeople's time, comprehensibility and usability of the results, and integration of the results with actual recorded sales.

4. Design a human/ERP solution that will enable the sales force to report large sales, new home center openings, etc. Again, consider the different customer types (large and small contractors and home center stores), demands on salespeople's time, comprehensibility and usability of the results, and integration of the results with actual recorded sales. Also consider how to track these unusual events and convince the sales force that the activity has merit.

5. Take up the debate over using a bolt-on for forecasting and inventory planning versus upgrading the ERP system's capability. List the pros and cons of each alternative. Make a recommendation and support it.

6. How would you address the issues involved in setting a dynamic reorder point and developing an order quantity for buyers to use?

7. What do you recommend the firm do with special orders? How should manufacturing be expected to handle these orders? Are there customer service issues to be considered if more specials are outsourced to other suppliers?

Index